Diversity and Super-Diversity

Selected Titles in the Georgetown University Round Table on Languages and Linguistics Series

The Usage-based Study of Language Learning and Multilingualism
LOURDES ORTEGA, ANDREA E. TYLER, HAE IN PARK, AND MARIKO UNO, EDITORS

Languages in Africa: Multilingualism, Language Policy, and Education
ELIZABETH C. ZSIGA, ONE TLALE BOYER, AND RUTH KRAMER, EDITORS

Discourse 2.0: Language and New Media
DEBORAH TANNEN AND ANNA MARIE TRESTER, EDITORS

Telling Stories: Language, Narrative, and Social Life
DEBORAH SCHIFFRIN, ANNA DE FINA, AND ANASTASIA NYLUND, EDITORS

Sustaining Linguistic Diversity: Endangered and Minority Languages and Language Varieties
KENDALL A. KING, NATALIE SCHILLING-ESTES, LYN FOGLE, JIA JACKIE LOU, AND BARBARA SOUKUP, EDITORS

DIVERSITY AND SUPER-DIVERSITY

Sociocultural Linguistic Perspectives

Anna De Fina, Didem Ikizoglu, and Jeremy Wegner, Editors

GEORGETOWN UNIVERSITY PRESS
Washington, DC

Library of Congress Cataloging-in-Publication Data

Names: Georgetown University Round Table on Languages and Linguistics (2015 : Washington, D.C.), author | De Fina, Anna, editor | Ikizoglu, Didem, editor | Wegner, Jeremy, editor
Title: Diversity and Super-Diversity : Sociocultural Linguistic Perspectives / Anna De Fina, Didem Ikizoglu, and Jeremy Wegner, editors.
Other titles: Georgetown University round table on languages and linguistics series (2004)
Description: Washington, DC : Georgetown University Press, 2017. | Series: Georgetown University Round Table on Languages and Linguistics series | The chapters that comprise this volume are based on papers presented at the 2015 Georgetown University Roundtable on Language and Linguistics whose theme was "Diversity and Super-Diversity: Sociocultural Linguistic Perspectives." The volume is a collection of works by the plenary speakers as well as papers that we regard as most representative of the issues presented and discussed at that exciting event, which saw the confluence of presentations by scholars from twenty different countries--Introduction. | Includes bibliographical references and index.
Identifiers: LCCN 2016027071 | ISBN 9781626164222 (pb) | ISBN 9781626164215 (hc) | ISBN 9781626164239 (eb)
Subjects: LCSH: Sociolinguistics--Congresses. | Multilingualism--Congresses.
Classification: LCC P40 .G466 2015 | DDC 306.44--dc23
LC record available at https://lccn.loc.gov/2016027071

∞ This book is printed on acid-free paper meeting the requirements of the American National Standard for Permanence in Paper for Printed Library Materials.

18 17 9 8 7 6 5 4 3 2 First printing

Printed in the United States of America

Cover design by Pam Pease.
Cover image courtesy of iStock.

Contents

Introduction

ANNA DE FINA, DIDEM IKIZOGLU, AND JEREMY WEGNER

THE CHAPTERS THAT COMPOSE this volume are based on papers presented at the 2015 Georgetown University Roundtable on Language and Linguistics whose theme was 'Diversity and Super-Diversity: Sociocultural Linguistic Perspectives.' The volume is a collection of works by the plenary speakers as well as papers that we regard as most representative of the issues presented and discussed at that exciting event, which saw the confluence of presentations by scholars from twenty different countries.

We devoted GURT 2015, and now this volume, to super-diversity because we feel the need to introduce (or at least widen) the discussion of the theoretical and methodological challenges that this phenomenon poses to sociocultural linguists in the United States. Although important work in this area is being carried out on this side of the Atlantic, the main contributions to the study of super-diversity have, up until now, come from scholars in Europe, Asia, and Africa. The reasons for this are apparent in the sudden and radical changes that globalization has brought to Europe, Asia, and Africa and the manner in which it has radically intensified the movement and contact of people throughout those areas of the world. Globalization has increased population flows in unprecedented ways, such that urban centers have been transformed into sites of encounter for groups and communities that are highly diverse in terms of origins, cultural practices, and languages.

This has become particularly salient in parts of the world that had, until recently, been culturally, linguistically, and ethnically homogeneous. Technological advancement and global connectedness have also contributed to diversity as they intensify contact and exchange between peoples who are often spatially distant and culturally distinct from one another. New technologies have allowed for massive access to globalized phenomena, thus exposing people to a great variety of linguistic and cultural models. The proliferation of new media creates new communicative genres and hybrid semiotic practices; thus we find ourselves living in a world in which contact and interaction (physical or virtual) between diverse peoples, languages, cultural models, media, and practices are the norm.

These changes and developments have deeply affected the ways people use language to communicate in all contexts of life and indeed in all countries, thus calling for a rethinking of the traditional concepts and methodologies underlying the practice of sociocultural linguistics. Recent work in the field has started to give substance to this realization, *problematizing* the conception of languages as well-bound, separate codes, *complicating* traditional associations between languages and social identities, and *emphasizing* the interconnectedness of communicative events and practices at various scales resulting from the embedding of languages (and other semiotic resources) within new physical landscapes and mediated practices. These themes and new preoccupations were elaborated in the papers presented at GURT 2015 and we want to give greater reach to these reflections.

Due to constraints of space and scope, this introduction does not contend any particular notion of what 'super-diversity' actually means (see Vertovec 2013; Budach and de-Saint Georges, forthcoming), or whether the phenomena designated as such are new or old, or even whether or not sociolinguistics is equipped with the means to account for them. An entire volume devoted to this debate would not be sufficient to resolve such questions at this point. Our aim here is modest: we intend to highlight main themes and issues running through the different chapters and to highlight the contributions of each of the authors to the study of super-diversity. Most of all, we want to open the door to further reflection and discussion.

The chapters presented revolve around significant issues in the debate over super-diversity: namely, the way late-modern identities should be studied and represented and the role of mobility and complexity in the constitution of such identities; the emergence of complex language practices among super-diverse populations and the coexistence of conviviality and conflict within those; changing and ever-evolving definitions of speech communities and the impact of new technologies in the ways in which they get constructed, circulated, and negotiated; the impact of super-diversity in state-controlled policies and in the realm of education.

The themes of identity, complexity, and mobility are the focus of the first three chapters of the volume. In chapter 1, "Chronotopic Identities: On the Timespace Organization of Who We Are," Jan Blommaert and Anna De Fina argue for a rethinking of ideas and constructs about identity in the era of super-diversity. They propose the Bakhtinian notion of the *chronotope* as a source of inspiration for the development of an approach to identities that avoids "simplifications by taking into account the complex interactions between practice, iteration, and creativity in social life." The authors point out that the concept of the chronotope "enables sociolinguists to avoid the analytical separation of behavior and context," which is not matched by the experiences of people engaged in semiotic activities in that chronotopes invoke orders of indexicality valid in specific timespace frames and invite an analytical focus that goes deeper and deeper into identity and practice configurations. The equal focus accorded to temporal and spatial structure in the framing of practices highlights the intersection and convergence of multiple frames and time scales in interaction, revealing the inadequacy of traditional sociolinguistic notions of 'scenes,' 'situations,' and 'contexts.' From this perspective, human interaction is organized according to the chronotopes invoked by specific timespace configurations that reflect elements of subordinate and superordinate frames at both micro and macro scales.

The theme of chronotopic relations is also central to the chapter by Ruth Wodak and Markus Rheindorf, "'Whose Story?': Narratives of Persecution, Flight, and Survival Told by the Children of Austrian Holocaust Survivors." Focusing on narratives inherited by the descendants of Holocaust survivors, the authors address the phenomenon of 'collective memory,' defined as "a collection of traces of events that are significant for the historical trajectory of a specific group, endowed with the capacity to relive these shared memories on the occasion of rites, celebrations and public festivities" (Halbwachs 1985). Such traces of events bear significance that transcends the individual. As Wodak and Rheindorf point out, this is a process whereby history is constructed. One startling finding of this study is that stories relating events from 1938 and 1945 lack temporal reference, instead relying on places and spaces rather than time to situate events. The authors argue that this constitutes a 'change of chronotope,' from the temporally ordered events "before Hitler" to "the timeless space of war, flight, and persecution." The connectedness of identities, space, and time is taken up in a different direction in chapter 3, "Linguistic Landscape: Interpreting and Expanding Language Diversities" by Elana Shohamy. The author argues for the usefulness of a Linguistic Landscape perspective to capture the ways in which social and linguistic identities are negotiated and fought over in concrete public spaces. She traces the emergence of more sophisticated versions of the LL approach in response to the complexities of super-diverse environments by showing how LL studies have gone through phases that can be characterized as 1) quantitative, 2) multimodal, 3) anti-homogenizing, 4) focused locality (e.g., neighborhoods rather than cities), and 5) activist. Indeed, the author argues for a broader, more nuanced approach to Linguistic Landscapes that accounts for the multiplicity of symbolic processes through which public spaces are constructed by diverse inhabitants. She supports the active involvement of researchers, such that situations studied are changed by design as a result of their participation. The LL approach is illustrated through the analysis of struggles over identity and visibility in the case of minority languages in Israel.

The next chapters explore the emergence of complex language practices among super-diverse populations and the coexistence of conviviality and conflict within those. In chapter 4, "A Competence for Negotiating Diversity and Unpredictability in Global Contact Zones," Suresh Canagarajah challenges traditional notions of communicative competence associated with homogeneity, uniformity, and therefore unity, and argues instead for a new perspective that shifts from 'immobile languages' to 'mobile (semiotic) resources.' From this standpoint, according to the author, "mobility is at the heart of language." Drawing data from a study of foreign-born professionals in the UK, he highlights these multilinguals' development of a language competence that is rooted in "spatial repertoires"; that is, of linguistic features and elements deeply embedded within socioculturally defined spaces, rather than in a rigid acquisition of the second language system. In the next chapter, "The Strategic Use of Address Terms in Multilingual Interactions during Family Mealtimes," Fatma Said and Zhu Hua investigate linguistic diversity from the standpoint of language learning, interculturality, and socialization. Specifically, they examine the interactions of a single transnational family residing in Newcastle, UK, whose members have different birth places and different linguistic repertoires. The authors find that the family members make use of terms of address in creative ways that highlight the bidirectional nature of socialization processes, particularly in the case where parents and children are faced with a variety of linguistic and identity repertoires. In such situations, both the tensions between different "home cultures" and the desire to come to a harmonious synthesis of different identities play a role. The authors examine how negotiations that take place among family members over these different forces play out in the use of terms of address in a variety of Arabic, which is itself mixed. Like Canagarajah, Adrian Blackledge, Angela Creese, and Rachel Hu highlight the role of conviviality and the avoidance of tension in the translanguaging exchanges taking place at the Birmingham Bull Ring Indoor Market (García 2009). Reflecting on data from an ethnographic study conducted in that context, the authors note that "the day-to-day practices of buying and selling in Birmingham indoor market were, as far as we could see during four months of observation, normally characterized by good humor, conviviality, generosity of spirit, and people's willingness to get on with other people." In the chapter "Everyday Encounters in the Marketplace: Translanguaging in the Super-Diverse City," the authors analyze various strategies used by customers and sellers to communicate with each other despite their lack of competence in one another's languages, from gestural resources to the learning of key words and phrases. The analysis exposes the problems inherent in approaches to language competence that define it as "full command of the syntactic, lexical and phonetic system of a language," thus highlighting the need to learn from super-diverse contexts how people concretely operate within complex multilingual and multicultural environments.

The three subsequent chapters turn to ideological constructions concerning linguistic phenomena within speech communities: how, on the one hand, normative and prescriptive ideologies still prevent many people from embracing the complexity and plurality of linguistic experiences, and, on the other hand, new technologies continue to change the way ideas about language are circulated and negotiated. In chapter 7, "(In)convenient Fictions: Ideologies of Multilingual Competence as Resource for Recognizability," Elizabeth Miller takes issue with terms such as multilingualism, plurilingualism, multivocality, and interlingualism, which continue to characterize languages and cultures as if they were individual unitary entities that can be pluralized. Instead, she argues that researchers should reorient to the burgeoning complexity of communicative practices that make use of 'extreme mixedness' as needed. However, based on a study of adult migrant business owners in the United States, the author also shows that these traditional views and hierarchies of language distinctiveness remain active as frames for self-understanding. Miller found that interviewees referenced traditional categories (ethnicity, nationality, culture, etc.) in such a way as to position themselves as certain 'types' of people through the labels available to them, effectively "co-constructing particular identities in the process of responding to interview questions." In the subsequent chapter, Anastasia Nylund advocates for working toward greater understanding of intragroup diversity and the role of individual and community ideologies in discourse. In particular, she focuses on the metalinguistic discourse of African American speakers in a diverse community undergoing rapid social change, analyzing how *metasociolinguistic* stancetaking—that is, stancetaking toward ideas about language's role in society—is enacted through constructed dialogue. She finds that stances toward self and other are frequently in opposition, highlighting a tension in the broader social discourses regarding (African American) speech in the community. In chapter 9, "Citizen Sociolinguistics: A New Media Methodology for Understanding Language and Social Life," Betsy Rymes, Geeta Aneja, Andrea Leone-Pizzighella, Mark Lewis, and Robert Moore advocate a 'citizen sociolinguistic' approach to super-diversity, arguing that in sociocultural linguistics "the sophistication of the research subjects and their own detailed understandings of their language practices has often been overlooked in favor of the interpretations of their researchers." In contrast to this, the authors investigate the sociocultural ideologies (or folk theories) held by participants in order to better understand the perspectives and assumptions that shape and motivate their interactions in everyday life. The chapter presents a series of studies of metalinguistic comments on different speech phenomena on Youtube in order to illustrate both how people construct linguistic phenomena and how new technologies have provided folk ideologies about language with new forms of communication and circulation. The authors view "the circulation and exchange of samples of observed speech and metacommentary upon them as a social activity in its own right, one that is centrally constitutive of non-face-to-face online communities."

The final two chapters engage with the way state-controlled educational institutions and language policies respond to diversity and super-diversity. In "Recasting Diversity in Language Education in Postcolonial Late-Capitalist Societies," Luisa Martín Rojo, Virginia Unamuno, Inmaculada Sánchez, and Christine Anthonissen reflect on ways in which various late-capitalist and postcolonial regimes recast new forms of diversity through the implementation of language education policies and programs. They examine these policies in a variety of educational scenarios involving migrants or minority populations in postcolonial states, from South Africa, to Spain, to Argentina, to the United States. They consider different kinds of language programs, examining various dimensions of the educational processes (from linguistic policies to local practices in classrooms) and arguing that former inequalities, prejudices, and social hierarchies are still active and even amplified in many apparently liberal societies today. Indeed, while states proclaim their willingness to open up to multilingual policies and linguistic inclusion, in reality the kind of multilingualism that they finance and push for in most cases involves the preparation of members of the elite for the needs of a globalized labor force and the exclusion of less-privileged students. The chapter also discusses resistance to discriminatory policies, through the case of the Intercultural Bilingual Education program addressed to indigenous local groups, to show how members of those communities disrupted state policies by taking charge of the program. In the last chapter, "Diversity in School: Monolingual Ideologies versus Multilingual Practices," Anna De Fina examines the case of an inner-city school in Palermo, Sicily, to illustrate the impact of super-diversity on Italian educational institutions. Analyzing data collected in an ethnographic project conducted in a fifth-grade classroom in which Sicilian children were enrolled together with children from Tunisia, Morocco, Sri-Lanka, and Bengal, De Fina shows the tensions between the multilingual and multicultural reality of children and the prevailing monolingual/monocultural norm implemented by teachers and more generally by the Italian state programs. Children were found to engage in a variety of translanguaging practices involving both foreign and local languages and both teachers and children showed a keen interest in the diverse linguistic and social experiences represented in the classroom. But such practices were inscribed into what Goffman defines "back regions" of interaction—that is, spaces that were not officially sanctioned—and almost never entered the "front regions" of teacher-student communication. This research confirms the existence of a push and pull of opposing trends and forces in globalized societies.

It is our hope that the works collected in this volume will be instrumental in stimulating further research and theoretical reflection on diversity and super-diversity.

References

Budach, Gabriele, and Ingrid de-Saint Georges. Forthcoming. "Superdiversity and Language." In *Routledge Handbook on Migration and Language*, edited by Suresh Canagarajah. Florence, KY: Taylor and Francis.

García, Ofelia. 2009. "Education, Multilingualism, and Translanguaging in the 21st Century." In *Social Justice through Multilingual Education*, edited by Tove Skutnabb-Kangas, Robert Phillipson, Ajit K. Mohanty, and Minati Panda, 140–58. Bristol, Eng.: Multilingual Matters.

Vertovec, Steven. 2007. "Super-Diversity and Its Implications." *Ethnic and Racial Studies* 30 (6): 1024–54.

Chapter 1

Chronotopic Identities

On the Timespace Organization of Who We Are

JAN BLOMMAERT AND ANNA DE FINA

SUPER-DIVERSITY OFFERS SCHOLARS a broad range of opportunities to revise and rethink parts of their conceptual vocabulary in attempts to arrive at more sensitive and accurate tools for thought and analysis. The recognition of a reality that might, in some respects and to some degree, have always been there but was never enregistered in theoretical and methodological frameworks might, in fact, be seen as the most productive outcome of the current debates over whether or not super-diversity is "new." The perspective is indeed new, but it also allows us to return to old issues armed with some fresh ideas (cf. Blommaert 2015c; Silverstein 2015; Arnaut 2016; Parkin 2016). In what follows, we take these ideas to issues of identity.

Reflections and theorizations on identity within sociolinguistics and discourse analysis in the last two decades have moved more and more toward context-sensitive, social constructionist understandings (see Bucholtz and Hall 2005; Benwell and Stokoe 2006; De Fina, Schiffrin, and Bamberg 2006; De Fina 2011). Yet, even within these new paradigms, identities are often still understood in dichotomous terms as *either* micro *or* macro, individual or social, local or global, etc., with hyphenations allowing for a limited degree of complexity, and with language separated from specific identities by "and" (see, e.g., papers in Preece 2016). In this chapter we explore the Bakhtinian notion of the *chronotope* as a source of inspiration for the development of an approach to identities that avoids such simplifications by taking into account the complex interactions between practice, iteration, and creativity in social life. We shall elaborate on the following central idea: It is possible to see and describe much of what is observed as contemporary identity work as being chronotopically organized. Indeed, it is organized in, or at least with reference to, specific timespace configurations which are nonrandom and compelling as 'contexts.'

We intend to illustrate how a view of identities as chronotopic can offer invaluable insights into the complexities of identity issues in super-diverse social environments, and how it fits within a renewed sociolinguistic paradigm that stresses ethnographic, practice-oriented approaches to communication and discourse, aimed at the most minute aspects of identity practices operating as indexicals for large-scale 'structuring' characteristics of social practice—a nano-politics of identity so to speak (cf. Parkin 2016; Rampton 2006). We shall do this largely in a dialogue with some classic sociological statements on these topics, as a way to show the advantages of our mode of analysis over more sweeping and generalizing approaches.

Chronotopes and Sociology

In their seminal study on the unequally accessible cultural capital of French university students, Bourdieu and Passeron make the following remark: "Sans doute, les étudiants vivent et entendent vivre dans un temps et un espace originaux" (Undoubtedly, students live and expect to live in an original time and space) (1964, 48). The specific time they live in is measured by the academic year, with its semesters, lecturing times, and exam sessions. And the way they live is relaxed, slightly anarchic, and down to themselves when it comes to organizing their days, weeks, and months—"le temps flottant de la vie universitaire" (the fluid time of university life) (51). The specific spaces include, of course, the university campus, its buildings, lecture halls and staff offices; but also "des quartiers, des cafés, des chambres 'd'étudiants' " ("'student' neighborhoods, cafés, and rooms"), cinemas, dance halls, libraries, theaters, and so forth; the Parisian Quartier Latin, of course, serves as a textbook example here (51).

It is no miracle, then, that a walk through the Quartier Latin during the academic year would reveal a specific demographic pattern—a dense concentration of young people, who would be students, and middle-aged men, who would be senior academics—different from, say, people shopping along the fashion stores on the Champs Elysées or taking the commuter trains out of Paris at 5 p.m. According to Bourdieu and Passeron, due to these specific timespace givens, students acquire a sense of shared experience, which, invariably, becomes an important part of their autobiographies later in life—"in my student days," "we met when we were students," etc. The specific timespace of student life involves particular activities, discourses, and interaction patterns; role relationships and identity formation modes; particular ways of conduct and consumption; of taste development and so forth, most of which are new, demand procedures of discovery and learning, and involve the mobilization of existing cultural and social capital in the (differential) process of acquiring new capital. References to similar timespace elements (a charismatic or dramatically incompetent lecturer, a particular café, or a then-popular movie or piece of music) create a shared sense of cohort belonging with others, which coexists with preexisting belongings to social groups and which enters into posterior forms of belonging. In that sense, our student days do not compensate for or replace preexisting class memberships (which the book documents at length), and neither constitute the sole bedrock for posterior identity formation. Rather, in Bourdieu and Passeron's view, our student identity represents a relatively superficial phenomenon, "plus proche de l'agrégat sans consistence que du groupe professionnel" (closer to an aggregate without consistency than to a professional group) (1964, 56), let alone "un groupe social homogène, indépendant et intégré" (a homogenous, autonomous and integrated social group) (49), which reproduces underlying (class) differences while constructing one new layer of shared biographical experience. Thus, while students share almost identical experiences and develop particular and similar identities during their days at the university, the meanings and effects of these shared experiences will differ according to the more fundamental social and cultural identity profiles they "brought along" to university life.

Probably without being aware of it, Bourdieu and Passeron provided us with one of the most precise empirical descriptions of what Bakhtin calls a "chronotope," (a notion that he applies to works of literature), which he defines as follows: "We will give the name *chronotope* [literally 'timespace'], to the intrinsic connectedness of temporal and spatial relationships that are artistically expressed in literature" (1981, 84–85). Indeed, Bakhtin coined this term to point toward the inseparability of time and space in human social action and to the effects of this inseparability on it. In his work he identifies the "literary artistic chronotope" where "spatial and temporal indicators are fused into one carefully thought-out, concrete whole," such that the chronotope could be seen as "a formally constitutive category of literature" (84). It is thanks to this concept of chronotope that Bakhtin was able to address the co-occurrence of events from different times and places in novels, the fact that shifts between chronotopes involve shifts of an entire range of features and generate specific effects. He saw the interplay of different chronotopes as an important aspect of the novel's heteroglossia, part of the different "verbal-ideological belief systems" that were in dialogue in a novel, because every chronotope referred to socially shared, and differential, complexes of value attributed to specific forms of identity, as expressed (in a novel for example) in the description of the looks, behavior, actions, and speech of certain characters, enacted in specific timespace frames. Importantly, Bakhtin assumes also that chronotopes involve specific forms of agency and identity: specific patterns of social behavior "belong," so to speak, to particular timespace configurations; and when they "fit," they respond to existing frames of recognizable identity, while when they don't they are "out of place," "out of order," or transgressive (see Blommaert 2015a for a discussion).

In a more contemporary and applied vocabulary, we would say that chronotopes invoke orders of indexicality valid in a specific timespace frame (cf. Blommaert 2005, 73). Specific timespace configurations enable, allow, and sanction specific modes of behavior as positive, desired, or compulsory (and disqualify deviations from that order in negative terms), and this happens through the deployment and appraisal of chronotopically relevant indexicals—indexicals that acquire a certain recognizable value when deployed within a particular timespace configuration.

Through these lenses, one can, for example, also read Goffman's (1963) *Behavior in Public Spaces* as a study of the orders of indexicality operating in public spaces and not elsewhere, while his description of poker players in *Encounters* can be read as a study of the orders of indexicality valid in places such as the poker rooms of

Atlantic City or Las Vegas (Goffman 1961). Howard Becker's (1963) *Outsiders*—jazz musicians and marihuana users—also organize their behavior and the criteria for evaluating behavior determining different degrees of membership in their "deviant" community, within the clearly demarcated timespace configurations of the 1940s–1950s American-metropolitan jazz clubs. Studies of doctor-patient interaction show that these are also typically set in the highly specific, regimented, and asymmetrical timespace configurations of medical centers and consultation times therein (Cicourel 2002).[1]

In such timespace configurations, Goffman situates specific actors enacting specific roles (poker players must be strangers and can never have met each other elsewhere; they gather just to play poker and do that competently), specific, relatively strict "rules of engagement," and normative assumptions (focus on the game, play the game by its rules), as well as identity judgments (a "superb" poker player). Like Bourdieu and Passeron, Becker, and others, Goffman describes the indexical organization of specific chronotopes: the ways in which particular socially ratified behavior depends on timespace configurations, or more broadly, the ways in which specific forms of identity enactment are conditioned by the timespace configurations in which they occur. The "gatherings" described in *Behavior in Public Places* are such timespace configurations, and the specific modes of behavior Goffman describes and analyzes are the ones that "fit" those particular configurations. The careful description of such nonrandom chronotopic connections, by the way, bears a well-known academic label: ethnography.

Chronotopes as Identity Frames

A shorthand term such as *chronotope* enables us to avoid an analytical separation of behavior and context, which is not matched by the experiences of people engaged in such activities. In its most simple formulation, the idea we develop here is that the actual practices performed in our identity work often demand specific timespace conditions as shown by the fact that changes in timespace arrangements trigger complex and sometimes massive shifts in roles, discourses, modes of interaction, dress, codes of conduct and criteria for judgment of appropriate versus inappropriate behavior, and so forth. We see this factor as a constraint on what is possible in the way of identity work—a *framing* constraint not always accurately identified in studies on identity.

Let us take a rather simple example: a group of colleagues who share their 9 to 5 daytime in the same office; all of them have mutually known names and roles, often hierarchically layered, and specific shared codes of conduct that govern their interactions (the shortcut term for such codes is often "professionalism"). Men are dressed in suits and neckties, ladies wear similar formal professional dress. The group, however, has developed a weekly tradition of "happy hour." Every Thursday after work, they jointly leave the office and walk to a nearby pub for a drink or two. The moment they leave their office building, men take off their neckties, and the tone, topics, and genres of talk they engage in with each other change dramatically—a Goffmanian frame shift of sorts. "Professional" and job-focused talk may be exchanged for banter, small talk about family life, joke-cracking, or flirting. And the roles and relationships change as well: the office "boss" may no longer be the "coolest" person, and a very competent worker may turn into a very incompetent drinker or joke-teller. We see the same people engaging in entirely different social practices and relationships, embodying entirely different roles and identities grafted onto or mobilized alongside existing ones (the boss in some way remains the boss even during happy hour)—all of it due to a change in the timespace configuration in which they move, which in turn changes the frame within which behavior is produced, evaluated, and understood. "Happy hour" behavior is intolerable during office hours, and office behavior is intolerable in the pub ("No job talk!")—timespace reordering involves a complete reordering of the normative codes of conduct and redefines the space of what is possible and allowable in performing identity work. Such phenomena, once we start looking for them, occur constantly. In fact, one may be hard pressed to come up with modes of social conduct that are not conditioned by nonrandom timespace arrangements. Our suggestion here is to take this kind of "context" seriously—that is, that we need to address it in a systematic and meticulous way and see what purchase it has. Doing so will increase the accuracy of our analyses of the dynamic and changing nature of social life and of the groups that organize it.

At the most basic level, it is good to point out that the chronotopic nature of specific forms of identity is part of common sense understandings about the way groups and cultures function. Thus, chronotope-based constructs are already entrenched in our everyday vocabularies. For example, when we speak of "youth culture," we obviously speak (be it with perplexing vagueness even in published work) about a complex of recognizable cultural phenomena attributed to a specific period in human lives—"youth"—which is often also specific to a place or a region. For example, Talcott Parsons's discussion of American youth culture differs from that of French youth culture offered at the same time by Bourdieu and Passeron (Parsons 1970, 155–82). Youth culture, therefore, is always a chronotopically conditioned object of study.

Identifying a phenomenon such as youth culture in terms of its chronotopic conditions involves and explains certain things. It involves generalizability. If specific forms of cultural practice mark specific periods of life, all such periods must have their own forms of cultural practice. In other words, a chronotopic qualification such as youth culture could (and perhaps must) be extended to any other form of cultural practice describable as tied to and conditioned by specific timespace configurations. In fact, there is nothing more specific to youth culture than, say, to the culture of young parents, or of mature professionals, or of retired senior citizens. In each case we shall see specific forms of practice and identity construction conditioned by the particular stage of life of the ones who enact them, usually involving trajectories through specific places (think of schools for teenagers or kindergarten for young parents). And just as youth cultures typically set themselves apart by specific forms of jargon and slang (now both in spoken and written forms), other age groups similarly display such discursive and sociolinguistic characteristics.

Generalizability, in turn, implies fractality. There is no reason why chronotopic cultural practices would be confined to the "big" stages of life only, because even within narrower timespans we can see nonrandom co-occurrences of timespace configurations and forms of cultural practice and identity enactment. Think of the timeframe of a week, for instance, in which specific days would be reserved for "work" (involving specific trajectories through time and space) and others for, say, religious services, family meetings, shopping, and leisure activities. The timeframe of a single day in such a week, in turn, can be broken down into smaller chronotopic units, with activities such as "breakfast," "dropping kids off at school," "going to work," "being at work," "returning from work," and eventually "watching TV in bed" all marked by nonrandom collocations of time, space, and behavioral modes. The rules of macroscopic conduct also apply to microscopic behavior. In the same way, while societies recognize particular chronotopic arrangements as defining big groupings based on chronotopic conditions such as those characterized by commonality of age or profession, participants in smaller or less homogenous communities can identify other kinds of chronotopic arrangements as relevant to group identities at different and progressively more micro levels, such as schools, classrooms, or peer groups.

These considerations explain why and how a chronotopic view of identities can be used as a tool for better accounting for the complex identity work that goes on within communities and to relate it more specifically to times, spaces, and practices without resorting to simplistic dichotomies between macro and micro contexts. This means that we must surrender the perceived clarity of existing and widely used identity categories and diacritics in order to gain analytical accuracy and precision.

Classroom Chronotopes and Super-Diverse Identity Work

Let us illustrate the deep embedding of identities within, and sensitivity toward, timespace arrangements by means of elements of analysis taken from an ethnographic study of a small community of practice. In so doing, we shall also sense the advantages of transcending the existing, *prima facie* obvious, identity categories and diacritics. The community in question is a super-diverse fifth-grade classroom in an inner-city school in Sicily (for a description of the project see De Fina 2015 and chapter 11 of this volume). The class was comprised of eighteen children (ten boys and eight girls) aged ten or eleven. Origins and mother tongues in the class varied, as seven boys and four girls were born in Sicily of Italian parents, five were born abroad of foreign parents and two were born in Sicily of Tunisian parents. Among the foreign-born children, three girls were from Bangladesh and one was from Sri Lanka, and one boy was from Morocco. Among the Sicilian children, one girl was a special-needs student. The class had two regular teachers and one special-needs teacher.

A traditional sociolinguistic approach to identities in this classroom would focus on teacher-students identities as basic to communication and as driving the analysis of interactions. However, a closer look at the daily practices of this community reveals how central timespace configurations are to its actual social organization, as well as how such timespace configurations affect relevant identity categories, roles, and negotiations regarding the practices performed by the group.

If we start by looking at temporal structure, we can easily see how chronotopes define the scenarios and the conditions within which identity work takes place. Daily lessons are regularly divided into activities that take up specific times (for example math lessons and foreign language lessons have the same duration but happen on different days) and require particular space configurations (desks aligned in certain ways, occupied by students sitting in places assigned to them by the teachers, teachers sitting or standing at the front center table or going around from desk to desk).

These timespace configurations are constitutive of what Goffman calls "front regions"—scenarios of interaction recognized as primary and official (1959, 106–60). Because of the routine and ritualized nature of these activities and interactions, expectations about roles and identities are rather fixed, since the rules of the game are similar for students and teachers in different schools in different times and space. Thus, for example, in terms of linguistic resources, the roles of student and teacher are strongly connected with the use of Italian as the official language. Deviation from such a rule leads to the potential attribution of identities that hold negative connotations for the deviant participant (such as 'bad,' 'undisciplined,' or, as in the case we will see below, 'ignorant' student). An example of these kinds of chronotopic role-behavior expectations can be found below. Note that utterances in Sicilian are transcribed in italics.

Example 1

1.	T1	((to Antonio)): Quand'è che ti sei andato a tagliare i capelli.
2.	Antonio	*Duminica.*
3.	T1	*Du-mi-ni-ca,*
4.		((voices)) @@@@@
5.	T1	*Du-minica*!
6.		*Duminica*@@@
7.		((voices)) @@@@

Translation

1.	T1	((to Antonio)): When did you go to cut your hair.
2.	Antonio	*Sunday.*
3.	T1	*Sun-day.*
4.		((voices)) @@@@@
5.	T1	*Sun-day.*
6.		*Sunday*@@@
7.		((voices)) @@@@

In this fragment Antonio answers a question posed by the teacher in Italian (line 1), with an utterance in Sicilian dialect (line 2). The use of Sicilian instantly provokes a reaction from the teacher, who imitates Antonio's response (lines 3, 5, and 6) while at the same time inciting laughter from the rest of the class (lines 4 and 7) and producing laughter herself (line 6). The teacher's reaction is immediately understood as a challenge to Antonio's identity thanks to the fixed, well-established (and historically sedimented) associations between official classroom discourse (which is expected within the timespace frame given) and Italian and the related indexical significance of dialect in this context. Since a child who does not speak proper Italian is regarded as unfit for interaction with a teacher, indexical associations of dialect with ignorance and lack of sophistication immediately arise.

However, this community of practice engages in many different types of activities and interactions whose recurrence in time and space also shape specific orders of indexicality associated with them. These are represented, for example, by "back region" activities. First, it must be noted that timespace configurations change completely in back regions (such as those created in peer communication during lessons) with respect to front space activities. For example, in back regions the timing of talk is affected by the disruption of role hierarchy that is implicit in these interactions. Talk needs to be uttered in spurts, at particular intervals of time (when teachers are not looking), and in whispers. Relevant space configurations for peer-to-peer talk include closer proximity between two interactants, single desks, and neighboring desks as focal points rather than the front table where the teacher speaks. In a sense, space is reconfigured even though no physical displacement of objects is taking place. Simultaneously, though, back regions may become front regions when school activities change, as in the case of breaks when students and teachers may move freely around the room, the position of desks can be altered, and certain particular desks may assume prominence as meeting places for the different groups that organize peer interaction. When children are on break, for example, the rules of the game also change completely and so do their inventories of relevant identities and the indexical associations that arise from linguistic (and other kinds of) behavior. Because behavior that has been cemented in back regions depends much more on specific routines and practices established by individual communities, as researchers we need to pay special attention to what happens there.

During back region exchanges and during all events in which peer-to-peer interaction is predominant, the way uses of linguistic resources are interpreted in terms of identity displays changes completely with respect to teacher-student interactions. For example, in this class neither the use of dialect nor of Italian seemed to regularly invoke specific indexicalities for all children. However, considering the sheer amount of speech in dialect versus Italian, dialect seemed to divide children along gender lines, while the type of uses of dialect also divided children along ethnic lines. So when males spoke in Sicilian the choice may have been relevant or not in terms of identity claims, while when foreign-born girls used Sicilian, inferences on their identity presentations always arose. In the case of both males and females, again, the possible indexicalitites related to dialect use are closely linked with activities and timespace arrangements. In the case of boys, for example, when they were in a "play" frame (with all the possible configurations in terms of proxemics, behavior timing, etc.), dialect may have been simply an unmarked choice, but if they were in a "fight" frame (with associated timespace arrangements) dialect became indexical of greater aggression and greater "manliness."

Let us look at an example. In the following fragment, Manlio and Nino have been involved in a fight during a back stage exchange.

Example 2

1.	Nino	*Chista è a me' matita stava disegnando io*!
2.	Manlio	((screaming)): MAESTRA MI FAI DARE LA MATITA DA NINO?
3.		Maestra G! ci stava disegnando Carlo!
4.	Nino	Mae non è quella è quella!
5.	Teacher	Tu l'hai finito il tuo disegno, TI SBRIGHI?
6.	Nino	E Manlio finiscila! *Tinni vai?*
7.	Manlio	*Suca!*
8.		(...)
9.	Manlio	*A cu ci rici suca?*
10.	Nino	*Suca a cu' ci u rici a* (...)
11.		(...)
12.	Nino	*Puo' ammuttari quanto vuoi tanto* (...)
13.	Manlio	*Nino è 'na munnizza!*

Translation

1.	Nino	*This is my pencil I was drawing with it!*
2.	Manlio	((screaming)) TEACHER CAN YOU TELL NINO TO GIVE ME THAT PENCIL?
3.		Teacher G! Carlo was drawing with it!
4.	Nino	Teacher it's not that! It's that!
5.	Teacher	You have finished your drawing, WILL YOU HURRY?
6.	Nino	And Manlio stop it! *Go away!*
7.	Manlio	*Fuck you!*
8.		(...)
9.	Manlio	*Who did you say fuck to?*
10.	Nino	*Who are you saying fuck you to* (...)
11.		(...)
12.	Nino	*You can push as much as you want* (...)
13.	Manlio	*Nino is trash!*

At the beginning, Manlio and Nino were fighting over a pencil. As we see when Manlio enters the front stage to address the teacher (whom he calls by her first name in line 3), he switches from dialect into Italian and Nino does the same. As Nino gets back to his fight with Manlio he starts in Italian but then continues in Sicilian when he goes from asking Manlio to stop, to ordering him to go away. The fight escalates into insults (lines 7–13) which are all exchanged in Sicilian. Given the presence of many similar instances in the recordings, it can be concluded that dialect is used in these cases to convey a "true man" identity.

At the same time, the entire exchange will be seen as constituting a breach of normal order in the front stage activity because children have broken rules that relate to proper behavior, which involves the invasion of each other's space (through the fight over the pencil), of the teacher's space (through screaming), and of the regular time frame of the lesson as they have spoken when they are supposed to be silent. Thus, while they can be cast as real men in their own sphere of action, they appear as troublesome disturbers in the official sphere of front stage interaction.

The existence of front stage and back stage regions in this community points to two important phenomena: the presence of reified and socially dominant chronotopes and chronotopic identities (the typical/acceptable teacher or student identity) which is widely recognized, and liminal ones (defined and developed in the back regions), but also to the *coexistence and interaction* of these regions and identities within communities. A full understanding of what goes on in the social processes observed here must consider all these possible interactions as constitutive of the life of such community, since no single "line" of regulated conduct suffices to explain these processes.

These examples illustrate how complex the relations between identities and contexts are but also how the conveying and negotiation of identities depends on recognizable and iterative timespace-behavior configurations. Above, we pointed toward the generalizability and fractality of chronotopic frames. We can add another item at this point: their ability to *interact*. The macroscopic chronotopes intersect and co-occur together with the microscopic ones and with several others in between, and the different chronotopic frames need to be constantly balanced against each other. (As observed above, the boss remains the boss during happy hour or the teacher may remain the teacher during breaks but they still need to "fit" into the happy hour or break frame.) And to go back to our example of the chronotope of youth culture, when we take a long and hard look at it in practice, we can see how it is composed of a large quantity of more specific chronotopic arrangements. Students, for instance, can perform much of their student practices from Monday till Friday in a university town, but perform their practices of friendship, family life, love relationships, entertainment, and local community involvement during the weekend in their home town. Throughout the week, however, both spaces are connected in intricate ways through various types of interactions, from mentioning names "from elsewhere" during a conversation to phone texting and social media contacts.

And this is dynamic as well: The freshman student will organize his/her life differently from the senior and more experienced student, just as the junior professional will act differently from the "old hands" (and note that the transition from newcomer to old hand can happen very quickly—the literature on the experiences of frontline soldiers in the Great War is replete with stories of "aging" overnight during their first battle). In the same way, children from the classroom we discussed can enact old and new identities in a bus that takes them to a school trip or in an entirely different space: a public auditorium where a competition among schools takes place.

Chronotopes shed light on various forms of cultural globalization in which local and global resources are blended in complex packages of indexically super-rich stuff. Hip-hop is a prime example, of course (Pennycook 2007; Westinen 2014), where the global AAVE templates of the genre are mixed with deep sociolinguistic locality—often strictly local dialects—and lyrics that bespeak the (chronotopic) condition of local youth-in-the-margins. Chronotopes, thus, also involve numerous scalar distinctions, which can be seen as the features that enable relatively unproblematic co-occurrences rather than conflictual ones. The appropriation of music and songs from different parts of the globe into very local contexts is an important element of identity work for youth in their play frames, while it would be read as an index of deviant identities in the context of a math lesson. As the singing of hip-hop songs can be used to project coolness and worldliness among young people belonging to peer groups across the globe, the singing of an American song performed *sotto voce* in Sicilian dialect during a lesson by a Moroccan boy can constitute a parallel act of affirmation of a worldly and young persona.

Conclusions: Back to Sociological Theory

The chronotopic nature of cultural practices helps us to get a precise grip on a number of other things as well, and this is where we need to return to our sociological classics. It may help us rethink *generations*, *anachronisms*, and *obsolete* cultural practices, for instance.

Except for census sociology, generations are notoriously fuzzy and puzzling units of sociocultural analysis. As Bourdieu and Passeron point out, the joint experience, several years long, of being a student in the same university and program does not cancel the power of reproduction of inequalities across "generations." Thus upper-class and working-class people may have attended the same schools, the same lectures, and the same movie or theater performances, and spent time in the same cafés and neighborhoods—none of that would reshuffle the transgenerational cards of social class difference, for the same experiences have different meanings and effects depending on this slower process of transmission and social dynamics. The "generation" of social class, therefore, is a slower and longer one than that of, say, intellectuals, engineers, or jazz lovers.

We would suggest that we can get a more precise grip on generations when we consider what was said above: that at any point in time, we organize our lives within interacting macroscopic and microscopic chronotopes. This means that at any point, our cultural repertoires might contain obsolete elements that no longer fit into the social order we now incorporate. Middle-aged people typically still have (and upon request, can perform) a vocabulary of slang obscenities developed during adolescence and hugely functional at that stage of life as symbolic capital for "cool" or "streetwise" peer group identities, but for the deployment of which very little occasion can be found in life at present. Similarly, many people still know small bits of mathematics jargon, of Latin and ancient Greek, learned in high school but never used again since the last day of school. Such resources remain in the repertoire and can, perhaps, be invoked on nostalgic storytelling occasions, but would have very little other function or value. As we move through "generations," the cultural stuff that defined the chronotopic arrangements of earlier stages remains in our repertoire, but becomes obsolete.

In that sense, the coexistence and interaction of chronotopes in cultural practices can also provide a basis for understanding *sociocultural change*. Entirely new phenomena are often tackled by means of very old and obsolete cultural resources—they are often managed by means of anachronisms, in other words. Thus, the key social identifier on Facebook (something entirely new, see further) is "friends"—one of the oldest notions in the vocabulary of social relations anywhere. The entirely new social community configuration of Facebook "friends" is thus anachronistically addressed and molded in the terms of an entirely different social community configuration.

Change can also be detected in the emergence of new phenomena within fixed chronotopic frames. As we discussed above, some models of social organization and interaction become more fixed and dominant than others, especially if they are supported by institutional structures of power. Thus good/bad student or teacher identities are based on relatively stable chronotopically organized practices and behaviors. And yet, when we analyze those practices with serious ethnographic precision we may see signs of change and perturbation of the social order. Such changes may be signaled by the appearance of new roles and new behaviors within well-structured, traditional activities. For example, Carnival celebrations in many European countries imply the dressing of children in clothes that evoke traditional figures in their culture, the consumption of certain foods, and the development of certain activities. The arrival of girls in a saree combined with the performance of bhangra dances and the eating of 'exotic' foods in a Sicilian school point to the possibility of change happening within the molds of established chronotopes.

At the same time, change can be conceptualized in different ways in different social groupings at different scales. New events, processes, and phenomena can be normal for a younger generation and simultaneously abnormal for an older one, while it is the older one that holds, in many social domains, the power to define, regulate, and judge these new things, and will typically do this by taking refuge in old, obsolete concepts or discourses. Such anachronisms are often the stuff of public debate and social conflict, as when the Baby Boomers are blamed for the creation of economic bubbles and overspending, the Woodstock generation is getting crucified for their tolerance of soft drugs, or the *soixante-huitards* (those who were students during the May 1968 revolt) are coming under attack for a lofty leftism or the "decay" of the moral order. It is this layered (heteroglossic) copresence of chronotopically organized practices, in a sometimes unbalanced and anachronistic way, that may lead us toward the finer grain of social order and social conflict.

What exactly is contested across generations? And how exactly does this contestation operate? Those are questions we might begin to explore now. Similarly, an awareness of the layered copresence of such practices may enable us to get a more precise understanding of the complex balance between "thick" and "light" communities and forms of membership therein. In earlier work, we pointed toward the—in our view increasing—importance of "light" communities on social media (i.e., communities not formed by the "thick" bounds of nationality, ethnicity, gender, class, and so forth but rather by the transient criteria of lifestyle, taste, and political inclination; see Blommaert and Varis 2015), where people gather and jointly act while focusing on objects, meanings, and practices.

Such "light" groups were never really privileged by sociology: the Durkheimian and Parsonian tradition displayed a marked preference, precisely, for the mechanisms of cohesion and integration that brought multiple disparate light communities together into a thick community—the nation, the tribe, the region, the family, the religious community, etc. (cf. Durkheim 1885; Parsons 1970; Lukes 1973). And we have seen above how Bourdieu and Passeron disqualify students as an "aggregate without consistency" that could surely not qualify as a "real" social group. Bourdieu and Passeron argue that a serious sociological study of students, due to the ephemeral character of this community, should not address the student community in isolation, for it could never be seen as entirely autonomous with respect to the larger, deeper forces of social class distinction (Bourdieu and Passeron 1964, 56). Thus, while students could be studied as a group, they could not be studied as a *group in itself*; the "groupness" of students must, rather, be constantly checked as to its features and characteristics against the thick community structures upon which it was grafted.

We can considerably refine Bourdieu and Passeron's relatively rudimentary base-superstructure model by paying attention to the specific chronotopic organization of behavior judged to be characteristic of specific groups. It would help us to see that the thick structures, while perhaps determining, are not necessarily dominant in explaining the social valuation of cultural practices typical of light communities, for the precise mode of valuation will be an effect of the specific chronotopic arrangements we address.

The largest social space on earth these days is the virtual space. And it is entirely new as a sociological and anthropological fact. We already mentioned how entirely new social environments such as social media are often approached from within anachronistic modes of social imagination; and the world of social analysis does not differ too much from that of lay practices in this respect. We can only point toward the possibility of an extraordinarily interesting line of research in the vein sketched here. There are specific timespace challenges raised by online culture: Contrary to the social imagination of classical sociology and anthropology, the social practices developed online involve no physical copresence but a copresence in a shared "virtual" space of unknown scale-dimensions, involve often an unknown number of participants (also often of unknown identities), combined with a stretchable time frame in which temporal copresence is not absent but complemented by an almost unlimited archivability of online communicative material. Thus, determining the specific chronotopic nature of cultural practices in a virtual cultural sphere promises to be a stimulating and thought-provoking exercise. Issues of scale—the internet is an immense social space—will call for ethnographic precision in analysis, so as to avoid rapid but unfounded generalizations of the kind "Facebook is a family of two billion people." Using a far more refined research tool, directed with great precision at the specific context-situatedness of any form of social practice, must help us ditch such sociological (as well as political) illusions and replace them with a more complex, but also far more accurate, image of what really goes on in that colossal social space, what exactly contributes to modes of social organization there, and how patterns of organization change over time.

Notes

This paper considerably revises, expands, and elaborates an argument sketched in earlier working papers (Blommaert 2015b; De Fina 2015), in turn building on Blommaert and Varis (2015). We are grateful to Ben Rampton, Piia Varis, Ico Maly, Jef Van der Aa, Max Spotti, Rob Moore, Sjaak Kroon, and Jos Swanenberg for numerous discussions on the topics covered in this paper.

1. Symbolic interactionism—a sociological discipline now nearly forgotten—provides fertile material for chronotopically organized identity work, and rereading some of these classic studies while building our argument was inspiring. The hardcore ethnographic stance of symbolic interactions, as we can see, points directly to the inevitable relevance of spacetime configurations for understanding social behavior. See Blumer (1969) for an influential discussion of symbolic interactionism.

References

Arnaut, Karel. 2016. "Superdiversity: Elements of an Emerging Perspective." In *Language and Superdiversity*, edited by Karel Arnaut, Jan Blommaert, Ben Rampton, and Massimiliano Spotti, 49–70. New York: Routledge.

Bakhtin, Mikhail M. 1981. *The Dialogic Imagination*. Edited by Michael Holquist. Austin: University of Texas Press.

Becker, Howard. 1963. *Outsiders: Studies in the Sociology of Deviance*. Glencoe, IL: Free Press.

Benwell, Bethan, and Elizabeth Stokoe. 2006. *Discourse and Identity*. Edinburgh: Edinburgh University Press.

Blommaert, Jan. 2005. *Discourse: A Critical Introduction*. Cambridge: Cambridge University Press.

———. 2015a. "Chronotopes, Scale and Complexity in the Study of Language in Society." *Annual Review of Anthropology* 44:105–116.

———. 2015b. "Chronotopic Identities." *Tilburg Papers in Culture Studies* 144. https://www.tilburguniversity.edu/upload/83e91218-34c2-4cdd-9fe3-b5a587c690e7_TPCS_144_Blommaert.pdf.

———. 2015c. "Commentary: Superdiversity Old and New." *Language & Communication* 44:82–88.

Blommaert, Jan, and Pia Varis. 2015. "Enoughness, Accent and Light Communities: Essays on Contemporary Identities." *Tilburg Papers in Culture Studies*, paper 139. https://www.tilburguniversity.edu/upload/5c7b6e63-e661-4147-a1e9-ca881ca41664_TPCS_139_Blommaert-Varis.pdf.

Blumer, H. 1969. *Symbolic Interactionism: Perspective and Method*. Berkeley: University of California Press.

Bourdieu, Pierre, and Jean–Claude Passeron. 1964. *Les Héritiers: Les Etudiants et la Culture*. Paris: Minuit. Reprinted in 1985. Page references are to the 1964 edition.

Bucholtz, Mary and Kira Hall. 2005. "Identity and Interaction: A Sociocultural Linguistic Approach." *Discourse Studies* 74 (5): 585–614.

Cicourel, Aaron. 2002. *Le Raisonnement Médical*. Edited by Pierre Bourdieu and Yves Winkin. Paris: Seuil.

De Fina, Anna. 2011. "Discourse and Identity." In *Discourse Studies: A Multidisciplinary Introduction*, edited by Teun A. van Dijk, 263–82. London: Sage.

———. 2015. "Ethnography as Complexifying Lenses." *Tilburg Papers in Culture Studies*, paper 146. https://www.tilburguniversity.edu/upload/fdf6bb3c-b036-49fb-a558-ce42026ed3ef_TPCS_146_DeFina.pdf.

———. 2016. "Diversity in School: Monolingual Ideologies Versus Multilingual Practices." In *Diversity and Super-Diversity: Sociocultural Linguistic Perspectives*, edited by Anna De Fina, Didem Ikizoglu, and Jeremy Wegner, in press. Washington, DC: Georgetown University Press.

De Fina, Anna, Deborah Schiffrin, and Michael Bamberg, eds. 2006. *Discourse and Identity*. Cambridge: Cambridge University Press.

Durkheim, Emile. 1885. *Les Règles de la Méthode Sociologique*. Paris: Flammarion. Reprinted in 2010. Page references are to the 1885 edition.

Goffman, Erving. 1959. *The Presentation of Self in Everyday Life*. New York: Anchor Books.

———. 1961. *Encounters: Two Studies in the Sociology of Interaction*. Indianapolis: Bobbs-Merrill.

———. 1963. *Behavior in Public Places: Notes on the Organization of Gatherings*. New York: Free Press.

Lukes, Steven. 1973. *Emile Durkheim: His Life and Work – A Historical and Critical Study*. Harmondsworth, Eng.: Penguin.

Parkin, David. 2016. "From Multilingual Classification to Translingual Ontology: A Turning Point." In *Language and Superdiversity*, edited by Karel Arnaut, Jan Blommaert, Ben Rampton, and Massimiliano Spotti, 71–88. New York: Routledge.

Parsons, Talcott. 1970. *Social Structure and Personality*. New York: Free Press.

Preece, Sian, ed. 2016. *The Routledge Handbook of Language and Identity*. London: Routledge.

Rampton, Ben. 2006. *Language in Late Modernity: Interactions in an Urban School*. Cambridge: Cambridge University Press.

Silverstein, Michael. 2015. "How Language Communities Intersect: Is 'Superdiversity' an Incremental or Transformative Condition?" *Language and Communication* 44:7–18.

Pennycook, Alastair. 2007. *Global Englishes and Transcultural Flows*. London: Routledge.

Westinen, Elina. 2014. "The Discursive Construction of Authenticity: Resources, Scales and Polycentricity in Finnish Hip Hop Culture." Ph.D. diss., Tilburg University and University of Jyväskylä.

Chapter 2

"Whose Story?"

Narratives of Persecution, Flight, and Survival Told by the Children of Austrian Holocaust Survivors

RUTH WODAK AND MARKUS RHEINDORF

SINCE 1999, A GROUP of descendants of former Austrian resistance fighters and refugees, born between 1940 and 1955, has held biannual meetings in Vienna. They call these meetings *Kinderjause* (a compound of German *Kinder* [children] and *Jause* [a casual meeting for tea, cake, or sandwiches]) in reminiscence of their common past. They share a past in the sense that in their childhood and youth they were an objectively marginalized social group due to their political stance and/or because of the re-migration of their parents.

The network they maintain was at no time relevant to their professions or careers. Almost all of them received higher education and studied at university. Some of them were able to achieve relevant, even prominent positions in society in their respective professional and political fields of action. There are striking parallels in their choices of profession: many are medical doctors, psychotherapists, scientists, teachers, artists, architects, and journalists. In most of their biographies, pivotal years in Austrian history (1965, 1968, 1986, and 2000) were also years of intense political activity.[1]

Their parents, most of them Jewish and resistance fighters or resistant in other ways, communists, or so-called "revolutionary socialists" (i.e., Trotskyites), were incarcerated in the National Socialists' concentration camps or were forced to leave Austria and became politicized in their exile. Their biographies differ hugely and their trajectories transcend European borders—ranging from exile in France, Belgium, England, China, or the Soviet Union, to the international brigades in Spain, enlisting in one of the Allied Armies or the Jugoslav Freedom Battalion, to imprisonment in numerous concentration camps and many other places of resistance and persecution. Many of those who returned from exile were not welcomed in Austria—many

Austrians did not want to hear about Nazi atrocities, felt guilty, or were frightened that they would have to return the stolen (i.e., Aryanized) homes, goods, or professional positions (Berger 2007; Knight 1988; Ziegler and Kannonier-Finster 1997; Maimann 1994; Kuschey 2008).

This paper draws on data collected during a research project in which twenty-nine semistructured and ten in-depth interviews were conducted with a subsample of this group, covering the biography of their parents, their flight and forced displacement, deportation and imprisonment, their own educational and professional biographies, their visions, and the charge placed upon them—often allegedly—by their parents to carry on the political work, the "never again."

We focus on the interviewees' narratives about flight and forced displacement of their parents (i.e., the remembered memories—or rather the retold tellings of memories—in the context of postwar Austria; Wodak et al. 1990) and analyze the timespace configurations (i.e., the particular chronotopes of their narratives; Bakhtin 1981; see related work in De Fina 2003a, 2003b). In other words, we are guided by the following research questions: How do the members of this group narrate their parents' biographies between 1938 and 1945? And how do they work through the cognitive dissonance of growing up in a country that had persecuted and displaced their parents, a place associated with the traumatic experiences of their parents? Our research is thus intimately linked to research on politics of the past, of memory, and of commemoration (Wodak et al. 1994; Uhl 2008).[2]

Following a brief description of our sample and the discourse-theoretical framework, we turn to the systematic analysis of narrative sequences. Due to the scope of this paper, we briefly summarize the initial corpus-linguistic analysis that allowed us to select topically salient narrative sequences by semantic macrostructures, and have to neglect details of the quantitative analysis. In the concluding discussion we argue that such studies on the intergenerational trauma of flight and persecution are of particular relevance today in light of the presence of more than sixty million refugees worldwide and the difficulties that even wealthy countries such as EU member states supposedly have finding adequate accommodation for refugees.

The Sample

Some of the interviewees were born in exile. In some of those countries of birth, the children were relatively safe, while in others (e.g., France) they survived the first years of their life in hiding and under false names. Some met a particularly tragic fate, their communist parents falling victim to Stalinist terror in the Soviet Union or deportation to Siberia. Some of our interviewees were born in such circumstances and survived the banishment.

Most of the interviewees were born after 1945. In particular, the Jewish children among them had no grandparents, which was rare even in the postwar generation. While they grew up in socially marginalized circumstances, they did so in an intellectually privileged environment: Their parents saw themselves not as victims but as victors in the worldwide struggle between fascism and freedom. Their children were their hope, they saw in them the future of the world, and that world (from a communist or socialist perspective) was a ubiquitous topic of discussion at home, with friends, and in the child and youth organizations in which most of our interviewees were also socialized. The distinct trauma of their parents, through persecution, imprisonment, resistance, and years of war in Allied or underground armies, was rarely if at all spoken about in the family or youth organizations. Indeed, postwar silence surrounded the narratives of the victims as well as the perpetrators (Wodak 2011; Schröter 2013), although, of course, reasons for silence varied significantly.

Toward the end of the 1960s, almost everyone in the group was active in the student movement, many in leading roles. It was only in the 1970s, when the first of them entered their professions, developed individual life plans, and the Left outside the Parliament fragmented into many parts, that the decade-long cohesion of the group *Kinderjause* partly dissolved, only to tighten again ten years later under the impression of the Waldheim controversy (Wodak et al. 1990; Mitten 1992).[3] At this time, many of them became actively engaged in the newly founded Green Movement, and some even took political positions.

Our sampling criteria consisted of the following elements:

- Gender
- Jewish or non-Jewish
- Parents: resistance, flight, forced displacement, exile or imprisonment, underground
- Born during or after the war (in AUT, CH, F, GB, SU)[4]

Tables 2.1 and 2.2 below summarize the sample distribution.

Table 2.1. Sample distribution

No. of interviews (semistructured)	Second generation	Third generation
Total	29 (2 siblings)	11
Male	19	6
Female	10	5
Jewish	20	
Parent(s) fled into exile	20	
Parent(s) imprisoned	15	
Active in the resistance	23	

Table 2.2. Sample distribution by date of birth

No. of interviews (semistructured)	Second generation
Total	29 (2 siblings)
Born 1939–1944	14
Born 1945–1946	3
Born 1947–1953	12

The semistructured interviews were conducted by experienced interviewers, the in-depth interviews by E. B. and R. W. All interviews were first transcribed broadly in their entirety, while important segments were closely transcribed where necessary for the detailed qualitative analysis (see below). The interviewees were asked about their childhood, school years, reasons for choice of profession, their political involvement, and their opinions about the sociopolitical development of postwar Austria. Interspersed were questions about the biographies of their parents and grandparents. We focused specifically on the information that the children had received about the flight and persecution of their parents, how these had survived and where, and in which kind of contexts—if at all—the family had talked about the Nazi terror, the oppression, persecution, and flight or deportation. Moreover, we focused on the effect and impact the narratives of such traumatic experiences had had on the interviewees, how they had coped with this knowledge, and with whom they had shared this information. In the in-depth interviews, moreover, it was possible to challenge the obvious absence of much information, of what had remained unsaid and how the children, finally, assessed their parents' lives and decisions when struggling for survival. For example, did the interviewees perceive their parents as victims or heroes? How did they reconcile the many contradictory emotions and impressions accompanying such fragmented and frequently tragic lives?

Theoretical Framework

Memories, History, and Narrative

The analysis of narratives (i.e., narrative structures, characteristic patterns, actors, and actions) allows insight into socially grounded and shared "collective stories." In particular, personal, traumatic events are usually framed and recounted in narratives. They serve to place fragmentary, incomprehensible events in a quasi-coherent framework that is not simply individually but socially "meaningful." We would thus expect members of a social group with a shared past—whether known to each other personally or not—to use similar narratives or a similar repertoire of narrative elements to give meaning to this past. The history emerging from biographical interviews as a post-factum and meaning-infused narrative is thus always a construction: Contemporary historiography highlights the lack of reliability in narrated memories with respect to the "historical truth," but this does not invalidate interviews or narrated memories as subjects of scientific inquiry; quite the opposite, it opens them to qualitative research into the individual and collective (discursive) construction of history through life stories. Accepted histories are thus the result of a social process through which it is decided which stories about past events can carry the majority's values and perception of the world, and are thus accepted as memories—which makes this process a field of conflict and controversy (Heer et al. 2008).

Investigating this interplay is about relationships between facts, interpretations of events, and the collective and subjective experience. Histories consist of such normatively established relations, of interpretations of connections between people, places, events, and actions in time (i.e., narratives). Collective memory could thus be termed a collection of traces of events that are significant for the historical trajectory of a specific group, endowed with the capacity to relive these shared memories on the occasion of rites, celebrations, and public festivities (Halbwachs 1985). This approach has been applied to groups of various sizes, ranging from transnational commemorative communities to nationalism, social groups, and the family as a unit of social cohesion (Achugar 2016; Keppler 1994; Welzer 2001).

As a conceptual framework for our linguistic analysis, we draw on Bakhtin's notion of the chronotope as "a unit of analysis for studying language according to the ratio and characteristics of the temporal and spatial categories represented" (1981, 425). Insofar as the chronotope is both a cognitive concept and a feature of narrative, it provides a conceptual frame to discuss the complex interplay between the wider cultural context, shared cultural norms and discourses, personal experience, and the situational context of telling a story to an audience. The chronotope of a particular narrative is defined by the way in which the telling of events is "deformed" (Holquist 1990, 113)—that is, does not follow chronology or other accepted forms of narrative. In the telling of any story, Bakhtin argues, the construction of meaning must negotiate a chronotope, making it an "ideological index" (1981, 258). This observation points to the significance of chronotopes in narratives as a social practice through which memories are scripted and shared, thus bridging the individual and collective. Among members of a social group, and in a particular setting, the specific character of a shared chronotope is seen as plausible, common sense, even natural. Precisely because time and space are such basic, fundamental aspects of human experience, the way they are indexed in narratives carries the weight of the seemingly self-evident.

While Bakhtin's claim to a "cognitive" aspect of the chronotope remains relatively vague compared to the textual analysis, more recent discourse analysis proposes socio-cognitive approaches to stored memories and stories: Van Dijk (2009) suggests that every linguistic perception and evaluation is based on a previous filtering through cognitive schemata. Perceptions are fitted, understood, and remembered according to these internalized schemata (or memory patterns). Through this, however, they are also changed according to the respective collective and subjective experiences. Such schemata are not biological but acquired through socialization (Reisigl and Wodak 2001; Wodak and Reisigl 2015).

Remembering the Holocaust

Holocaust narratives, Schiffrin (2003, 538–39) argues, as intertextually linked, generic narratives, may present a (partial) solution to the conundrum of having no words to describe the unspeakable: "Because of the radical break between trauma and culture, victims often cannot find categories of thought or words to contain or give shape to their experience" (Schiffrin 2002, 313). Arguably more so than in most narrative situations, the authenticity and credibility of the teller/telling rest primarily on personal experience and thus on a correspondingly positioned (i.e., "performed") narrative voice. The means of this positioning are manifold and yet typical: "Credibility, i.e. the possibility for a story or a narrator to be accepted as truthful, is often based on the idea of the primacy of personal experience over other forms of experience and knowledge, hence the widely held view of narrative as a privileged genre for communicating personal experience. . . . Embedding narratives into accounts increases their plausibility and . . . people gain credibility through narratives because these contain many details and give particular vividness to the reconstruction of facts" (De Fina and Georgakopoulou 2012, 137). The accounts into which the narratives about the Holocaust, the persecution, flight, and return of their parents are embedded by the interviewees are also accounts of the circumstances of their *knowing* or rather *not-knowing*. This is often realized through disclaimers such as "I don't really know," "I was not there," or "I actually know very little," realizing the opposite of story ownership (i.e., "story dis-ownership").

We are, moreover, dealing with "retellings" or "retold stories" characterized by specific features distinguishing them from other narratives: They are often short, succinctly formulated, devoid of detail, and abstract (typified and functionalized actors). In their retellings, they also become increasingly intertextual, use certain culturally established, shared, and thus discursively available patterns (including phrasings), and are in this sense *metanarratives* (Schiffrin 2006, 275). They are a special kind of social construct insofar as they reflect well-known and shared narratives and build on them (De Fina and Georgakopoulou 2012, 149). Indeed, we encountered similar stories as metonymic examples of Nazi atrocities such as a narrative on life as a prisoner: One of the SS guards throws the prisoner's cap over the fence and then cruelly threatens to shoot him if he does not climb over the fence to retrieve it, an escape attempt for all to see. Escape attempts, of course, imply a death penalty. Since both of the prisoner's actions will give the SS guard reason to murder him, the prisoner is caught in a lethal double bind.

In the process of their retelling, narratives often develop into two types: *generic* or *scenic narratives*. Narratives become generic through decontextualization, losing their specifics (De Fina and Georgakopoulou 2012, 108; see "generic accounts" in Baynham 2005, 15). More specifically, it is a well-documented fact that narratives about the Holocaust, flight, and persecution during World War II often take generic forms, even in the case of never-publicized family stories. This happens in the course of "retellings," as even the second telling of a narrative already shows narrative patterns and scenarios shared across speakers, often providing a way for the person telling the story to come to terms with traumatic events. Schiffrin recognizes in this a general function of narratives as a means of making the world meaningful, explainable, and manageable to oneself and others (2002, 313).

In retelling, narratives may also become "scenic narratives" that rely on a specific kind of detailing (e.g., quoted or enacted dialogue) for their authenticity while also maintaining their decontextualized character (Wodak 1986). In scenic narratives, the interviewee performs the incident by reenacting the experience via direct quotations and elaborating the complication of the story. A polyphonous text emerges, containing many voices: those of the parents, perpetrators, and victims, as well as bystanders. Frequently, scenic narratives are missing the orientation at the outset and a coda at the end. Many emotions are expressed, via intonation, code-switching, hesitation, pause, or indeed, by embarrassed laughter or crying. The teller relives the experience as told by their father or mother. In both cases, the underlying process can be understood as entextualization or textualization: "The process of rendering discourse extractable, of making a stretch of linguistic production into a unit—a text—that can be lifted out of its interactional setting" (Bauman and Briggs 1990, 70).

This allows the telling of lived experience to become "text" and thus to be used and reused in many different contexts (Jacquemet 2005, 202). Public or publicized narratives have strong influence even on very private stories (e.g., family histories), in the sense of the above-mentioned intertextuality: Narrative is one of the social practices through which individual and collective memories are negotiated and constructed among social groups (Achugar 2007, 523). Norrick (1997) refers to these as "familiar tales," while Bruner (2001, 29) recognizes in them an underlying interlinking or "entrenchment" of narrative(s) in culture.

Methodology

Working with an extensive corpus of interview material, we feel that it is a sound research strategy to integrate quantitative and qualitative methods, using results obtained through the former to guide the application of the latter. We used corpus linguistics to identify semantic macrostructures in the interviews (second generation only). Macrostructures define the global coherence of discourse (in the sense of constituting the semantic basis for a range of pragmatic aspects such as implicit and explicit categorizations, tacit knowledge, conclusion rules, and narrative settings) and contribute to the local coherence between propositions (van Dijk 2009, 4–5). While the semantic macrostructures of discourse underlying a single text, as demonstrated by van Dijk (2009), can be reconstructed by qualitative analysis of same text, corpus-linguistic analyses may provide an alternative approach to more extensive material.

We first identified keywords by frequencies, then calculated keyness in relation to a reference corpus of biographical interviews also conducted in Austria using WordSmith software. The keywords were then clustered into semantic fields to identify semantic macrostructures. The clusters indicate 1) the centrality of family, especially mother, father, and grandparents; 2) the explicit addressing of the narrative situation; 3) the importance of political terms, organizations, and figures; 4) events and experiences related to persecution, emigration, flight, and return; and 5) historical reference points such as dates, places, and events. In contrast, work, career, and personal life play a subordinate role. The homogeneity of these macrostructures across the corpus is also remarkable: The items with the highest overall keyness occur in 100 percent of the interviews, and more than 50 percent of the words with significant keyness occur in over 66 percent of the interviews.

The reference corpus allows relating keyness to frequency as a more specific measure of specificity of semantic macrostructures. It shows how the *Kinderjause* interviews differ from the reference corpus between a measure of 1 (the highest ratio; i.e., frequency in our corpus matching keyness 100 percent) to 0 (the lowest possible ratio; i.e., frequency—no matter how high—is identical in both corpora). In table 2.3. below, frequency serves as a secondary indicator to determine salience.

Table 2.3. Keywords sorted for keyness/frequency-ratio and frequency (rank 1—25)

Keyword	Frequency	% of texts containing	Keyness in relation to reference corpus
Kommunistisch(e/n), Kommunist(en/in), KPÖ, KP – *Communist(s), Communist Party of Austria*	679	100	679
Jüdische, Jude(n), Jüdin, Jüdisch(en), Judentum – *Jewish, Jew(s), Jewishness*	425	100	425
FÖJ – *Free Austrian Youth*	189	96	189
Nazi(s) – *National Socialists*	92	75	92
Linke(n), links – *Leftist(s), left*	91	69	91
verfolgen, verfolgt – *Persecute, persecuted*	82	92	82
Stubenbastei (name of Viennese school)	79	77	79
Israel	76	62	76
Sowjetunion – *Soviet Union*	69	62	69
Moskau – *Moscow*	60	42	60
Lager – *Camp*	58	62	58
Peter (name)	53	62	53
Emigration, emigriert – *Emigration, emigrated*	52	44	52
Identität – *Identity*	48	65	48
Tod – *Death*	46	62	46
Milieu	38	50	38
Auschwitz	37	38	37
Sturmvögel (youth association)	36	52	36
Dachau	35	31	35
Umgekommen – *Perish*	33	62	33
Mauthausen	32	31	32
Stalin	32	58	32
Außenseiter – *Outsider*	31	38	31
Gewerkschaft – *Union*	30	15	30
Kinderland (program to send children to safety)	30	42	30

Adjusted for the keyness-to-frequency ratio, nineteen macrostructures were identified. The highest salience was found for

1. political organizations, movements, and parties, represented in part metonymically by historical figures and leaders (Marx, Stalin, Kreisky);
2. Jewishness/being Jewish;
3. persecution, imprisonment, and death (and the places associated);
4. emigration, flight (and the countries or cities associated);
5. Nazis, the Gestapo, and National Socialism as such; and
6. identity and the self in relation to country/nation, family, heritage, and politics.

Also significant with a ratio of at least 0.75 are references to

7. fear;
8. memory, memories, and remembering;
9. resistance, struggle, and fight;
10. return, arriving, and having survived;
11. the invasion and annexation of Austria; and
12. extended family.[5]

This allows a more differentiated understanding of the salient semantic macrostructures in our corpus: for example, while close family members appear with very high frequency, this of itself is not significant for biographical interviews. In this paper, we focus mainly on the macrostructure of persecution and flight (3 and 4 in our list) in order to explore the individual and shared chronotopes as well as forms of telling and retelling. As elaborated above, we assume that such patterns allow insight into the many ways in which the interviewees cope with the traumatic pasts of their parents and of their own positionings, assessment of the life stories of their parents, and their narratives' relevance for the present, for identification or distancing from the past and their parents' political mission and beliefs. Moreover, the impact of the more general postwar silencing in Austrian society could be, we argue, observed.

Results

Narrative Veil

Remarkably, the situation and conditions of telling are continually foregrounded and negotiated for the narratives in our data: These conditions are presented like a veil of not-knowing or not-knowing-well, of partly remembering and not-having-been-told, framing the narratives of flight, persecution, and imprisonment themselves as a metacommentary. In the words of Erich,[6] recounting and quoting the command of silence—even of never-knowing—placed upon him by his mother: "You may never mention this [...] you may never know about this." Whether anything, how much, what, and when anything was actually told our interviewees by their parents differs widely in each case.

This narrative veil is constructed through the ways in which the narrators relate themselves, the "I" of the respective narrative, to the contents narrated—typically stories told by their parents. It is noteworthy that it seems to be of relatively little importance what and how much was actually recounted by their parents; the veil is always constructed around and throughout the narratives. This is illustrated by a quantitative analysis of the (verb) collocates of first-person personal pronouns in our data (see tables 2.4. and 2.5. below).

In relation to previous research on Holocaust narratives told by survivors—for which both "story ownership" and the authenticity that comes with it are highly relevant—we thus see a stark contrast. The interviewees continually emphasize that their parents' stories are not their own, that they were not "there," did "not experience" them, "know nothing" or "next to nothing." The function and positioning within the narrative is thus analogous to "ownership" in the sense of a framing meta-narrative used particularly at the beginning and ending of narrative passages, but is also used intermittently as a form of reassurance—here an assurance of not laying claim to the story—vis-à-vis the audience (i.e., the interviewers), but to the opposite effect.

The linguistic means used to this effect are devices indicating vagueness as highlighted in the following passage:

Table 2.4. Verbal processes in interviewees' self-representation (I, me, my, mine; we, us)

Process	Agents	Patients
Verbal	17	75
Material	41	36
Mental	28	186
Relational	—	19

Table 2.5. Collocates in interviewees' self-representation (I, me, my, mine; we, us)

Collocate	Frequency
Wissen – *Know*	41
Erzählen – *Tell*	31
Glauben – *Believe*	28
Erinnern – *Remember*	27
Sagen – *Say*	22
Denken – *Think*	15
Eindruck – *Impression*	12
Fragen – *Ask, question*	11
Beschäftigen – *Trouble, occupy one's mind*	9
Sehen – *See*	8
Wundern – *Wonder*	4

Example 1

> It was a topic, not only but still largely in a *very general form.* The concrete story I *know very little.* I know that my parents fled from Austria in June 1938 and actually meant to go to France, but went via Italy. They did send their whole luggage to France, *as far as I know,* but my mother went to the Swiss consul in Italy. *Why, I don't know,* however, and she bribed him with jewelry, as she told me, and thereby got entry into Switzerland. Then my parents spent the wartime from 1938 to 45 in Switzerland. My father was lucky not being imprisoned like most others. *I really don't know anything specific, it was never this concrete.* (Peter)

Knowing and certainty are commented on as taboos imposed, in some cases, by the interviewees' parents, right after telling.

Example 2

> My mother told me things and then: "Seal of silence, you may never speak about this, you may never mention this." . . . "You must not do anything to know, this someone or that someone came back." But we did not go into this afterwards, because we said this exceptional situation should not revisited after the war. "But it was him and it was her, but you may never know this." (Erich)

The paradoxical, indeed impossible command imposed on the narrator as a child is never to tell, indeed never to know, what his mother just told him. Indeed, deontic modality as in the above commands and prohibitions characterizes the narrative framing of many interviews in our corpus. Speaking from such a position, of course, contaminates the epistemic modality of storytelling.

"Narrative affectivity," according to De Fina and Georgakopoulou (2012, 65), is highly significant insofar as it not only frames the narrative but also gives it coherence by involving the narrator as a character in the story he or she is telling. The disclaimers we identified are, indeed, "story openings" and as such "consequential for what is going to come" (49). It is at these critical junctures in the narratives (i.e., junctures between the told world—which has two timeframes: recounting memories told by their parents and recounting being told—and the world of telling—the interview), that we find the narrators performing the *narrative veil.* Our narrators position themselves in two worlds, but also have to relate to a third: the traumatic experiences of their parents. It is this world at two removes that they narrate as people who were never there, who were told nothing, little, or not enough, and who are now called on to tell someone else's stories, which they only know very vaguely or were even told to forget.

Retold Stories

Such "retold stories" or "retellings" sometimes rise to a level of generic quality that the narrators themselves cannot help but notice and comment on (De Fina and Georgakopoulou 2012, 49). One of our interviewees, in reflecting on her lack of certainty and authenticity of the stories she told, referred to them as "family legends."

Example 3

> That was the first time I realized how many family legends are being told. For example: my father's flight. My father had been arrested as a communist and could only leave the country with great difficulty, after the Nazis were already here. After the annexation, he was helped by a Nazi lawyer. Even he always said that, who then gave him his passport and said "I envy you for being able to leave." That is one of those; that is something of a mythologizing of the charming Viennese. Because my parents grew up in Vienna before the Holocaust and were very patriotic Austrians. [. . .] This legend, for example: All of them, all the Jews were taken out of the trains at the border as a rule, just to pester them, keeping them there so long that the train would leave without them and they had to take the next train. My father, and I by the way could never imagine this, is supposed to—according to family legend—to have run after the train, jumping on it and reaching Brussels, and no one was there, because people already knew that if you told them you would arrive by this train or that train, they wouldn't be. That was a family legend. I always found it funny, above all because I always saw my father as not doing any sports and could never imagine him at 30 jumping after a train. Ok. Then I read the letters and my father's first letter came from Brussels and did not mention running after a train or almost missing a train. (Sabine)

This narrative is representative of our interviewees' retelling of their parents' narratives—questioning the authenticity of generic, retold stories and one's ability to really know what happened while retelling the stories verbatim—and also illustrates another characteristic: the focus on places (and space in general) rather than time (and dates specifically).

Sabine goes on to describe the "funny" and sometimes "a little heroic" wartime stories of her parents, emphasizing stock elements: "We were getting married in the middle of the war and there was an air raid. And we were going to the movies and there was an air raid but we still went to the movies." The interlinking of private, family stories and generic, publicized stories is characteristic of coping with exile and emigration experience.

The narratives of persecution and, sometimes, also of support and help from friends or strangers, whether scenic or generic, are always situated in space rather than time, as in the following account of a death march:

Example 4

> Toni always told me how she was hidden when she had Typhus. How Viola, her Polish friend and a doctor, cut the tattooed number from her arm because she had been sentenced to death. How they fed her and made her well again. How they marched. That was the march from Auschwitz to Ravensbrück . . . that was a little heroic. . . . Friends and comrades, who were also communists, on this march equipped her with everything. It was winter and they gave her clothes. And more and more they threw away all those things because they could no longer carry them. (Sabine)

Timeless Places in Private and/or Public Discourse

Analysis of key elements in the narratives shows that certain macrostructures or topics are not simply treated euphemistically or vaguely (as by nominalization or passivation) but also through the verbal processes used to progress the narrative. In terms of a broad categorization as by Systemic Functional Linguistics (Matthiessen and Halliday 1997), the narrators rarely speak of perpetrators performing actions (material processes) and, if so, not in relation to victims; they speak of victims not as fleeing but as arriving at, travelling from or, most frequently, as simply being in places (relational processes). These lexico-grammatical choices inform the above-noted prevalence of space over time.

A closer quantitative and qualitative analysis of narrative passages related to World War II and the Holocaust—in contrast to events before and after—shows that very few specific temporal references (e.g., dates) are used and that most temporal referencing is vague and relational (e.g., "then," "back then," "now," "later," "before," "after"). This pattern is so consistent that we see a quantitative cluster of specific dates leading up to 1938, the beginning of the war and flight for many, as a significant rupture in normal spacetime experience; similarly, we see a second cluster of dates beginning with 1945, the end of the war, anchoring the narratives in a specific time again. Between these caesuras, however, the narratives largely lack temporal specificity. At the same time, the events during this time are linked to specific as well as generic places ("the camp" or "a camp"). In the particular chronotope of the analyzed narratives, these are places outside of time, particularly outside of official historical chronology and military history. They become metonymic, condensing the many movements during the respective "journey"; in many ways, they are all similar, encompassing a range of different activities in order to survive—which the interviewees have not been told about in any detail and which are thus left to imagination.

The loss of time can also be measured quantitatively, showing peaks at biographically significant dates (1938, 1945, and 1968; see figure 2.1) as well as the absence of absolute temporal reference between 1938 and 1945 (see figure 2.2).

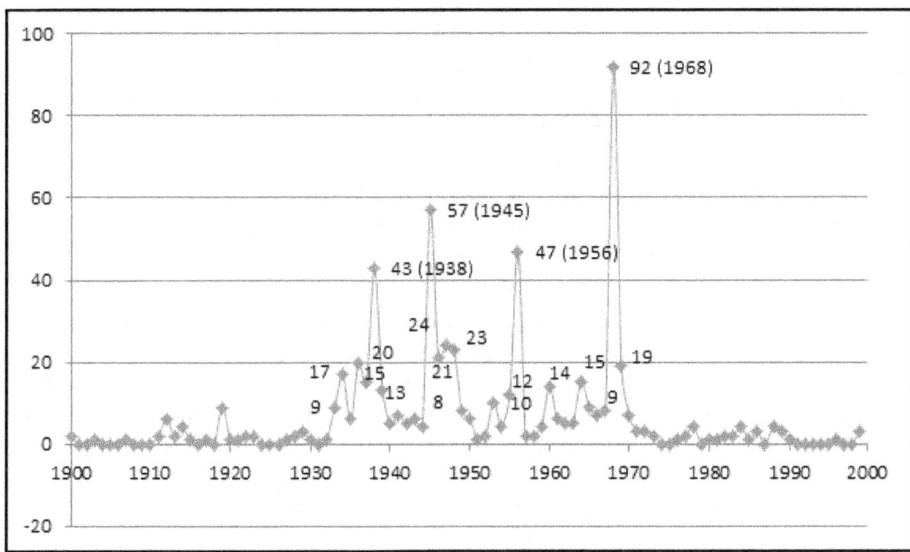

Figure 2.1. Temporal reference in the narratives (days, weeks, months, or years, all dates)

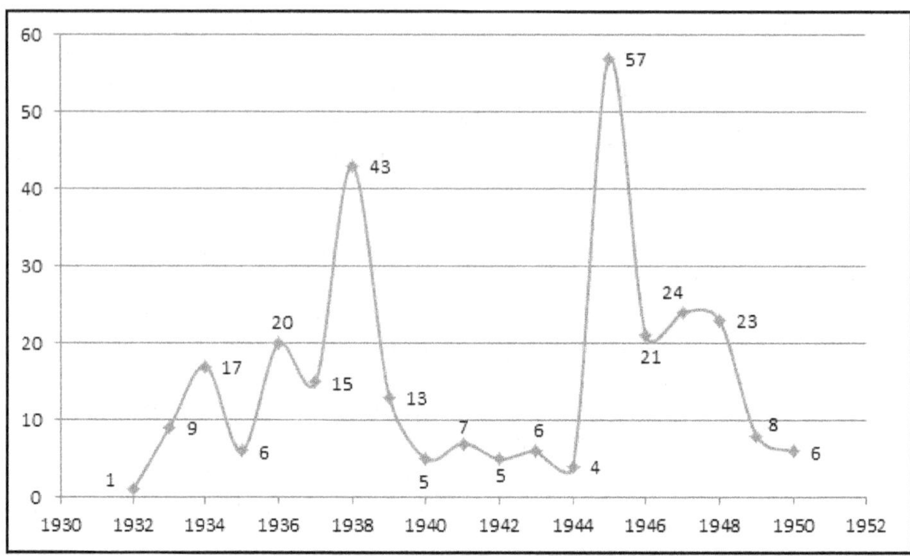

Figure 2.2. Temporal reference in the narratives (days, weeks, months, or years 1930 to 1950)

Within those temporal boundaries of 1938 and 1945, virtually all temporal reference is relative, vague, or expressed through spatial reference. Even the Holocaust itself is thus envisaged as a static place and space, very much like previous research has documented it for *being-in-the-war* or *being-imprisoned-in-a-camp* for World War II. In such places, metonymically representing what are often very complex configurations of personal experience, ideology, historical events, and public discourse, narratives can condense into poignant, scenic narratives.

In her research on the construction of time and space as orientation elements in narratives that recount disorienting experiences, De Fina (2003a) investigated orientation management in storytelling and argued that such elements connect narrators and interlocutors to both micro- and macro-social contexts. Because narrative provides a tool for configuring experience in particular ways, the detailed linguistic analysis of what Bakhtin terms chronotopes thus allows analysis to trace links between narratives and social contexts, but it also gives access to a specific group's shared experiential world referenced through the narratives—which may or may not correspond to that of other groups.

While previous research on "orientation" (Labov and Waletzky 1967) or "positioning" by the narrator (Bamberg 1997; Wortham 2001) had posited temporal ordering as a basic principle of narrative organization, De Fina convincingly shows that this does not, in fact, apply to all narratives and that the relationship and relative weight of time and space in narrative depends on social context, teller, content, etc. Orientation is thus not a matter of simply providing content but an occasion for narrators to negotiate and build shared understandings of experiences in specific contexts (De Fina 2003a, 370–72).

In most narratives and hence the standard view of narrative, the narrator is in control of the telling and orientation sections and clauses function to identify time and place. Narrators who are lost, however, in the sense that they struggle to reconstruct complex spatial and time movements in the story based on limited information and knowledge (De Fina 2003a, 371–72), will show different linguistic behavior. Precision in some passages, by contrast, is symbolically significant in such narratives of disorientation. Narrators use it to mark the beginnings of significant passages, often told as scenic narratives, with detailed time references in sharp contrast with subsequent references that are either absent or vague. We are thus dealing with a group-specific epistemic community and a temporally abstracted chronotope that is at least partly disconnected from the official, consensual historical discourse about 1938 to 1945 in Austria.

The change from another chronotope to the timeless space of war, flight, and persecution is apparent in the following passage. The interviewee here invests great effort in giving precise dates, but abruptly stops with the reference "before Hitler invaded."

Example 5

> She **left home** very early and was very young then as she worked in this communist something, **there, there**, and did all sorts of things. She then after 1934, I assume, I don't know, no, that must have been around 1935, 1936, **there** she was then locked up as a communist, the communists were already illegal then, since 1934, but that must have been a little later. She was born in 1913, so she was, I think, 24 or so, that would have been 1936 or so then, yes, that's about right. She then, relatively shortly before Hitler invaded, was released and that is why at once—she was known because of that and would have been in danger—and she then, with a forged passport that she got from the party, went first to **Switzerland**, which she felt was terrible, because she was working **in the house of some rich Jewish family there,** but my mother is so not into housework things that I cannot imagine that at all. She found that terrible, she hates **Switzerland** since then and then she **went to England** and there she worked **in this Austrian Center, where** they also had a magazine and **there** she sort of began with her journalistic work, which she then later continued. (Peter)

This change of chronotope is evident in all narratives of flight, persecution, and emigration we analyzed. These are, in fact, narrated as a sequence of places and states (of being in a place), typically named as metonyms and/or euphemisms for the flight. This form of narration reflects the situation of refugees during wartime, making it from one place to another for safety. As narrative, however, it deviates from accepted historiographical discourse in Austria, which strongly focuses on dates and moments in time (turning points, individual decisions, etc.; see Kühberger 2015). It does not match earlier discourse either, in which Austrians' roles in National Socialism were downplayed or indeed denied. The fact that flight and persecution, even imprisonment, are narrated as a series of states rather than something done to the interviewees' parents, does not simply avoid blaming the perpetrators, it more comprehensively deletes them as a way of dealing with trauma (Zajde 2011). Even in these absences and silences, trauma is inscribed into these narratives and passed on with them. War and all its horrors thus become a place one could hope to leave, as expressed in the following.

Example 6

> **Out of the war** they only, well I knew, my father was, would even have had a visa **to Brazil**. He learnt Portuguese and <u>then</u>, as far as I know, he voluntarily said, No, he is not going **there**, but going **out of the country**. He went **to Belgium**. They were <u>always</u> in this kind of, such Jewish organizations. This having a safety net **in a foreign country**. My father's brother was <u>already</u> **there** and was **there**, I think, <u>already</u> in love with a Belgian woman. Insofar my father **there**—Well, my mother was **in Spain** and <u>then</u>, then she could not **come back**, but **to Spain** she also went **from France**. She did not come **from Austria**, but she was <u>already</u> **in France** <u>before that</u>. I believe, <u>in 35</u> she <u>already</u> went **to France**, because she had a cousin **there**. She then went **to Spain**, <u>then</u> she said, that she actually wanted **back to Vienna** <u>one more time</u> to convince her father, to leave, but the Communist Party, so my mother told it, took away their passports **in Spain**. (Gregor)

Here, euphemistic references imply tacit knowledge (Zappavigna 2013): To "go to Spain" in the above context means to take an active part in the armed fight against fascism; to "be at Morzinplatz" (as referred to in another narrative) means to be incarcerated, questioned, and likely tortured by the Gestapo. Frequently, this knowledge characterizes the historical and political frame of reference for the *Kinderjause* group. In part, it corresponds to the frame of reference shared by the majority in Austria: "to be a Russian prisoner of war" or "to be a Yugoslavian prisoner of war" entails very specific experiences for former Wehrmacht soldiers as per generic narratives. Such references outline places that are inscribed into the collective memory and discourse in Austria, passed on through numerous narratives and experiences, denoting pain and suffering that are no longer mentioned.

In part, such referencing or naming of places is problematic even in the shared framework. This is illustrated by repairs and renaming in the narratives. One interviewee spoke with matter-of-factness about the murder of her parents, creating distance through expressing irritation over terminology.

Example 7

> That is, so to speak, the family on my father's side. On my mother's side, both of course died **in the Holocaust**, **Shoah** or whatever you want to call it, my grandfather however died here **in Vienna**, but allegedly, he was allegedly hit in the pogroms with a stone on the head or so, there **in Steyr**, so that he died, and my grandmother was taken **to Maly Trostinec** and murdered **there**. I cannot speak about this very well (*chokes dramatically, as if on her own words*). (Edith)

Discussion

Regarding the commonalities of the *Kinderjause* group, we note that dealing with their parent's stories is a common experience. We see shared understandings and shared knowledge, but also a specific way of talking about time and space that has become part of their common discourse. In sum, we were able to show that the *Kinderjause* interviewees employ a range of narrative strategies in dealing with their parents' persecution, resistance to Naziism, and struggle for survival during World War II, each of which serves a particular function:

- Generic narratives metonymically represent atrocities;
- Retellings manifest and comment on the family dynamics of passing on remembrance;
- Narrative veiling focuses on the narrator's epistemic uncertainty in remembering, acknowledging both the silences surrounding their parents' past as well as limitations of their own will/interest to "know"; and
- The chronotope of timeless space deletes perpetrators and the day-to-day struggle of survival; scenic narrations serve as entry points to emotional trauma.

On the level of linguistic realizations/means, temporal reference is not used for orientation in the narrative segments relating to the period between 1938 and 1945. In absence of time as the default way of narrative sequencing, spatial reference provides a means of marking story episodes with specific events, evaluations, and or resolutions. The narrators often struggle at these transition points. Although space and relational or vague time reference are also combined, space is often the only element of orientation or works as an anchoring device for any time reference. In the narratives of flight and persecution, orientation is expressed either through generic relational forms (then, later, before) or is more meaningfully anchored to space in the sense that it is told as a sequence of being in specific places, of states rather than movements. While official discourse about this period in history is oriented and aligned with events or dates along a temporal as well as spatial dimension, the interviewees' retold narratives about war and the Holocaust are focused on the spatial dimension—to the point where these places and spaces metonymically and euphemistically represent perpetrators and persecution.

Notes

1. These dates were all connected with scandals related to Austria's Nazi past: 1965, T. Borodajkiewicz, a professor at the Business University in Vienna, was reported to have made explicit anti-Semitic utterances during his lectures. After much debate, demonstrations, and a trial, he was suspended. 1968 was the year of the Student's Movement as well as the occupation of former CSSR by Soviet troops. 1986 was the year of the 'Waldheim Affair,' and in 2000 the so-called black-blue government was installed in Austria, a coalition between the conservative party (ÖVP) and the right-wing populist Austrian Freedom Party (FPÖ). This coalition caused a huge scandal across the European Union (see Wodak et al. 1990; Wodak 2011; Wodak and Pelinka 2002 for more details).
2. In addition to linguists (Ruth Wodak, Markus Rheindorf), the team of researchers included historiographer Helene Maimann and psychiatrist Ernst Berger.
3. Above all in the FÖJ (Freie Österreichische Jugend—Free Austrian Youth, a movement associated with the Communist Party in Austria) but in some cases also the VSM (Verein Sozialistischer Mittelschüler—Association of Socialist Middle Schoolers) and VSSTÖ (Verband Sozialistischer Studenten—Association of Socialist Students), yet others in Haschomer Hatzair, the leftist-zionist youth movement, or the Jewish sports club Hakoah.

4. In 1986, former UN Secretary General Kurt Waldheim became a symbol for the typically "Austrian" way of (not) coping with the Nazi past of Austria and with the active involvement of many Austrians as Nazi perpetrators. Postwar, the hegemonic narrative stated that all Austrians had been victims of Nazi occupation; indeed, Austria had ceased to exist as an autonomous state. During the 1986 election campaign for Austrian president, in which Waldheim stood as candidate for the conservative People's Party, the Austrian weekly *Profil* launched the information that Waldheim had been stationed in Saloniki, Greece, as personal translator of the infamous Wehrmacht general Löhr. Thus, it followed, he must have known about the atrocious war crimes committed against Greek civilians and the deportation of thousands of Greek Jews to Auschwitz—which he had denied previously and argued that he had "forgotten" to mention this period of his life in his autobiography. The subsequent international scandal forced many to confront—for the first time in explicit ways—the perpetrator and bystander roles in which their families had been involved (e.g., Wodak et al. 1990; Mitten 1992). The "victim myth" was challenged, and the hegemonic identity narrative slowly changed in the 1990s.
5. Medium significance of a ratio below 0.75 but higher than 0.5 are: 13) childhood, growing up, and youth; 14) reading and books; 15) home, having a home, Austria, and society; and 16) close family including mother, father, and siblings. Of low significance with a ratio below 0.5 are the macrostructures 17) war, military events; 18) their own children; 19) school, studies and studying, graduating, and teachers; and 20) god(s) and religion.
6. For ethical reasons, the names of our interviewees are anonymized.

References

Achugar, Mariana. 2007. "Between Remembering and Forgetting: Uruguayan Military Discourse about Human Rights (1976–2004)." *Discourse & Society* 18 (5): 521–47.

———. 2016. *Discursive Processes of Intergenerational Transmission of Recent History*. Basingstoke, Eng.: Palgrave.

Bakhtin, Michael. 1981. *The Dialogic Imagination: Four Essays*. Translated by Caryl Emerson and Michael Holquist. Edited by Michael Holquist. Austin: University of Texas Press.

Bamberg, Michael. 1997. "Positioning between Structure and Performance." *Journal of Narrative and Life History* 7 (1-4): 335–42.

Bauman, Richard, and Charles L. Briggs. 1990. "Poetics and Performance as Critical Perspectives on Language and Social Life." *Annual Review of Anthropology* 19:59–88.

Baynham, Mike. 2005. "Network and Agency in the Migrations Stories of Moroccan Women." In *Dislocations/Relocations. Narratives of Displacement*, edited by Mike Baynham and Anna De Fina, 11–35. Manchester: St. Jerome.

Berger, Ernst, ed. 2007. *Verfolgte Kindheit – Kinder und Jugendliche als Opfer der NS-Sozialverwaltung*. Vienna: Böhlau.

Bruner, Jerome. 2001. "Self-making and world-making." In *Narrative and Identity. Studies in Autobiography, Self and Culture*, edited by Jens Brockmeier and Donal Carbaugh, 25–38. Amsterdam: John Benjamins.

De Fina, Anna. 2003a. "Crossing Borders: Time, Space, and Disorientation in Narrative." *Narrative Inquiry* 13 (2): 367–91.

———. 2003b. *Identity in Narrative: A Study of Immigrant Discourse*. Amsterdam: John Benjamins.

De Fina, Anna, and Alexandra Georgakopoulou. 2012. *Analyzing Narrative. Discourse and Sociolinguistic Perspectives*. Cambridge: Cambridge University Press.

Halbwachs, Maurice. 1985. *Das kollektive Gedächtnis*. Frankfurt: Suhrkamp.

Heer, Hannes, Walter Manoschek, Alexander Pollak, and Ruth Wodak, eds. 2008. *The Discursive Construction of History: Remembering the Wehrmacht's War of Annihilation*. Basingstoke, Eng.: Palgrave.

Holquist, Michael. 1990. *Dialogism: Bakhtin and His World*. London: Methuen.

Jacquemet, Marco. 2005. "The Registration Interview. Restricting Refugees' Narrative Performances." In *Dislocations/Relocations. Narratives of Displacement*, edited by Mike Baynham and Anna De Fina, 194–216. Manchester: St. Jerome.

Keppler, Angela. 1994. *Tischgespräche. Über Formen Kommunikativer Vergemeinschaftung am Beispiel der Konversation in Familien*. Frankfurt: Suhrkamp.

Knight, Robert. 1988. *"Ich bin dafür, die Sache in die Länge zu ziehen." Die Wortprotokolle der Österreichischen Bundesregierung von 1945-1952 über die Entschädigung der Juden*. Frankfurt: Fischer.

Kuschey, Bernhard. 2008. *Die Wodaks. Exil und Rückkehr*. Vienna: New Academic Press.

Kühberger, Christoph. 2015. "Hitler: Personalisation in Historical Representation and No End." *Public History Weekly* 3 (10). DOI:dx.doi.org/10.1515/phw-2015-3764.

Labov, William, and Joshua Waletzky. 1967. "Narrative Analysis: Oral Versions of Personal Experience." In *Essays on the Verbal and Visual Arts. Proceedings of the 1966 Annual Spring Meeting of the American Ethnological Society*, edited by June Helm, 12–44. Seattle: University of Washington Press.

Maimann, Helene. 1994. *Politik im Wartesaal. Österreichische Exilpolitik in Großbritannien 1938-1945*. Vienna: Böhlau.

Matthiessen, Christian M. I. M., and Michael A. K. Halliday. 1997. *Systemic Functional Grammar: A First Step into the Theory*. Beijing: Higher Education Press.

Mitten, Richard. 1992. *The Politics of the Antisemitic Prejudice. The Waldheim Phenomenon in Austria*. Boulder: Westview.

Norrick, Neal R. 1997. "Twice-Told Tales: Collaborative Narration of Familiar Stories." *Language in Society* 26 (2): 199–220.

Reisigl, Martin, and Ruth Wodak. 2001. *Discourse and Discrimination. Rhetorics of Racism and Antisemitism*. London: Routledge.

Schiffrin, Deborah. 2002. "Mother and Friends in a Holocaust Life Story." *Language in Society* 31:309–53.

———. 2003. "We Knew That's It: Retelling the Turning Point of a Narrative." *Discourse Studies* 5 (4): 535–61.

———. 2006. *In other words: Variation in Reference and Narrative*. Cambridge: Cambridge University Press.

Schröter, Melanie. 2013. *Silence and Concealment in Political Discourse*. Discourse Approaches to Politics, Society and Culture. Amsterdam: Benjamins.

Uhl, Heidemarie. 2008. "Interpreting the 'War of Annihilation.'" In *The Discursive Construction of History: Remembering the Wehrmacht's War of Annihilation*, edited by Hannes Heer, Walter Manoschek, Alexander Pollak, and Ruth Wodak, 251–66. Basingstoke, Eng.: Palgrave.

van Dijk, Teun A. 2009. "Semantic Macro-structures and Knowledge Frames in Discourse Comprehension." In *Cognitive Processes in Comprehension*, edited by Marcel A. Just and Patricia A. Carpenter, 3–32. New York: Psychology Press.

Welzer, Harald. 2001. *Das soziale Gedächtnis. Geschichte, Erinnerung, Tradierung*. Hamburg: Hamburger Edition.

Wodak, Ruth. 1986. *Language Behavior in Therapy Groups*. Los Angeles: University of California Press.

———. 2011. "Suppression of the Nazi Past, Coded Languages, and Discourses of Silence. Applying the Discourse-Historical Approach to Post-War Anti-Semitism in Austria." In *Political Language in the Age of Extremes*, edited by Willibald Steinmetz, 351–79. Oxford: Oxford University Press.

Wodak, Ruth, Florian Menz, Richard Mitten, and Frank Stein. 1994. *Die Sprache der Vergangenheiten. Öffentliches Gedenken in österreichischen und deutschen Medien*. Frankfurt: Suhrkamp.

Wodak, Ruth, Peter Novak, Johanna Pelikan, Helmut Gruber, Rudolf de Cillia, and Richard Mitten. 1990. *'Wir sind alle unschuldige Täter!' Diskurshistorische Studien zum Nachkriegsantisemitismus*. Frankfurt: Suhrkamp.

Wodak, Ruth, and Anton Pelinka, eds. 2002. *The Haider Phenomenon in Austria*. Boulder: Transaction Press.

Wodak, Ruth, and Martin Reisigl. 2015. "Discourse and Racism." In *Handbook of Discourse Analysis 2nd Edition*, edited by Heidi Hamilton, Deborah Tannen, and Deborah Schiffrin, 576–96. Oxford: Wiley-Blackwell.

Wortham, Stanton. 2001. *Narratives in Action. A Strategy for Research and Analysis*. New York: Teachers College Press.

Zajde, Nathalie. 2011. "Die Schoah als Paradigma des psychischen Traumas." In *Holocaust und Trauma. Kritische Perspektiven zur Entstehung und Wirkung eines Paradigmas. Tel Aviver Jahrbuch für deutsche Geschichte 39*, edited by José Brunner and Nathalie Zajde, 185–206. Göttingen, Ger.: Wallenstein.

Zappavigna, Michele. 2013. *Tacit Knowledge and Spoken Discourse*. London: Bloomsbury.

Ziegler, Meinrad, and Waltraud Kannonier-Finster. 1997. *Österreichisches Gedächtnis. Über Erinnern und Vergessen der NS-Vergangenheit*. Vienna: Böhlau.

Chapter 3

Linguistic Landscape

Interpreting and Expanding Language Diversities

ELANA SHOHAMY

IT WAS A SPECIAL opportunity for me to be invited to deliver a plenary at the GURT 2015 conference, eight years after presenting a plenary at GURT 2007 on the related theme of Sustaining Linguistic Diversity: Endangered and Minority Languages and Language Varieties. The title of the 2007 plenary was: *Oppressive Methods of Suppressing Diversities for Hebrew Revival* (Shohamy 2008). The main question addressed then was: How far should we go with language revival before the revived becomes so powerful that it swallows all the other languages, especially when it is supported by strong ideology? In that paper I presented archival data, mostly from the 1930s, to point at the aggressive and harsh methods used to revive the Hebrew language in Israel. Some of the methods were the tracking of people's use of the Hebrew language at home as well as in public spaces, checking their oral language proficiency in Hebrew through informal tests conducted at their homes, nominating Hebrew language supervisors in hospitals to track patients' use of Hebrew while hospitalized, eradicating all the newspapers which were publishing in 'other languages,' and massive calls for shifting language patterns to Hebrew only. I argued there that most of these acts could be considered violations of personal rights, as most people could not comply with the harsh demands of using only Hebrew in all domains of life right after migration. This resulted in many people becoming silent and dysfunctional in public places and their own homes while trying to communicate with their children.

These acts were part of the widespread ideology of the Zionist movement to suppress the language diversity that existed at the time for all immigrants to Palestine who used mostly territorial and/or Jewish languages, as very few learned spoken Hebrew in the places they came from. Thus the demand for a total language shift to one single language that most people did not know was motivated by the belief that one ideologically uniformed language is required, as it will create strong unity, cohesion, and collective identity. I turned to my own family, collecting documents about their patterns of acquiring the Hebrew language. This was part of a study that examined the cost that individuals paid for the revival of Hebrew. Those who managed to acquire Hebrew were mostly men who were literate in reading Hebrew, as many had learned it as part of reading the prayer book and could shift more easily to spoken Hebrew. Most women, on the other hand, were not literate in Hebrew, so the shift was difficult, if not impossible. With time, and especially since Hebrew had become the medium of instruction in schools, Hebrew became a dominant language among the communities residing in Palestine at the time and later in Israel, and it is a dominant language widely used in all domains of life. The diversity that existed during the thirties, before and after, was eradicated within one or two generations. Figures 3.1a and 3.1b show the massive campaign used to force 'Hebrew only' as the state-mandated language while shaming, bashing, and suppressing all the other languages of the immigrants.

Figure 3.1a. Posters showing the bright future of Hebrew and the dark future of all other languages

Many of those who could not function in Hebrew had proficiency in a number of other languages, usually territorial and Jewish languages, but these languages turned out to be of no value in relation to Hebrew, which was the only ideologically recognized language considered prestigious and valuable in the new context. The situation, in fact, continues today, as the many immigrants to Israel are using languages such as Russian, French, Amharic, English, Spanish, Tigrinya, Nepalese, Tagalog, and many more that are devalued and decontextualized, especially in schools where Hebrew is the only medium of instruction. In addition, Arabic, which is a language used by Arabs living in Israel, although official, is considered a minority language, with its 20 percent of Arabic speakers. It is used as the main home and public language in everyday life as well as the main medium of instruction in all Arab schools. Although Arabs also learn Hebrew from a very young age, they have

Figure 3.1b. Hebrew suppressing all 'other' languages

difficulties in higher education, as Hebrew (and English) are the only languages used in all universities in Israel.

The archival data I collected for the 2007 paper stimulated me to examine further the methods for reviving languages and the widespread phenomenon of suppressing language diversity, especially in immigration contexts. That led me to go deeper into the study of my family, who arrived in Palestine in the 1930s not speaking Hebrew; this is where I could detect, in individuals' biographies, the "victims" and "winners" of the Hebrew-only ideology. I will now provide a short description of their language biographies, pointing to the mixed patterns of acquiring Hebrew and how the privileged ones in terms of Hebrew were successful in life while the others were marginalized from participation in society. They were all multilingual in a number of languages, but not in Hebrew, the only 'good' language to know in that place and time. I focus on four members of my family: my grandfather, grandmother, mother, and father. Their pictures are displayed below (figures 3.2a and b and 3.3a and b).

My grandfather, Baruch Ostrovski, emigrated from the Ukraine to New York in 1905. In New York he became the principal of a Yiddish school that believed Yiddish should be the language used in the Jewish state (a "Yiddishist"). He then immigrated to Palestine in 1930 and by then went along with the idea that Hebrew should be the main language of the Jewish state. He continued to use Yiddish at home but Hebrew only in all public spaces. He knew how to read Hebrew before he immigrated to Palestine so the shift to spoken Hebrew was relatively easy. I refer to him as a 'winner' as he was very successful when he arrived in Palestine. He became the mayor of the town of Raanana, a newly founded town, and held this position for thirty years.

My mother, Shoshana Ostrovski Goldberg, was born in New York, spoke Yiddish until age five, learned English in school, and moved to Palestine with her parents when she was fourteen. She learned Hebrew by being tutored by a private teacher intensively in Hebrew and at school, where Hebrew became the medium of instruction. She moved to the United States in 1939 for a short time that lasted until 1950 (due to the Second World War). She used English at home and Hebrew in public spaces and became an English teacher; I view her as a 'winner.'

My grandmother, Feiga Ostrovski, was born in the Ukraine and spoke Yiddish only; she then immigrated to New York at age seventeen, learned some English, and translanguaged with Yiddish and English most of her life, although Yiddish was always her stronger language. She followed Baruch to Palestine in 1930 and continued to speak Yiddish all her life and did not acquire Hebrew. I view her as a 'loser,' a victim to the Hebrew language who could not function outside of home.

My father, Leon Goldberg, was born in Poland, where he spoke Yiddish. He immigrated to New York when he was nine as a child laborer while his parents stayed in Poland and died in the Holocaust; he would visit them every few years until the Second World War broke out. He spoke Yiddish and English in New York and moved to Israel with my mother in 1950. He continued to speak English and acquired very minimal level of Hebrew, mostly oral. The cost for him was that he never had a permanent job, and was marginalized in many ways, both for his minimal Hebrew and because he was not an ideological Zionist, but had moved to Israel

◆ **Figure 3.2a.** My grandfather, the mayor, giving a speech

◆ **Figure 3.2b.** In a typical posed picture of the high officials

to follow my mother. Additionally, English in the '50s after the British left was not considered a prestigious global language like it is now. He is characterized by me as a 'loser,' a victim of the language.

The above contextualization is necessary in order to understand the notion of diversity at the time. The example of Hebrew is especially striking, since when Jewish people started arriving in the area, hardly anybody knew or used Hebrew. Thus eradicating language diversity for the sake of monolingual policy, a totally subtractive ideology, can be viewed as a more extreme policy than in other situations of imposing monolingualism in nation states where national languages had already been dominant. In the case of Hebrew, people could not turn to it, as it was, to some

Figure 3.3a. My mother and father in the United States

extent, a language in the making. This changed after the establishment of Israel as a state in 1948.

Diversity in the current age is recognized in more positive ways, as it is reflected in various multilingual policies that encourage the learning and use of a variety of different languages as well as in the vast, expanding research and literature on multilingualism. The advantages of bi- and multilingualism are becoming more apparent, although ample controversies persist. It is becoming more clear that the learning of new languages in education systems also calls for maintenance of home languages in schools and in society. While officially, one language is the medium of instruction in schools, there is less denial of the place of home languages and linguistic diversity. Terms such as translanguaging are not foreign in many educational systems and in society. This does not mean that controversies about multilingualism do not exist in Israel, as strong Hebrew ideologies are still promoted by policy makers in the educational systems

Figure 3.3b. My grandmother Feiga Ostrovski in Israel with my sister on the left and me on the right

using one language as the medium of instruction in all Jewish schools and in language testing. In the midst of this transformation it is clear that language is still an object of strong battles about linguistic uniformity versus diversity and there is still relatively limited research that examines the benefits and costs of policies.

Linguistic Landscape: A Tool for Examining Diversity

The chapter now will examine multiple facets of diversity via the lens of Linguistic Landscape (LL) in order to delve deeper into the multiple levels, facets, and depths of diversity. The chapter will show how LL is a useful tool for diversity that exposes us to directions that are unique, as it focuses on public spaces as arenas of language use, representation, and controversy. The research and findings that will be reported here will demonstrate how the public space enables a broader and deeper view of language diversity. However, LL in spaces and places has been mostly overlooked in the research about diversity in spite of the fact that languages in public spaces are widespread and essential elements of language ecology everywhere and have been for some time (Coulmas 2009).

In the past decade, LLs, referring to languages posted and displayed in the public spaces, have been introduced as a major arena of research in sociolinguistics and applied linguistics, focusing mostly on multilingualism and its diverse representations. LL offers a unique way to examine multiple dimensions of diversity as it cannot be equated with what people speak or use at home. LL mostly deals with the languages that people choose to *represent* themselves, hence the reference to LL as "symbolic construction of the public space" (Ben Rafael et al. 2006).

In the remainder of this chapter, I examine how LL is used as a measure of diversity—that is, how individuals and institutions represent themselves in public spaces via diverse languages and other devices. The questions addressed are: How can we connect LL with the new definitions of language that have emerged in the past decade? Does LL contribute to the expansion of diversity in terms of identity, participation, and social justice, and if so, how? How can engagement with LL contribute to a greater awareness of diversity, activism, and social justice? The data used here are based on a number of research studies, conducted with some of my colleagues, and especially with Dr. Shoshi Waksman. The different studies are arranged according to categories that attempt to document the development of the field of LL in the past decade.

A major assumption with regards to languages in public spaces is that spaces are empty, and different types of LL and other devices turn spaces into 'places' via signs, announcements, graffiti, and instructions posted in streets, homes, cities, buildings, markets, neighborhoods, etc. While languages in public spaces seem random, research in LL has shown that LL is in fact systematic and anchored in theories of politics, policy, economics, geography, law, linguistics, migration, urbanism, bodies, architecture, education, culture, justice, power, and change. LL research describes, identifies, and interprets patterns of various forms of LL in public spaces and uses multiple research methods such as quantitative, interpretive, historical, ethnographic, and case studies to interpret the motives, pressures, ideologies, impacts, reactions, and decisions of institutions and people regarding LL within the above-mentioned disciplines.

A case in point is the study related to the revival of Hebrew issue discussed above (Shohamy 2008), where LL was used as a major tool for imposing the Hebrew language in major cities in the 1930s. The introduction and imposition of 'Hebrew-only' ideology was manifested in public spaces to play down and suppress other languages. In the LL study it was shown how Hebrew ideologues viewed the public space as instrumental in convincing those who did not know the language to learn it. Constructing the spaces as Hebrew-language landscapes served as a major strategy to spread the ideology of Hebrew and to convince people that Hebrew is in fact a dominant major language. Displaying Hebrew in public spaces was a major agenda of those responsible for imposing it. For example, in the archives, there is a description of young high school students who were assigned to go through city centers and erase all of the languages displayed other than Hebrew. Attitudes toward English were more tolerant during the time of the British Mandate, but that changed drastically after 1948 when the British left and Israel gained its independence. Activists sent threat letters to companies and institutions that did not use Hebrew on their signs, viewing those in other languages as violations, intrusions, and 'pollutions' of public spaces. The public space was a central arena where language battles were carried out, as LL was a major tool in these battles. LL was used as a tool to perpetuate ideology and contest language diversity, and hence to create homogenous language policy 'on the ground.' Thus the portrayal of the public space as a Hebrew space reflected the desire of policy makers to enforce the image that Hebrew is the norm. This policy was expected to create a feeling of 'otherness' of those who did not know Hebrew and hence motivate people to change their language patterns and make efforts to learn and use Hebrew.

In the rest of the chapter I will portray the main phases of the LL field in the past decade; these phases are mostly cumulative, but reflect general directions as seen through my own eyes and those of others.

LL Studies and Diversity

Phase 1: LL as Documenting Diversity

In what I refer to as Phase 1 of LL research, language diversity was measured via counting the number of languages represented in public spaces. The studies in that era were based on quantitative analyses of vast data on LL representations in towns and cities. The LL items were sampled and documented, marked and counted, followed by data analysis based on the frequency of the appearance of each language on the signs as a measure of diversity. Most studies differentiated between top-down and bottom-up signs, referring to signs displayed by institutions and corporations (top-down) versus those initiated by individuals on their shops, at homes, etc. (Ben Rafael et al. 2006). The results were then subject to theoretical explanations of the phenomenon. No attention was granted to the content of the signs, only to the languages that were displayed.

A case in point is the study by Ben Rafael and others (2006), which examined LL as a measure of diversity in Jewish and Arab towns in Israel. It was a large-scale study, examining patterns of multilingualism based on over one thousand signs, randomly collected. The results of the study revealed that each area in Israel is bilingual in a different language (see figure 3.4). In Jewish areas, Hebrew and English were the dominant languages, while very little attention was granted to Arabic; in Arab areas, Arabic and Hebrew were the dominant languages, and very little room was given to English; finally, in East Jerusalem, Arabic and English were dominant and very few, if any, signs were found in Hebrew and these were mostly the top-down variety. The theoretical interpretations of the study, taken mostly from the field of sociology, referred to theories of rational choice and market principles associated with status symbolism and globalization for the choice of English by Jews and Hebrew by Arabs, collective identity for national languages, and group identity for minority languages.

Conclusions and critique

Studies of the first phase point to the LLs of nations and big cities, which involve multiple factors. Therefore, interpretations of public space require a focus on a wide range of variables. LL perspectives need to be challenged, as arenas vary by their demography and background needs, and these vary drastically from one area to another. In the above study language, diversity patterns vary slightly from one area to another, and often with the internal and external immigration patterns. It is most likely that Jews, Israeli Arabs, and East Jerusalem Arabs are diverse within their subgroups as well. Indeed, a study by Shohamy and Abu Ghazaleh-Mahajneh (2012) demonstrates how specific towns differ from one another in regard to language use and representations. From this LL research we cannot determine how diverse or super-diverse countries are in terms of language representations, given the vast migration and movements of populations. The fact that a large number of languages known to be used in public spaces exists implies that a focus on nations and conclusions about 'the Arabs' or 'the Jews' overlooks internal diversity; thus there is a need to focus on smaller units of analysis in order to understand language representation in deeper ways.

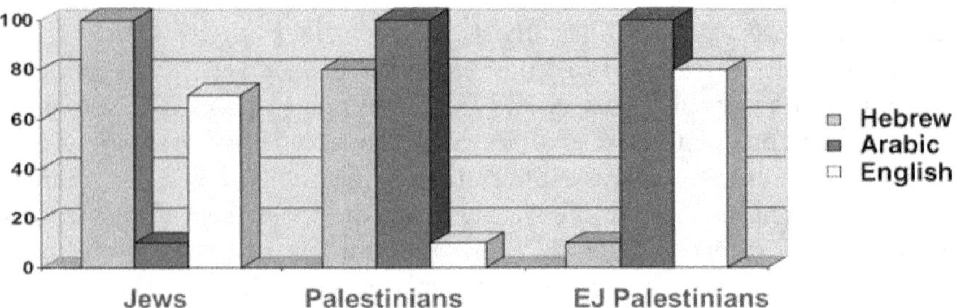

Figure 3.4. Frequencies of language representations in public spaces in Israel

Further, in large-scale studies the signs represented a relatively small number of languages compared to the known diversity from census data and reported data. For researchers there is a need to employ sampling methods that capture diversity in deeper ways. We can only describe whether one area is different from another. In addition, these kinds of studies focus mostly on representations of various languages, but it is debatable whether diversity is only about the number of languages, and not about deeper levels of diversity such as status, prestige, and official language policies (i.e., content and language variety as well as additional modalities). These methods take away from the depth of language diversity and ignore the complexities raised in the social world. In sum, numerical measurements may be necessary, but are not sufficient.

Phase 2: Expanding the LL Construct to Multimodality

Already in the early years of LL research it has become clear that a focus only on language does not provide meaningful interpretations of *languages* in public spaces, as there is a need to incorporate additional components beyond words. These additional components include images, graffiti, sounds, bodies, clothes, smells, movements, dance, objects, and people. Multimodality, as a discourse approach, was introduced to educational systems in a pivotal article by the researchers of The New London Group. Additional material about multimodality was introduced by Kress and van Leewan (1996), Jewitt and Triggs (2006), and Kress (2003).

In LL research people play a special role as actors and participants in different capacities. The introduction of people in LL is complex, as they interact with space and its derivatives. People also hang signs, display posters, design advertisements, and create websites. In addition, they are the ones who read, attend to, decipher, and interpret the displayed languages, and also those who choose to overlook, ignore, or erase them. While people at times act as agents for institutions, they also serve as those who read, contest, critique, and negotiate the public spaces. The specific roles of people as contesters and activists will be described in a number of studies on advancing various agendas of diversity as well as homogeneity.

In two studies we employed multimodal analysis to examine the tourist site Haapala, located at the center of Tel Aviv near the beach which commemorates the illegal migration of Jews to Palestine (Shohamy and Waksman 2009, 2010). The introduction of multimodality is rooted in our observation that focusing on language alone does not allow for a full analysis of semiotic practices at the site. Specifically, multimodality responded to the need to focus on the geographical location of the site, its placement, design, the ample photographs displayed on it in different places and their titles, the written signs and their explanations, the number of languages displayed, and the people who endow them with meaning and to whom the messages are intended. We showed that focusing on all of these sources together allows for a richer understanding of the meanings conveyed by the site (see Shohamy and Waksman 2009 for details). Figures 3.5a, 3.5b, and 3.5c display the multiple modalities of the site.

The second analysis of the same site (Shohamy and Waksman 2010) is anchored in theories of tourism (Jaworski and Thurlow 2010). The findings, based on the multimodal analysis, show that the messages delivered distinguished between four types of tourists: For those living in Israel, the message, in Hebrew only, was 'stay here.' For the Jewish tourists, the message was 'come join us here.' The idea transmitted to the non-Jewish visitors was 'support us but stay out' (given that Israel does not accept non-Jewish immigrants to Israel). Another group of visitors are Israeli Arabs, and although they are an integral part of the commemoration story, they are not mentioned on the site, or rather, are deleted, which in itself constitutes a strong message given the historical facts and the narrative of the site (see Shohamy and Waksman 2010 for more details).

Conclusions and critique

In this phase, LL expands diversity beyond language, but only to additional dimensions that are included on public-space displays; these additional components provide a more valid interpretation of diversity that is contextualized in broad spaces. Additional components provide us with opportunities to broaden the concepts and definitions of language, using a wider repertoire of modalities, such as texts, images, location, environment, people in practices, time, and ideology. Figure 3.6. shows the multiple factors that participate in the interpretation of one sign. The nexus analysis introduced by Scollon and Scollon (2003) is yet another method for expanding the definition of language into a broader and more diverse meaning as public spaces are embedded in geography and physical spaces.

Figure 3.5a. A photo of the Haapala site and its contexts

Figure 3.5b. Messages delivered via photos and images

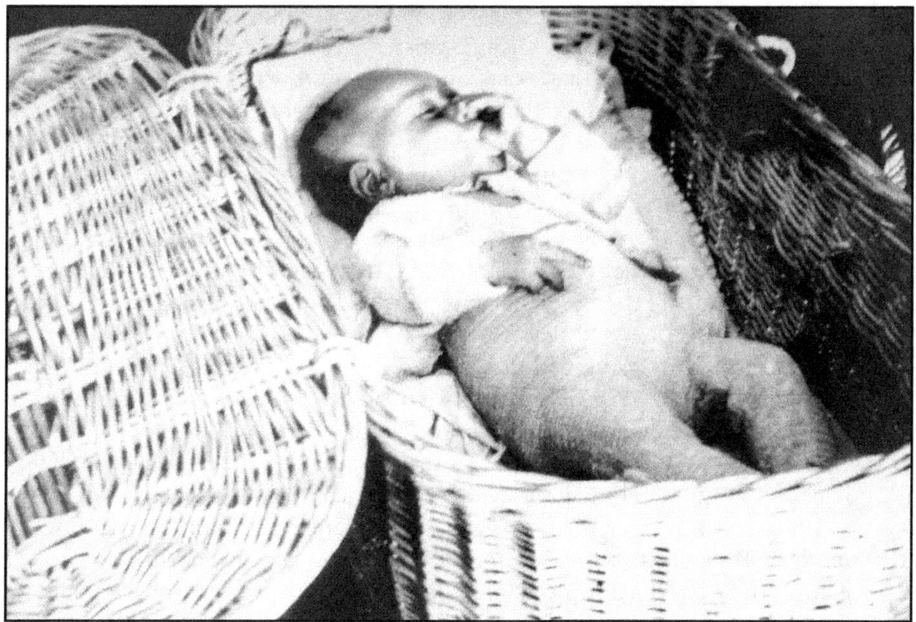

Figure 3.5c. Messages delivered via photos and images

Figure 3.6. Multiple factors participating in the interpretation of signs in public spaces

Phase 3: Language Diversity in the City: Contesting Homogeneity

The early focus on nations as units of analysis is important in terms of national language policy and generalities using statistics, yet the 'national lens' overlooks and ignores the rich diversity that exists on smaller levels especially in cities. Thus the next set of studies we conducted focused not only on smaller units that enable better and more valid conclusions but also deeper interpretation and a focus on the dialogue between different groups. The study on cities that is reported here also deals with contestation between the municipality imposing a homogenous identity on the city and people holding diverse views (Shohamy and Waksman 2012). In this study we gave attention to the role of people in LL research: On the one hand, the people are those who create the homogeneous policy and on the other they are also those who protest it.

In this study, we examined the LL policy of the city of Tel Aviv during the celebration of the centennial that took place in 2009 (Shohamy and Waksman 2010). The city was decorated widely with various LL-types of multimodal items that included new designs and writings of street names, introduced by the municipality; poems and songs in public spaces; and images and scripts of history.

In figure 3.7a we see the new signs which were erected for the centennial with no Arabic. In figure 3.7b we see Zionist poem about the new port. In figure 3.7c we see how even a parking lot was named Bazel to note the Jewish congress; and in figure 3.7d there is a display of a poster pointing to the hard physical work of those who arrived in Israel to build the country.

Figure 3.7a. Arabic is not included in the sign on the left; instead, there is information about the person emphasizing his contribution to the 'building of the nation,' which is only included in the Hebrew version

Figure 3.7b. Poetry reinforcing patriotic agendas displayed in public spaces

Figure 3.7c. A parking lot turned into Zionist propaganda referring to Bazel, where the first Jewish congress was held

Figure 3.7d. Images and scripts of Zionist history

The results of the analysis of the LL repertoire of Tel Aviv, a global multilingual and diverse city, tell a homogenous top-down story where languages and images follow a Hebrew-only language ideology as if all residents are of the same opinion about the history and current status of the city. In other words, no language diversity was seen in the top-down decorations done by the municipality. This phenomenon was perceived as a strong contradiction with the main characteristics of the city of Tel Aviv, which is viewed as global, heterogeneous, liberal, open, and drastically different from cities in other parts of the country, in such a way that it has led to the referring to the city as 'the country of Tel Aviv.' One wonders how this homogenous policy fits with the character of Tel Aviv in this day and age.

In order to understand the true story of the centennial, we looked at alternative LL items and the reactions of the residents. The findings demonstrate that different types of LL items were found in the public spaces pointing to a strong bottom-up LL policy created 'on the ground' where different forms of LL types were found. An opposition to the centennial was revealed in signs such as "100 years to Tel Aviv: Who is not included?" (figure 3.8a below); remapping of the city to include Arab towns of the past (figure 3.8b); narratives told by a person who lived in Palestine as a child and was expelled (figure 3.8c); graffiti stating the fact that other people used to live in this area (figure 3.8d); exhibits about the personal lives of residents of Jaffa (figure 3.8e); and the Arabic language visible in the port of Tel Aviv (figure 3.8f).

Figure 3.8a. "100 years to Tel Aviv: Who is not being counted?"

Figure 3.8b. Remapping the history of Tel Aviv and the Arab areas that existed in the past

Figure 3.8c. Narration of the story of the Nakba by a person who experienced it

The above LL items were instrumental in uncovering elements that were not shown by the municipality; thus, using LL, we were able to detect the diversity which was missing from the top-down policy. It was then that we observed how LL was instrumental in observing diversity up close, contesting the exclusion of othered people, their agendas and lack of participation in the top-down municipality program that did not include Arabs, refugees, asylum seekers, and others. For that analysis, multiple devices (which we refer to as LLs) were included, such as films, narratives, exhibits, graffiti, and more. These were LL tools to protest the top-down portrayal of the city by the municipality.

Figure 3.8d. Graffiti, a reminder of past history over centennial posters: "Here, in this very place, there used to be a Palestinian village that was destroyed"

Figure 3.8e. Exhibit about marginalization displayed in Jaffa: "Pain and rage about being marginalized: 'We should present ourselves in Tel Aviv and tell the "dictator" about his true nature; we need to tell people who live here that they are oppressed'"

Figure 3.8f. Decorating the city with Arabic (activist group Farhesia)

Conclusions and critique

The city is not a homogenous entity but rather consists of multiple voices in stark contrast with the LL messages posted by the municipality for the centennial. People do view this phenomenon and often refuse to accept the authority that is rewriting the city; thus, they contest and protest. Interestingly, for these contesting voices, protest is about utilizing *multiple* modes of LL in order to obtain recognition, not only of language diversity but also of people and what they represent. The top-down LL items represent homogenous views of the institutions while bottom-up items represent the diversity of views, perceptions, and opinions. These do not stand in isolation; rather, the LL emerges as a dynamic and contested construct led by people, and hence does not just "stand there" but rather develops from contestations and movements. The contestation does not take place in the LL signs alone; rather, it is expressed via multimodal devices. In these studies we could see that LL is further expanded to include signs in multiple languages, pictures, graffiti, photos, exhibits, biographies, oral narratives, films, public lectures, talk backs, virtual spaces, and more—as long as the people who initiate them view them to be sustainable, visible, and attractive to large audiences, and they can send strong and meaningful messages that the creators believe will have an influence and impact. LL then serves as a tool for contestation and protest by searching for alternative LL devices to reach particular goals. Thus we see that diversity is not necessarily only about languages; it includes the above-described devices as well as the Internet, which legitimizes and enables a richer repertoire of devices for protesting, objecting, and pointing to societal injustices.

The other findings from the focus on the city show that cities, similar to nations, have very centralized policies regarding the space of the city. For this reason, the diversity of the city, being smaller than a nation, enables contestation and at times even dialogue. One questions we may pose is: How big should the studied public space be in order to view and understand diversity'? If the city is too big, can we really hear the voices of communities? So far, we have learned that multimodality is a necessary component in any contestation beyond number of languages, and that we need to focus on history, environment, location, ethnicity, geography, and so on.

Phase 4: Expanding Diversity: Focus on Neighborhoods

Is the city too big to observe its diversity or is it the case that when we adopt smaller units we are able to see many more patterns of diversity? After all, there are those claiming that cities are similar to nations. Here are some words that are used to describe smaller units within and surrounding cities: quarters, ghettos, villages, enclaves, parishes, districts, areas, zones, regions, suburbs, communities, streets, and buildings.

Two neighborhoods were selected in order to examine diversity in smaller areas and neighborhood identities (Shohamy and Waksman, forthcoming).

The New Central Station neighborhood

The New Central Station neighborhood is a very diverse area linguistically and ethnically. This is where foreign workers, asylum seekers, and refugees and their families reside alongside Israelis who have been living there for some time. It is located in an area that historically is perceived as run-down and marginalized and as such attracted foreign workers, since rent as well as the price of food and other commodities is relatively low. In such neighborhoods, there is multilingualism in public spaces, which reflects the diversity of languages and people. The neighborhood is vibrant, dynamic, and reacts to everyday practices, including eating, walking, talking, and marrying (wedding ceremonies) rather than to explicit policies (except in institutions). There is in fact congruence between humans and language in the space. Most of the signs are bottom-up since, given the low status of this neighborhood, big corporations and even the municipality do not post signs, except for signs for mobile phones and internet communication. Figures 3.9a, 3.9b, 3.9c, and 3.9d show some of the diversity of the area.

The Ajami neighborhood in Jaffa

Jaffa is the other town that is adjacent to Tel Aviv, and it is the one that makes Tel Aviv-Jaffa a mixed area (i.e., where Arabs and Jews live together). Jaffa is considered the Arab area. At the end of 2009, the population of Jaffa consisted of 46,051 people, of whom 32,792 were Jewish and 13,259 were Arab. Yet, given that Tel Aviv is almost exclusively Jewish and that Jaffa is historically regarded as an Arab town in spite of numbers, the signs in the main center of the city are distributed as follows: 461 signs in Hebrew, 147 in English, and 82 in Arabic. (The large number of English signs is a result of the fact that Jaffa attracts a large number of tourists.)

Figure 3.9a. LL in central station

Figure 3.9b. LL in central station

Figure 3.9c. LL in central station

Figure 3.9d. People in new central station

Our research focuses on the neighborhood of Ajami where many Arabs live and where there is a flow of Jews who acquire houses, given its location near the beach. We interviewed people about their neighborhood identity and found that most of the reactions of the Arab residents whom we interviewed were not about languages but about the buildings. They overlooked the language, which would seem to be more important. The trauma was more about houses than about having to switch to Hebrew. Thus S. notes that "We are being bought by French immigrants who like this location." There was uncertainty and fear that 1948 would be repeated again. As to the neighborhood identity, S. says that her neighborhood is the street she lives on: "I have street identity as from this road, that includes three houses, I can see the old house where my grandfather used to live in before 1948."

Conclusions and critique

In immigrant neighborhoods, there is a multilingual richness reflecting the diversity of languages and people. Through vibrant, dynamic, everyday practices, languages react to life practices and not to explicit policy except in institutions. In Ajami, language, at this phase, is less important than buildings and places to live, as for the inhabitants these come first. People are bilingual in Arabic and Hebrew but are concerned about existential factors at this point, given the tensions with the many Jewish people who move to their neighborhood.

A deep sense of diversity can be obtained from the study of smaller places, which could become a means for understanding people and their environment and the meaning of diversity within history, present, and future. The two neighborhoods differ drastically, each embedded in a distinct set of variables. A deeper understanding of diversity needs to be cultivated ethnographically. Signs and various types of LL are important but one cannot ignore all the contextual variables that affect them.

Phase 5: Engagement in Diversity: Critical Awareness and Activism

The last phase reported here refers to a growing number of studies that apply LL research to education. One study that will be reported here was designed to examine whether engagement of high school students with LL activities will impact high school students' awareness of the public space (Havazki and Shohamy 2010). While the study incorporated both Jewish and Arab students, I will report here on the activities of the ten Arab students only. Each of the students was asked to take fifteen pictures of LL signs in their neighborhoods. As a pre-activity, students were asked to answer a questionnaire about the status and role of Arabic in Jaffa. The results showed that all of these students perceived Arabic to be an important and prestigious language in Jaffa. They then turned to perform the tasks of documenting the signs, analyzing them, and writing reactions about each of the signs.

The analysis showed that while the Arab students at the beginning of the study thought that Jaffa was an Arab city, they were astonished to see that in fact most signs appear in Hebrew and that their own language—Arabic—is marginalized. This realization resulted in anger and great disappointment, even toward the students' parents who so easily gave up their home languages. In other words, while the Arab students initially thought that Arabic was a majority language in Jaffa, they realized that judging by the signs, there is low representation of Arabic in the public space, even among their own families, parents, and the shops of Arab people they know. This awareness made them angry and unhappy, but at the same time, they reported that they want to change the situation, they plan to talk to their parents and make them aware and turn them into activists, wanting to change and transform the neighborhood. Actual engagement with LL data increases language awareness and has an impact on attitudes, which can lead to activism (Jewish students were less affected by the documenting tasks).

Here is a selection of some of the talk produced by the Arab students on this issue:

STUDENT 1 "And I ask myself why is English written before Arabic? Arabic is the second official language in Israel, isn't that so? And I live in a city where all inhabitants or most of them are Arabs or Arabic speakers."

STUDENT 2 "If Hebrew and English appear on the sign, at least they should add Arabic for the Arab inhabitants so they will understand the point of respect."

STUDENT 3 "I don't have any comments because look, from all of the ten signs I analyzed, this was [the only] restaurant sign which was written in Arabic and in Hebrew."

STUDENT 4 "This research reminds me of a research which was conducted in the U.S.A. on black and white dolls for little children, where the black girls chose the white dolls because even in their thoughts and hearts they thought white was more beautiful than black and that this was a symbol for beauty."

STUDENT 5 "This is a private sign that a person from Jaffa put, without any involvement of the state. This means that even Arabs slowly began to think that Hebrew was more beautiful and better, and sometimes they were ashamed of Arabic."

Conclusions and critique

Through actual engagement with LL tasks students have become aware of the sociolinguistic injustices and have started to develop a desire for change. These types of activities can be useful in encouraging awareness and activism among students and to involve many others—teachers, principals, university students, parents—who are engaged in diversity activities and research.

Conclusions, Implications

In this chapter I attempted to show how research in LL can be instrumental in understanding multiple facets of diversity. Each of the studies discussed represents a particular phase which can be instrumental in examining diversity and in fact these phases can be cumulative so that one does not preclude the other. In the study of phase 1 we see how diversity can be measured numerically and how the findings can be interpreted theoretically. It also shows that LLs are not confined to the languages people use in their speech; therefore, diversity can relate to representation or use two different constructs. In the second phase we can see that when it comes to the public space, focus on language only is not sufficient and that expanding the construct beyond words provides more valid data on the meanings of public spaces. In phase 3 we see how LLs in public space are not neutral; rather, that people react to the public space emotionally and with contestation, especially when they or other groups are excluded from the public space. They then ensure that their voices are heard as well and express themselves by employing multiple types of tools that are different than the tools that top-down institutions use, as they have the right to write in public spaces while those who object do not. The 'talking back' to the city is done using multiple devices, not only the traditional LL of signs but also exhibits, graffiti, images, sounds, films, narratives, and so on, which are more sustainable. I also showed how LL expands diversity in different directions—from simple language representation to understanding multiple modalities and a focus on different spaces as nations, cities, and neighborhoods, each with its own unique types of diversity and what is considered an LL embedded in these spaces. Finally, it was shown how LL is a useful engagement tool for students, to develop awareness and critical understanding of public spaces. A willingness to transform the space results from this engagement in documentation, analysis, and interpretation. Thus, LL research opens our eyes, or rather adds new eyes, to see the complexities and the potentials of a larger repertoire of languages, spaces, and people. It provides a deeper realization of the current diverse and super-diverse societies and their unique features.

References

Ben Rafael, Eliezer, Elana Shohamy, Muhammad Amara, and Nira Trumper-Hecht. 2006. "Linguistic Landscape as a Symbolic Construction of the Public Space: The Case of Israel." *International Journal of Multilingualism* 3 (1): 7–31.

Coulmas, Florian. 2009. "Linguistic Landscaping and the Seed of the Public Sphere." In *Linguistic Landscape: Expanding the Scenery*, edited by Elana Shohamy and Durk Gorter, 13–24. London: Routledge.

Havazki, Ricky, and Elana Shohamy. 2010. "Travel Diary in Jaffa: Development of Linguistic Landscape Awareness and Attitudes among Teenagers." MA thesis, Tel Aviv University.

Jaworski, Adam, and Crispin Thurlow, eds. 2010. *Semiotic Landscapes: Language, Image, Space*. Edinburgh: A&C Black.

Jewitt, Carey, and Teal Triggs. 2006. "Screens and the Social Landscape." *Visual Communication* 5 (2): 131–40.

Kintsch, Walter, and Teun A. van Dijk. 1978. "Toward a Model Text Comprehension and Production." *Psychological Review* 85:363–94.

Kress, Gunter. 2003. *Literacy in the New Media Age*. London: Routledge.

Kress, Gunte, and Toeh van Leeuwen. 1996. *Reading Images, the Grammar of Visual Design*. London: Routledge.

Lefebvre, Henri. 1996. *Writings on Cities*. Oxford: Blackwell.

The New London Group. 2000. "A Pedagogy of Multiliteracies, Designing Social Futures." In *Multiliteracies, Literacy Learning and the Design of Social Futures*, edited by Bill Cope and Mary Kalanzis, 9–37. London: Routledge.

Scollon, Ron, and Suzie W. Scollon. 2003. *Discourses in Place: Language in the Material World.* London: Routledge.

Shohamy, Elana. 2008. "At What Cost: Methods of Language Revival and Protection: Examples from Hebrew." In *Sustaining Linguistic Diversity: Endangered and Minority Languages and Language Varieties*, edited by Kendall A. King, Natalie Schilling-Estes, Lyn Fogle, Jia J. Lou, and Barbara Soukup, 348–71. Washington, DC: Georgetown University Press.

Shohamy, Elana, and Marwan Abu Ghazaleh-Mahajneh. 2012. "Linguistic Landscape as a Tool for Interpreting Language Vitality: Arabic as a 'Minority' Language in Israel." In *Minority Languages in the Linguistic Landscape*, edited by Durk Gorter, Heiko F. Marten, and Luk Mensel, 89–106. Basingstoke, Eng.: Palgrave-Macmillan.

Shohamy, Elana, and Shoshi Waksman. 2009. "Linguistic Landscape as an Ecological Arena: Modalities, Meanings, Negotiations, Education." In *Linguistic Landscape: Expanding the Scenery*, edited by Elana Shohamy and Durk Gorter, 313–31. London: Routledge.

———. 2010. "Building the Nation, Writing the Past." In *Semiotic Landscapes: Language, Image, Space*, edited by Adam Jaworski and Crispin Thurlow, 241–55. London: Continuum.

———. 2012. "Talking Back to the City of Tel Aviv Centennial: Ll Responses to Top-down Agendas." In *Linguistic Landscape, Multilingualism and Social Change*, edited by Christine Helot, Monica Barni, Rudi Janssens, and Carla Bagna, 109–26. Frankfurt am Main: Peter Lang.

Chapter 4

A Competence for Negotiating Diversity and Unpredictability in Global Contact Zones

SURESH CANAGARAJAH

AS LANGUAGE USE CHANGES in the context of super-diversity, there are new questions about what constitutes effective competence for communication. My ongoing research with multilingually skilled migrants suggests an orientation to competence that deviates from what dominant models in applied linguistics have theorized. The differences are so fundamental that they go to the heart of what we assume as intelligible and successful communication. This is the province of language ideology. The orientation of my subjects will make sense only if we consider the divergent language ideologies they bring to interactions in contexts of super-diversity. For this reason, I begin this chapter by examining how the language ideologies informing dominant models of language competence relate to super-diversity. I then articulate the needed changes in orientations to language competence to address intelligibility in spaces of super-diversity. From this theoretical framing, I analyze the data from my subjects to illustrate the features constituting their competence. The objective of this chapter is to retheorize competence for the age of super-diversity in order to design more relevant pedagogies.

Competing Language Ideologies

Though some might consider language ideology and language competence very divergent schools in linguistics, with the first belonging to critical anthropological work and the latter belonging to cognitive orientations, some scholars have made a case for their connection. Lourdes Ortega (2014) has argued, "Changes in ideologies go hand in hand with changes in the modus operandi by which disciplinary knowledge is generated" (48), as she examines the influence of monolingual ideologies on language competence models through the lingering dominance of the native-speaker construct. I continue this line of inquiry by examining ideologies relating to the efficiency and success of linguistic communication. I outline how dominant ideologies are challenged by emergent ideologies relating to super-diversity, calling for a different orientation to competence.

A traditional ideology that has explained the locus of language is the "one language=one place=one community" equation, known as the Herderian triad (Blommaert 2010). This ideology territorialized languages and provided ownership to specific communities. However, in super-diversity, each place is a meeting point of people from diverse communities with their own multilingual repertoires. Mary Louise Pratt's (1991) notion of contact zones is not a secondary space between the more primary "community." All communities are contact zones that involve interactions between diverse languages and cultures. It is not only that a community is in contact with other communities, adopting changes deriving from this ongoing history of interaction; the community itself constitutes members who bring with them diverse values, identities, and repertoires that are in contact. Pratt (1987) considers the Herderian triad a "linguistic utopia" designed to impose uniformity, control meaning, and ensure successful social interactions.

The Herderian triad has also influenced language competence to be theorized in terms of homogeneity, positing that the shared values, assumptions, and attitudes of the community ensure communicative success. Diversity is often treated as communicatively dysfunctional, presenting conflicting values that are difficult to negotiate. If diversity is acknowledged, it is treated as a part of social context that can be addressed as a feature of *performance* through one's underlying "universal" competence, as in Chomskyan linguistics. In this sense, diversity is relegated to a superficial contextual variability that is secondary to the more important grammatical competence that controls meaning. However, in super-diverse contexts, diversity is the norm, and central to communication. Furthermore, traditional language ideologies assume that shared grammatical norms ensure successful communication. Heterogeneity is treated as "variation" from an underlying homogeneity of norms, as in variationist sociolinguistics. However, such a language ideology is contradicted by super-diverse contexts where there are multiple grammatical norms brought in by the people in these interactions.

I borrow a fourth distinction in language ideologies from Blommaert's (2010) formulation. He argues that a sociolinguistics of globalization requires a shift of perspectives from "immobile languages" to "mobile resources" (41). The Herderian triad rooted languages in particular places. However, language resources travel across places through various human and nonhuman means. Mobility is at the heart of language if we consider how the formation of English is steeped in such processes. English was formed by the confluence of at least three dialects migrating from Continental Europe, and meshing with local languages like Celtic (Fennell 2004). It took a lot of ideological work for centuries to form these semiotic resources into a standardized language (Agha 2005). The term "resources" is also a meaningful shift from "language." It deconstructs language to bring out the diverse, fluid semiotic resources it is made of, in addition to treating language itself as one among many semiotic features (such as images, space, color, and the body). It also provides a functional orientation to language. We communicate not to confirm the language structure, but to perform important social functions through diverse semiotic features. This functional orientation also helps us rethink correctness. What is more important is the ability of people to achieve their communicative ends by shaping the language resources to suit their purposes.

A final traditional ideology is the belief in language structure as explaining one's capacity to communicate and ensuring successful communication. However, structure filters out spatiotemporal influence. We find more and more that migrants in super-diverse contexts align themselves with spatial resources to communicate successfully. In other words, they orchestrate the language resources they have in relation to the features of the communicative ecology (i.e., relevant social agents, objects, and setting) to achieve intelligibility and meaning. In doing so, they move from treating languages as structure to treating them as communication and a form of practice. Communication as practice goes beyond language structure to draw from diverse semiotic resources to perform activities required in particular spatial contexts. Often, migrants are able to perform such practices even if they don't have full and advanced proficiency in a particular language structure. Fast (2012) demonstrates how mobile European students have the proficiency to buy a bus ticket in English or order food in a restaurant in French, though they don't have proficiency in these languages for other functions. He argues that the students have developed competence in these communicative activities as practices, including the ensemble of required semiotic resources, the combination of which Pennycook and Otsuji (2015) label "spatial repertoires." Spatial repertoires constitute grammatical/lexical features embedded in the relevant social and material features of the setting to consider the multimodal resources that enable one to successfully conduct a communicative activity.

These ideological shifts have important consequences for how we redefine language competence. The territorializing and ownership ideologies presume that control is in the hands of the communicator. Language norms and meaning are defined in relation to native speakers and their communities, presumably reducing the misunderstanding and confusion that can result from the diversity of norms and communicative conventions. However, the ideology of contact assumes unpredictability of norms. Pennycook (2012) has illustrated the presence of unexpected languages in unexpected places in the context of mobility. Therefore, we have to define a competence for negotiating the unpredictability of language resources and norms in our everyday interactions in super-diversity.

We also realize that the dominant language ideologies assume grammatical mastery as the heart of competence. However, in contact situations where grammars from multiple languages might be at play, basing one's competence on grammatical mastery is unsustainable. How many grammars can we teach in order to prepare our students for the unpredictability of the contact zone? In the place of grammatical competence, situated performance is gaining more importance in contexts of contact. Firth (1996) shows how lingua-franca English speakers construct meaning in situationally relevant ways by drawing from diverse language and semiotic resources.

Interlocutors are intersubjectively constructing new grammars that index the shared meanings that shape their interactions.

A third consequence is that we have to shift from defining competence as propositional knowledge to procedural knowledge, to borrow terms introduced by Michael Byram (2008) for intercultural competence in globalization. Propositional knowledge is a competence based on the "what" of communication, while procedural knowledge is based on the "how." Competence based on a knowledge of grammar, norms, or conventions belong to the former. Such a knowledge is insufficient to deal with the diversity of norms in contact zones. As I will demonstrate below, interlocutors in contact zones assume multiplicity and variability of norms in each interaction. Rather than assuming a shared norm, they consider what they can "do" to negotiate these norms for meaning-making. This focus on strategies and practices is the domain of procedural knowledge.

Examining Dominant Models of Language Competence

In the context of the shifts articulated above, we can examine how existing models of competence relate to the challenges of communication in the contact zone. The dominant model is characterized by Michael Long (1997) as follows: "Most SLA [second language acquisition] researchers view the object of inquiry as in large part an internal, mental process: the acquisition of new (linguistic) knowledge" (319). At least three features stand out in this characterization of language competence: 1) It is a cognitive process; 2) It is a form of knowledge; 3) It is grammatical knowledge. For these reasons, the framework sustaining the model is rightly dubbed the "linguistic cognitive paradigm" (Ortega 2014, 33). It is informed by the structuralist legacy in grammar and the cognitive orientation of Chomskyan linguistics. As we have discussed above, this paradigm of propositional knowledge cannot cope with language interactions where diversity is the norm and unpredictability the nature.

We do have other models of competence that give more importance to social context and situated performance. Hymes's (1974) notion of *communicative competence* made a case for accommodating social context and the varying pragmatic and discourse norms in competence, without which the abstract grammatical knowledge would be meaningless. However, as Leung (2005) persuasively argues, this model too has been reduced to a form of propositional knowledge by practitioners and scholars. Rules such as "use pragmatic feature x in context y" fall under the structuralist principle of forming grammatical patterns out of the dynamism of language use. In order to account for super-diversity, communicative competence has to be developed from the ground up, encouraging situational and intersubjective negotiations of meaning in contexts of unpredictable norms.

An orientation to competence that values situated negotiations comes from conversation analysis (CA), which it labels *interactional competence*. This model is sensitive to the way interlocutors attend to the sequential moves of each other as they tailor their speech in relation to the situated interaction. However, the meaning-making practices of the interlocutors are evaluated in relation to the preexisting grammatical norm of a language. The new indexicals emerging out of these interactions are perceived as error or mistake when they deviate from standard English (see Firth and Wagner 1997 for a critique). Such model is also too focused on grammatical norms, overlooking the role of semiotic resources and ecological contexts in meaning-making practices.

The type of competence that is fully practice based and orients to diversity as the norm and unpredictability as the expectation is perhaps similar to what some scholars have called *strategic competence* (Canale and Swain 1980). Strategic competence is the ability to come up with effective practices to repair potential communication breakdowns or unanticipated problems in the interaction. It captures the dexterity of the speaker to deal with contexts where no norms are shared. This competence is demonstrated when one creatively uses the limited semiotic resources one has and draws from the ecological conditions to make languages work for interlocutors with divergent norms in unpredictable contexts.

There are many emergent models of competence that provide more space for social practices in communication, labeled "alternative approaches to second language acquisition" in an edited book of that title (see Atkinson 2011a). A list of such approaches is:

Sociocognitive orientation (Atkinson 2011b)

Sociocultural theory (Lantolf 2011)

Language socialization (Duff and Talmy 2011)

Ecological orientations (van Lier 2004)

Usage-based approaches (Ortega 2014)

Complexity theory (Larsen-Freeman 2011)

Though it is beyond the scope of this chapter to discuss each of them in detail, we can identify some assumptions that don't make them suitable for super-diversity. To some extent, all these models are still working along the notion of competence for one language at a time. What we need for contact zones is a competence that transcends individual languages, a translingual competence perhaps, that enables one to deal with the unpredictable mix of languages. Furthermore, though all these models address the "mind-world-body" connection (Atkinson et al. 2007, 171) remarkably well, they filter out the information on practices in order to focus on cognition as the locus of this competence. In some ways, they consider how social practices help internalize the language norms more effectively rather than study the practices for their own sake. I will now proceed to identify the practices and language ideologies emerging from multilinguals in contact zones to demonstrate the practice-based model that would account for their procedural knowledge to negotiate diversity and unpredictability. While illustrating the distinct language ideologies they bring to multilingual interactions, the data analysis will also help elaborate the strategies multilinguals adopt to succeed in communication. However, a few caveats first. A practice-based view does not perceive grammatical norms or the cognitive domain as irrelevant. It rather explains how practices constantly generate grammatical norms. In this sense, it is against the notion of grammar as preconstructed or stable. Similarly, it perceives cognition as shaped by practices, with social and contextual information embedded in cognitive processes. This model is thus against the Cartesian divide of the mind and body or cognition and environment. It is beyond the scope of this article to review the fascinating ways cognition is currently reconceived as embodied and embedded (see Atkinson 2011b for a review).

The endeavor in this study is to explore if there are patterns and models at the level of practice that explain people's competence for successful communication in contact zones. This is to answer Pennycook's (2010) call to develop a "grammar of practice" that has been ignored in our quest to seek abstract grammars of language located in cognition. However, I find the notion of "grammar" falling into the structuralist trap of establishing an abstract system removed from spatiotemporal information. The type of model I seek is a heuristic or template of practices interlocutors might use in order to negotiate meaning in a situated manner by responding to the challenges and resources in each context. Such practices have been categorized into two types by Schatzki (1996): "dispersed" and "integrated." The former are exploratory practices deployed to negotiate unexpected communicative situations to establish mutual footing and seek commonalties. The latter are sedimented and emerge through repeated interactions, integrated with particular social activities and communicative genres to become routine. However, one has to be cautious in starting with such integrated practices in the contact zone, as they may not be shared by the interlocutors. One has to adopt dispersed practices to establish common frames of reference before adopting integrated practices if they turn out to be shared. Dispersed practices can of course lead to integrated practices.

To be successful, a practice-based approach relies on the willingness of people to collaborate with each other to achieve shared meanings and norms across their diversity. This sense of collaboration is especially important in contact zones because interlocutors cannot depend on grammar to resolve their communicative problems. Reviewing empirical studies on lingua-franca English interactions, Seidlhofer (2004) observes that multilinguals display an ethos of solidarity, consensus, and supportiveness to help each other succeed in communication. Scholars in cultural studies are also beginning to theorize forms of "everyday conviviality" (Gilroy 2004) in super-diverse settings, where people are willing to collaborate with each other in social activity. Perhaps there is a new ethic and language ideology coming into prominence through globalization and mobility. However, this ethic is not new. Some have theorized this sense of collaboration as the defining feature of human communication. Labeling this as a *cooperative principle*, Tomasello (2008) observes that "at some point in human evolution, individuals who could engage with one another collaboratively with joint intentions, joint attention, and cooperative motives were at an adaptive advantage" (8). Note that what is shared is not a homogeneous grammar, but intentions, attention, and motives. Perhaps a qualification is in order. In arguing against ideologies of homogeneity and sharedness, I am not opposing all forms of commonalty, but only those which posit uniform values, norms, or conventions as essential for communicative success. Shared objectives in communication are what bring us together to interact and motivate collaboration in achieving meaning across our differences.

Research Context

The data analyzed in this article come from the project "Skilled Migration and Global English: Language, Development, and the African Professional" carried out between February 2010 and 2011. A multidisciplinary group of scholars from the following universities collaborated with me in obtaining data: universities of Bristol, Leeds, and York (UK); University of Sydney (Australia); University of Cape Town (South Africa); and the universities of Wisconsin and Washington (USA). The focus of our inquiry was how language skills facilitate success for skilled migrants in their professions in host communities and, in turn, influence productive contributions for development activities.

This study focused on different destination countries (USA, UK, Australia, and South Africa) where English is the dominant national language. The interview subjects come from sub-Saharan Africa. Skilled professionals are defined as those holding a baccalaureate or comparable educational degree, and working in a profession that requires credentialized skills. The informants come from a range of professions, with most from the fields of education, health care, and management. For data-gathering purposes, field workers focused on urban settings close to their universities. The study involved a total of sixty-six participants. The objective was to obtain in-depth narratives and opinions on the ways skilled migrants negotiate language differences in professional contexts. The research method involved face-to-face, telephone, and email interviews. All face-to-face and telephone interviews were audio-recorded and transcribed. Each interview ran for around forty-five to ninety minutes. The aim of these interviews was to elicit the participants' language ideologies through metapragmatic statements on their interactions in workplace settings. The study is limited by the fact that we didn't observe actual interactions, which data is important to assess the uptake of the practices our subjects discuss. The self-reported data may also not be corroborated by practice. However, the participants' metapragmatic statements reveal their language ideologies, which would play a significant role in the practices they adopt.

Though the semistructured interviews involved eighteen questions, I limit the discussion below to responses to a focal question: "Do you experience any tensions between the variety of English you speak and the other varieties spoken in the host community? How do you handle these differences? Would you say that these have any implications for your work and social life?" In retrospect, the question is influenced by the dominant language ideology that diversity results in tension, though our intention was to elicit the negotiation strategies our subjects use to deal with diversity and unpredictability. As we will see below, almost everyone contested the assumption that the difference in their English should result in tensions. Furthermore, though we focused on negotiations in English, they expanded the perspective to multilingualism by sharing how they negotiated other languages as well in their work experience or drew from their multilingual competence to negotiate English. The narratives and opinions from the interview data were then coded, along the principles of grounded theory to identify the orientations of the subjects to their communicative practices.

Procedural Competence

Exploratory Practices

The responses of our subjects pointed us first to their understanding of contact zone interactions. GHM's (Uganda, female, school administrator in Bristol) response is typical of why most subjects contested our expectation of tensions. She says, "I don't feel any tension about my ability to communicate in English and I think that it is sloppy when people say that they do not understand a person due to accent etcetera, as I speak a little of many different languages and try my best to communicate with everybody and expect all to do likewise." GHM looks down on people who complain about language difference because she assumes that they should be willing to collaborate with her in making the communication succeed. This is conveyed by her statement that she would "try [her] best to communicate with everybody and expect all to do likewise." It is also clear that she expects this collaborative disposition despite the "fragmented multilingualism" (Blommaert 2010, 9) she claims as her formal competence (i.e., note "a little of many different languages").

It also became evident that for many the ability to achieve meaning despite diversity was not a competence developed after migration. DB (Zimbabwe, female, researcher in Penn State) relates that it was such contact zone communication that had characterized her interactions in her home country before migration:

> We speak that language [Zulu] and may be may be somebody walks in and speaks Afrikaans you start speaking Afrikaans and a conversation can continue in three different languages, somebody speaks Afrikaans and I respond in Zulu and she responds in Tswana and continue talking, nothing unusual there. I understand what he says, she he understands what I'm saying, I understand what she say and he understands, so we all are engaged in a conversation. And there is nothing abnormal for us.

What DB depicts here is a conversation in three languages, with each interlocutor representing their contribution in their own language, while presumably using their receptive competence and other ecological resources to understand the other. Since this form of communication (a form of "polyglot dialogue"—see Posner 1991) departs radically from monolingual ideologies of successful communication, DB emphasizes at least twice that this is "nothing unusual" and "nothing abnormal for us." Such testimonies also convey to us that social and communicative realities of super-diversity are not new. They have been characteristic of other non-Western communities for centuries (Khubchandani 1997). Our subjects brought with them competencies and ideologies developed in their home communities to the newly emerging super-diverse contexts of the West.

How did our subjects negotiate this confusing diversity of languages? They focused on exploratory practices rather than grammatical norms. WG (Ethiopia, male, lecturer in Seattle) mentions, after contesting our assumption of tensions characterizing diversity, that he poses clarification questions and confirmation checks to negotiate understanding: "I've never experienced any tension. But when I feel there is a misunderstanding, I try to explain later or I try to ask, 'Do you understand what I am saying?' or 'What I mean by saying this?' or 'Do you understand me?' or, so. Yeah, I have never, you know, faced any tension amongst natives or natives here in terms of language communication." Conversation analysts have identified many such strategies that interlocutors use to achieve mutual understanding. Others, such as rephrasing and back channeling, also came up in our data.

Amare (Ethiopia, female, nurse in Seattle), while acknowledging that she has experienced some misunderstanding because of her accent, narrates how she focuses on negotiation strategies to resolve these problems: "And then later after I understood that it was an accent problem, I just took it easy and I try to improve. I try to improve and make myself clear what I am saying or I will try to say it slowly and clearly. So that way we can have common understanding." Thus Amare indicates that she improves to achieve common understanding by talking more slowly and clearly. Note that she doesn't try to acquire native-speaker accent to resolve the miscommunication.

TW (Zimbabwe, male, juvenile prison officer in Sheffield) narrates how fellow migrants adopted mutual attentiveness to understand each other: "Most people listen intently when they are speaking to each other because they know that this is not our country and we are bound to make mistakes in the way we say some words." Though TW displays traces of native-speaker ideology in treating his differences as "mistakes," it is clear that resolving miscommunication depends on practices such as listening intently rather than adopting native speaker norms.

Some refer to the well-known exploratory strategy in lingua franca situations identified by Firth (1996)—the "let it pass" principle. When they face misunderstanding, multilinguals don't stop the flow of communication by being judgmental. They let it pass. If the problematic item is important, it will come up again, perhaps with more contextual information, helping the interlocutor decode its meaning. Consider EV's (Zimbabwe, male, social worker in Sheffield) explanation:

> People don't want to be seen as though they are rude, lest they are accused of racism or harassment. Even on occasions when you have genuinely not understood what someone has said, you just let it pass. You may follow it up with an email just to be sure. At work, I always follow everything that I have said whether in a meeting or elsewhere with an email to forestall the chances of someone saying that they misunderstood what I was saying or to blame it on my accent.

EV does adopt a compensatory strategy of sending an email to confirm that his message was understood despite the 'let it pass' strategy of his interlocutor.

Sedimented Practices

While the strategies above were situational and exploratory, intended to negotiate miscommunication, certain other strategies emerged as routinized. These strategies constituted a heuristic rather than a sequentially ordered rule. The strategies were adopted as relevant for the interaction. I list each of them below and illustrate them from the data.

Start from your positionality

It became evident that the subjects didn't look for a neutral or common starting point for their interactions at the contact zone. They started with, and even maintained, their own norms and voices. Consider NN's (Zimbabwe, male, teacher in Sheffield) testimony:

NN: I live at a school so I have got very strong bonds with other teachers. Our college is outside town and there are houses there for teachers who want to live there. I think as a community, we are very united, maybe it's because we are isolated from the other communities and we just have to get along well. It could also be because the majority if not all of us who live here are foreigners, the other guys are from South Africa, India, and Trinidad, so it is easy for us to get together really. We speak different English, we speak it differently but we understand each other. We don't need an interpreter, which is good and over the years we have grown to understand each clearly than maybe was the case at first.

I: Do you experience any tensions between the variety of English you speak, and the other varieties spoken in the community? How do you handle these differences? Would you say that these have any implications for your work and social life?

NN: No. Like I said I interact with other professionals from other countries but I haven't come across what I can say is tension between us or indeed with Britons. I can understand them perfectly and my students can understand me.

NN first states that the migrant teachers in this campus use their own varieties of English. It is clear from his statement that they are able to negotiate their difference without the assistance of interpreters or other resources to establish commonalty. The fact that they have established a community of practice of sorts, interacting in this isolated campus over a long time, might have also helped them in achieving mutual comprehension despite the grammatical heterogeneity. Since it is difficult for our interviewer to understand this possibility, he repeats the focal question almost verbatim. At this point, NN raises the claim one notch higher by saying that native speakers ("Britons") are also able to achieve this comprehension.

Negotiate on equal terms

We would expect misunderstanding and dysfunctionality (influenced by language ideologies of sharedness and homogeneity) if everyone maintained their own norms in communication. What helped our subjects achieve understanding was their ability to negotiate differences on equal terms. That is, they adopted a footing that was egalitarian and favored reciprocal practices for mutual negotiations. It is not that there were no power differences (stemming from professional or other social inequalities). It is simply that they adopted equal footing to negotiate meaning in that communicative context, as MA (Nigeria, male, university administrator at Penn State) explains: "It is a two-way street, because of my the combination of Nigerian and British accent and all sorts of things. People had to listen to me more closely to understand what I said, OK? With the same token, I had to listen more carefully to them in order to understand them, [. . .] It was both ways, so I will, just by paying more attention."

The notion that communication in the contact zones is a "two-way street" was a metaphor that came up often in our interviews. Consider the notion of mutual attentiveness expressed by TW above. This ethic is different from dominant language ideologies that treat communication as a one-way street, based on the norms of the "owners" of the language.

Focus on practices

In order to establish this footing and continue to negotiate differences, interlocutors focused on practices rather than form. In addition to the largely verbal strategies discussed earlier, subjects also mentioned diverse multimodal strategies that drew from the broader situational ecology. YG (Zimbabwe, female, social worker in York) mentions that she found it useful to look at the person in face-to-face interactions, perhaps detecting clues from gestures and facial expression and even lip reading, to help comprehension: "In terms of looking at every person while they talk, it helps, to understand. And asking for clarification." Another subject, YC (Ghana, male, graduate student in York), mentions how sometimes even conversational strategies such as confirmation checks and clarification requests may not help in understanding. On these occasions, YC depends on context (perhaps including the topic under discussion and the evolving sequence of talk) to decode meaning: "Some of them, if I say, 'Can you repeat that again?' And they say it, and you can't still hear it, you just assume that, you know, depending on the context... 'Oh, yeah, yeah, yeah, I get it.'"

Co-construct terms of engagement

Through such practices, the interlocutors may go on to establish shared indexicals. Though we didn't have evidence for this, as we didn't collect data on actual interactions, we did hear about interlocutors adopting diverse strategies to establish a shared context to negotiate meaning. In an insightful study, Planken (2005) demonstrates how establishing a shared context can help interlocutors in meaning-making activity. She reports that experienced sales personnel in Sweden and Finland construct a "safe space" for negotiating difference by joking about their own communicative peculiarities. She states: "It would seem that by pointing out and acknowledging cultural differences, participants try or create a temporary in-group of (fellow) non-natives, whose common ground is the fact that they differ culturally" (397). Once this space is constructed, they succeed in their professional interaction despite the fact that they are using a language that they are not native to and features differences. Note that the common ground is a paradox—it is based on their shared difference, not homogeneity.

The participants mention diverse strategies they adopted to construct this common ground. In some cases, they engage in metapragmatic discourse to alter the language ideologies adopted by their noncooperative interlocutors, as WT (Ethiopia, male, health professional in Seattle) describes: "For most of the time, it is not a problem unless others make an issue of it. Then, I may resort to a little bit of educating—depending on how much time or the need to being polite. Mostly it is situational, and requires just patience and tact, time permitting." In the interview, it emerged that the "educating" WT refers to involved metapragmatic discussion. He conveyed the need to adopt a cooperative ethic and negotiate difference rather than insisting on one's own norms. However, WT is careful to be diplomatic in thus changing the footing of their interaction. He doesn't want to be confrontational or offensive, especially if the interlocutors enjoy power, as in the case of native speakers.

Expand your repertoire

In adopting these strategies, our subjects were not being stubborn in holding on to their own norms and preferences. They were expanding their repertoires and reconfiguring their norms. Consider AM (Nigeria, male, university administrator at Penn State), who first came as a faculty member to Penn State, but has since moved on to an administrative position in global programs. Referring first to US norms, he says, "It used to be a barrier, it's no longer a barrier because naturally, right now, I can cope with any varieties of English. Because I deal with people who speak different accents, because I travel all over the world. And when in India, for example, then I'm in China, when I'm in Britain, and so now my ear is tuned towards different accents or what they call accent."

AM acknowledges that his accent posed some problems for native speakers in the beginning. However, his international travel and work requirement has expanded his repertoire so that he is able to negotiate the accents of others in India, China, and the UK. If he had been obsessed with acquiring US English alone, he would have been handicapped for international communication. It also appears from his statement that he has reconfigured his notion of norms beyond native-speaker English to a contact zone ideology that values negotiating diversity. Developing the competence to negotiate "any varieties of English" is more resourceful than adapting to only one powerful variety.

Interestingly, we found that there was a lot of learning taking place despite the practice of our subjects starting interactions with their own preferred language resources. They demonstrated a high language awareness as they decoded the norms of others and expanded their own repertoires by themselves in noneducational settings. OI (Sierra Leone, female, professor at Penn State) relates how she and her husband had an epiphany moment when they became aware of the American preference for diphthongs in contexts where they use a monophthong. Similarly, AC (female, Sierra Leone, administrator at Penn State) narrates how she and her husband became aware of the rhoticity in the Krio that they had omitted in their English, when they returned for a visit to Sierra Leone. In this sense, the procedural knowledge our subjects adopted to negotiate diversity in contact zones was not without implications for cognition and grammar. Through the practice-based negotiation of language, our subjects were developing a heightened metalinguistic competence. They were also treating language socialization as a "lifelong and lifewide" process (Duff 2008, 257).

We mustn't also think of these spaces of interaction as a democratic space devoid of power differences. What we see is that subjects renegotiate power in order to construct a footing favorable for constructing meaning despite diversity and unpredictability. TR (Zimbabwe, male, accountant in Sheffield) mentions that native speakers sometimes asked for repetitions in order to exert their power and make him feel incompetent:

> If someone asks me to repeat myself, I feel offended and slighted; it's as if someone is questioning my command of the language. I think the others feel the same way when I ask them to repeat themselves as well. It is a difficult situation to be in but once you have spent a few days with someone, you get used to the way they speak and get on with it. What I don't like is colleagues that I have worked for years asking me to constantly repeat myself, I find this to be annoying and frustrating as I always think that they should understand the way I speak as I have been with them for a while. It makes me think that they are reminding me that I am a foreigner and I don't talk like them.

For TR, this practice simply conveys his interlocutors' unwillingness to negotiate difference. Given the fact that they have worked with him for a while, he would expect them to be familiar with his language difference. TW (Zimbabwe, male, juvenile prison officer in Sheffield) recounts how even fellow migrants might ask for repetitions to make him feel inferior. Both TR and TW were critical of people who adopted this practice, conveying the importance of a cooperative ethic. Other subjects insist that they themselves rarely asked for repetitions, as they considered them an insult to the speaker. In situations where their interlocutors demonstrated thus their unwillingness to negotiate, our subjects would adopt the strategies of metapragmatic talk and other strategies to change the footing as suitable for a "two-way street" communication. If the interlocutors insist on exerting their power, such interactions would end in communicative failure.

Conclusion

How and where did our subjects develop this strategic competence for negotiating diversity and unpredictability? It emerged that they had developed this competence in their home countries, where similar conditions of diversity were present, as OI's (Sierra Leone, female, professor of English at Penn State) narrative explains:

> One thing I have realized personally for a while is that I always loved, may be because I grew up in a multilingual society where you always knew there were other languages all around you, and so you had a way of opening up to other things. I have a feeling that we, it is easier for us to translate and become something else and understand. But Americans tend to be so unique, language, so just like one language and sound one way.

OI is comparing the dispositions she was socialized into with those of Americans. She has developed a way of "opening up" to others, the capacity to "translate," and transmute her identities and preferences to perceive norms from her interlocutors' point of view (i.e., "become something else and understand"). Americans, on the other hand, insist on their own ("unique") norms and would prefer to maintain interactions in "one language and sound one way." I have elsewhere expanded on the dispositions that our subjects develop in diverse contact zones to practice and develop a language competence for diversity and unpredictability (Canagarajah 2013).

I like to think of these dispositions and language competence as something people are not born with but are socialized into. This is good news for native speakers or those who consider themselves monolinguals. They too can develop these dispositions, as all social spaces are contact zones. There are resources and environments for all of us to develop this language competence. It is the territorial and ownership-based ideologies identified earlier that have prevented those in the West from developing such dispositions. However, there is evidence of a shift in language ideologies in the West too. The ethic of collaboration is becoming more salient, as in the observations of cultural studies scholars such as Gilroy and others who talk about "everyday conviviality" in contexts of super-diversity. If not dominant, this is at least an emergent ideology that can contest the monolingual ideologies based on control, grammar, and propositional knowledge and socialize people into alternate communicative practices.

Teachers can cultivate these language ideologies and ethics to develop a competence for diversity among students. We can fashion pedagogical activities to develop a cooperative disposition among students, which would motivate them to collaborate with their interlocutors in constructing meaning. Furthermore, rather than being obsessed with grammar (in a single language at that), we should develop language awareness that would move students beyond languages to consider how they can draw from diverse semiotic systems and ecologies for meaning. Finally, we should encourage the notion of language socialization as ongoing. We should consider learning as part of language use, not preceding and separated from it. It is in this manner that students would try to figure out the norms of their unpredictable interlocutors and expand their repertoires for diversity. The language competence represented by our subjects, and its pedagogical applications, might help resolve the inconsistencies Kramsch identifies between language use in global contact zones and the pedagogies in our classrooms.

References

Agha, Asif. 2005. "Voice, Footing, Enregisterment." *Journal of Linguistic Anthropology* 15 (1): 38–59.

Atkinson, Dwight, ed. 2011a. *Alternative Approaches to Second Language Acquisition*. Abingdon, VA: Routledge.

———. 2011b. "A Sociocognitive Approach to Second Language Acquisition: How Mind, Body, and World Work Together in Learning Additional Languages." In *Alternative Approaches to Second Language Acquisition*, edited by Dwight Atkinson, 143–66. Abingdon, VA: Routledge.

Atkinson, Dwight, Eton Churchill, Takako Nishino, and Hanako Okada. 2007. "Alignment and Interaction in a Sociocognitive Approach in Second Language Acquisition." *Modern Language Journal* 91:169–88.

Blommaert, Jan. 2010. *The Sociolinguistics of Globalization*. Cambridge: Cambridge University Press.

Braunmüller, K. 2006. "On the Relevance of Receptive Multilingualism in a Globalised World: Theory, History and Evidence from Today's Scandinavia." Paper presented at the First Conference on Language Contact in Times of Globalization, University of Groningen, Germany, September 28.

Byram, Michael. 2008. *From Intercultural Education to Education for Intercultural Citizenship*. Clevedon, Eng.: Multilingual Matters.

Canagarajah, Suresh. 2013. *Translingual Practice: Global Englishes and Cosmopolitan Relations*. Abingdon, VA: Routledge.

Canale, Michael, and Merryl Swain. 1980. "Theoretical Bases of Communicative Approaches to Second Language Teaching and Testing." *Applied Linguistics* 1 (1): 1–47.

Duff, Patsy. 2008. "Language Socialization, Higher Education, and Work." In *Language socialization: Encyclopedia of Language and Education*, edited by Patsy Duff and Nancy Hornberger, 267–70. Boston: Springer.

Duff, Patsy, and Steven Talmy. 2011. "Language Socialization Approaches to Second Language Acquisition: Social, Cultural, and Linguistic Development in Additional Languages." In *Alternative Approaches to Second Language Acquisition*, edited by Dwight Atkinson, 94–116. Abingdon, VA: Routledge.

Fast, Hans. 2012. "Language-Use as Spatial Experience: Migrants' Non-fluent Participation in Stabilisations of Linguistic Practice." Master's thesis, Utrecht University, the Netherlands.

Firth, Alan. 1996. "The Discursive Accomplishment of Normality. On "Lingua Franca" English and Conversation Analysis." *Journal of Pragmatics* 26:237–59.

———. 2009. "Doing Not Being a Foreign Language Learner: English as a *Lingua Franca* in the Workplace and (Some) Implications for SLA." *International Review of Applied Linguistics* 47:127–56.

Firth, Alan, and Johannes Wagner. 1997. "On Discourse, Communication, and (Some) Fundamental Concepts in SLA Research." *Modern Language Journal* 81:285–300.

Gilroy, Paul. 2004. *After Empire: Melancholia or Convivial Culture?* London: Routledge.

Hymes, Dell. 1974. *Foundations in Sociolinguistics: An Ethnographic Approach.* Philadelphia: University of Pennsylvania Press.

Khubchandani, Lachman. 1997. *Revisualizing Boundaries: A Plurilingual Ethos.* New Delhi: Sage.

Lantolf, Jim. 2011. "The Sociocultural Approach to Second Language Acquisition: Sociocultural Theory, Second Language Acquisition, and Artificial L2 Development." In *Alternative Approaches to Second Language Acquisition*, edited by Dwight Atkinson, 24–47. Abingdon, VA: Routledge.

Larsen-Freeman, Diane. 2011. "A Complexity Theory Approach to Second Language Development/Acquisition." In *Alternative Approaches to Second Language Acquisition*, edited by Dwight Atkinson, 48–72. Abingdon, VA: Routledge.

Leung, Constance. 2005. "Convivial Communication: Recontextualizing Communicative Competence." *International Journal of Applied Linguistics* 15 (2): 119–44.

Long, Michael. 1997. "Construct Validity in SLA: A Response to Firth and Wagner." *Modern Language Journal* 81 (3): 318–23.

Ortega, Lourdes. 2014. "Ways Forward for a Bi/Multilingual Turn in SLA." In *The Multilingual Turn: Implications for SLA, TESOL, and Bilingual Education*, edited by Stephen May, 32–52. New York: Routledge.

Pennycook, Alastair. 2010. *Language as a Local Practice*. London: Routledge.

———. 2012. *Language and Mobility: Unexpected Places.* Clevedon, Eng.: Multilingual Matters.

Pennycook, Alastair, and Emi Otsuji. 2015. *Metrolingualism*. Abingdon, VA: Routledge.

Planken, Barbara. 2005. "Managing Rapport in Lingua Franca Sales Negotiations: A Comparison of Professional and Aspiring Negotiators." *English for Specific Purposes* 24:381–400.

Posner, Ronald. 1991. "Der polyglotte Dialog. Ein Humanistengespräch über Kommunikation im mehrsprachigen Europa Aufgezeichnet und ins Hochdeutsche gebracht." *Der Sprachreport* 91 (3): 6–10.

Pratt, Mary Louise. 1987. "Linguistic Utopias." In *The Linguistics of Writing: Arguments between Language and Literature*, edited by Nigel Fabb, Derek Attridge, Alan Durant, and Colin MacCabe, 48–66. Manchester: Manchester University Press.

———. 1991. "Arts of the Contact Zone." *Profession* 91:33–40.

Schatzki, Theodore. 1996. *Social Practice: A Wittgensteinian Approach to Human Activity and the Social.* New York: Cambridge University Press.

Seidlhofer, Barbara. 2004. "Research Perspectives on Teaching English as a Lingua Franca." *Annual Review of Applied Linguistics* 24:209–39.

Tomasello, Michael. 2008. *Origins of Human Communication*. Boston: MIT Press.

van Lier, Leo. 2004. *The Ecology and Semiotics of Language Learning: A Sociocultural Perspective*. Norwell, MA: Kluwer Academic Publishers.

Vertovec, Steven. 2007. "Super-Diversity and Its Implications." *Ethnic and Racial Studies* 30 (6): 1024–54.

Chapter 5

The Strategic Use of Address Terms in Multilingual Interactions during Family Mealtimes

FATMA SAID AND ZHU HUA

THE NOTION OF SUPER-DIVERSITY was proposed by Vertovec (2007) to address the changing nature of global migration characterized by "a dynamic interplay of variables among an increased number of new, small and scattered, multiple-origin, transnationally connected, socio-economically differentiated and legally stratified immigrants" (1024). The intention behind the introduction of this notion, as Meissner and Vertovec (2015) point out, is not to stress the existence of more ethnicities, but to recognize "multidimensional shifts in migration patterns" (541). This chapter aims to contribute to the debate on multidimensional shifts in migration patterns through an examination of multilingual practices, socialization and negotiation of cultural values among members of a family of second- and third-generation immigrants. The findings are based on a three-year study investigating mealtime routines and interactions of a multilingual Arabic-English-speaking family in London. Informed by a sociolinguistic, language socialization theoretical framework (see Ochs and Schieffelin 1984), this chapter focuses on the strategic use of address terms in the course of mealtime interactions (i.e., the way family members employ address terms to achieve a range of interactional goals). These analyses will help us better understand the role of multiple languages in the process of socialization and bring to the fore issues of cultural values and social relationships in the context of super-diversity.

Multilingual Practices at Home

Broadly speaking, multilingual practices within families of immigrant backgrounds have been researched from three interconnected perspectives: language learning, interculturality, and language socialization. In the last two decades, a great deal of literature and scholarly effort have focused on how to support learning of the so-called home, minority, community, or heritage languages. For example, the work in the area of family language policy (FLP, defined as "explicit and overt planning in relation to language use within the home among family members" by King, Fogle, and Logan-Terry [2008, 907]) has generated insights into the factors conducive to successful maintenance of the language(s) concerned. Some of the key factors which have been identified are: close family relational dynamics (Said and Zhu Hua, in press), intergenerational learning (Vidal and He 2015), supportive social networks with extended families and peers of similar backgrounds (Gomaa 2011), language policies and ideologies (Smagulov 2015), and frequent trips back to the parents' home country (Okita 2001). The recent establishment of the AILA research network 'Social and Affective Factors in Home Language Maintenance and Development' represents the latest effort to foster collaborations and exchange between scholars working on home language maintenance and development.

The second perspective, *interculturality*, examines how immigrant families construct, negotiate, and renew their sociocultural values and identities through multilingual interactions. As argued by Zhu Hua (2010), migration is among the most significant domains for examining changes (as well as tensions) in cultural dynamics and values, as the process of migration not only has a significant impact on the individuals and their family and group dynamics (Alba and Nee 2003), but also emphasizes individual and intergenerational differences in their allegiances and everyday practices. Studies of the use of multiple languages in family interactions in this respect have recently shifted from a traditional focus on different generations, different languages, and different sociocultural values (see Edwards 1994; Garcia and Diaz 1992; Li 1994; Paulston 1994) to an approach that sees multilingual practices as contextually contingent resources employed by multilingual speakers to both index and construct their everyday worlds and, in particular, their own (and new) sociocultural values, and their roles and identities, as well as those of others (Zhu Hua 2008). A small number of available studies on multilingual family interactions following this approach have argued that multilingual practices contribute to the emergence of new family relational dynamics and the development of sociocultural values (e.g., code-switching [Williams 2005; Zhu Hua 2008], use of address terms [Zhu Hua 2010; Song 2007], and metalanguaging [Zhu Hua 2010]).

The third perspective, language socialization, closely related to language learning and development and interculturality perspectives, investigates how language learning may relate to becoming a competent member of community. Language socialization (LS) refers to a dual process of socialization *through* language and socialization *into* language (Ochs and Schieffelin 1984). Although earlier LS research focused primarily on how children become competent members of their communities through language learning within social activities, LS research recognizes that socialization is a bidirectional process that involves both novices and experts taking on the roles of *socializer* and *socialized* in the course of joint activity. For example, Ochs and Schieffelin (2011) emphasize that "participation in communicative practices is promoted *but not determined* by a legacy of socially and culturally informed persons," suggesting that such practical participation provides opportunities for children to develop their own agency and personally innovative social practices (4). Recently, studies on multilingual LS have begun to emerge (see Bayley and Schecter 2003; for a review, see Baquedáno-Lopez and Kattan 2008) and explicate the complexity of socialization and the challenges faced by families in maintaining heritage languages and cultural values associated with their places of origins while learning the host/mainstream language and culture. One such challenge is the intergenerational differences in beliefs and perceptions about the roles of home in contrast to mainstream languages and language use, which often results in heightened metalinguistic awareness accompanied by constant, explicit discussion regarding which languages to use, when, to what extent and *why*, in family interaction. In another study (Said and Zhu Hua, in press), we report that, in the Arabic- and English-speaking multilingual family that we researched, one desirable family value, "being clever," is consistently referred to in its Arabic form, *shaatir*, despite constant blending and mixing of different languages. Additionally, an overall positive multilingual outlook in the family language policy and practice of this group assisted the children in navigating between their two languages. This poses the question of why one language is preferred over another by a speaker. Hence, in the following section, we discuss why we choose to focus on address terms in our attempt to find answers to the above question.

Address Terms

Address terms provide an opportunity to investigate the interrelatedness of language use, social relations and cultural values (Zhu Hua 2010). By definition, address terms (or *terms of address*) are "words or expressions used in interactive, dyadic and face-to-face situations to designate the addressee" (Braun 1988, 7). They vary from society to society and can be direct names (Mary), titles (Sir, Doctor), or terms that reflect the relationship between two people (mum, son).

In general, the study of these terms is concerned with the ways in which people address one another across various cultural and linguistic conventions and what these choices reveal about social hierarchies (Braun 1988; Brown and Gilman 1960). More specifically, from a sociolinguistic perspective (Farghal and Shakir 1994; Peoples and Bailey 2010), address terms are viewed as socially driven phenomena, as they mirror the complex social relations of individuals in a speech community (Paulston and Bruder 1976), thus illustrating the relative power and distance of speaker and hearer (Wood and Kroger 1991). In many cultures terms of address act as a means of politeness through which respect is shown to the 'face' of the addressee during conversation (Brown and Levinson 1978). Braun (1988) states that address term is socially meaningful, since "speakers have to choose between several variants; all of which are grammatically interchangeable forms and the variant chosen expresses social features of the dyad" (13). The expectation is that the choice of one over the other will index the attitudes and identities of the speaker, thus situating his or her relationship with the addressee. Therefore, the study of address terms is crucial in understanding how a given language provides tools as well as choices for its speakers to position themselves in relation to others.

Learning address terms in multilingual immigrant families is essential but often a complex process. Children need not only to acquire two or more distinct systems of address, but also to develop understanding of the roles that various terms of address (choices between languages and choices within a language) play in the establishment and maintenance of social relationships. For example, Song's (2007) study of Korean families in a midwestern US city examines how parents choose to socialize their Korean- and English-speaking bilingual children into particular Korean address terms that index hierarchies between speakers, addressees, and others referred to in discourse. She identifies a range of language socialization practices by parents, including defining relationships and introducing address terms to children when meeting strangers for the first time, animating children's voices, and recasting (repeating and correcting) their utterances, thus providing a model for the children in how to use each appropriately. The children in her study demonstrated bilingual creativity in negotiating their presentations of self, through code-switching to English or 'anglicizing' a Korean name (i.e., preferring one's first name with an English pronunciation) to avoid indexical meanings associated with Korean address terms.

Similarly, Zhu Hua (2010) investigates address term use within Chinese families living in the UK and examines how the socialization of such terms and associated metalanguage practices allowed family members to create new cultural and social identities as they navigate between Chinese and English cultures. The study argues that through language socialization, younger generations of immigrant families not only become familiar with the social, cultural, and linguistic norms of their community, but also play an active role in constructing and creating their own social and cultural identities. This chapter addresses questions of *how* and *why* some cultural values are socialized through a particular language by investigating the strategic use of address terms in the mealtime interactions of a multilingual Arabic- and English-speaking family.

The joint activity of family mealtimes has long fascinated anthropologists and linguists alike (see Blum-Kulka 1997; Mondada 2009; Said 2014; De Leon 2011; Snow and Beales 2006; Busch 2012). Mealtimes are seen, in many cultures, not only as a setting in which children get nourished but also as a context through which they are socialized by their parents (Bugge and Almås 2005; Douglas 1970, 1972). This chapter views the mealtime event as a 'cultural' site for socialization, in line with Ochs and Shohet (2006), who regard mealtimes as "historically durable, yet transformable, socially organized and organizing, and tempospatially situated arenas, which are laden with symbolic meanings and mediated by material artefacts" (35). Language, in the course of these joint interactional episodes, operates as a tool through which parents socialize their children (into culture, manners, morality, family rules, etc.) and through which children equally socialize their parents or refute their parents' socialization.

The Family Under Study & Arabic Address Terms

The data reported in this chapter are part of a longitudinal study that set out to investigate how a multilingual family made use of their multiple languages. The interactional data was collected through video recordings taken at mealtimes. The mother of the family was asked to be in charge of recording, except for the first one, for which the first author was present. The recordings were later transcribed, and after the data was anonymized, two independent Arabic-English bilingual speakers checked the transcription for accuracy. Data was transcribed according to LIDES (MacWhinney 2000), a system for multilingual data (see Appendix for transcription conventions). The system allows for multi-tiered transcription, in which the researcher can present the utterance first in the original language, and then offer a gloss, followed by a translation in English (Moyer and Turrell 2010).

The family of four live in London. The father is a second-generation Arab immigrant whose parents migrated to Newcastle from Algeria in the early 1950s. He is a multilingual speaker of Algerian Arabic and English and literate in Standard Arabic. Similarly, the mother is a second-generation immigrant whose parents migrated from South Yemen to Sheffield in the 1960s. She speaks Yemeni Arabic and English, understands Standard Arabic, but cannot read or write (any form of) Arabic. The boys, Hamid (age six) and Adam (age nine), speak Arabic (in this case a mixture of Yemeni and Algerian Arabic) and English. At the time of data collection, the children were learning French and Spanish in a language club after school during the week and attending an Algerian community school where they were learning Standard Arabic on Saturdays.

There are a number of features associated with Arabic address terms. First of all, in the Arabic language speakers usually address one another using first names (Ahmad, Laila), *teknonyms* (in some cultures this refers to a title given to someone, for example, father/mother of so-and-so), or kinship relations (e.g., my brother/sister). These forms of address are typically prefixed by a vocative marker/particle 'ya' meaning 'O,' which serves to attract the attention of a potential addressee while doubling up as a politeness marker, for example, *ya walad* (O boy).

Secondly, the Arabic kinship terms are categorized under the Sudanese kinship system (Schwimmer 1996). The latter is one of the more complex systems, since each relative is clearly defined (e.g. mother's sister is different from father's sister and mother's sister's son is distinct from father's sister's son). Typically, reference terms (e.g., sister) can be changed to address terms (e.g., my sister) by adding a pronoun suffix to the lexeme that describes the relationship between speaker and addressee. The pronoun suffix appears in the postconsonantal or the postvocalic position and can be the first person pronominal suffix: /-i/-y/, or /-a/ in some dialects, meaning my; for example, in Standard Arabic *umm-i* (my mum), *ibn-i* (my son), or *bint 'amm-i* (my father's brother's daughter). The same process takes place with other non-kin terms or words (for example, *sadeeq-i*, 'my friend').

Thirdly, Arabic address terms are known for a feature referred to as the "reverse role address term" (Rieschild 1998), or "bi-polar kin term" (Yassin 1977) or still the "inverse address term" (Braun 1988). Rieschild (1998) defines the feature as follows: "the senior (by generation, age, or relative social position) in a dyad addresses the junior by using the (usually kinship) vocative that juniors use to address seniors in that relationship" (917). The reverse-role address term only reflects the gender of the speaker, not that of the addressee. For example *ya Maama*, when used in its reverse role, means "O my daughter/son," and its function, as will be discussed below, is socially significant. The reverse role is also present in other languages such as Georgian, Turkish, Russian, Romanian, and Italian, and they share similar features and functions.[1]

Data and Findings

Overview

Out of the 490 utterances in the data, 165 (33 percent) contain address terms of various types such as kinship, reverse role (bipolar), proper names, and endearment address terms. In total there are 21 different address terms. Among 7 kinship terms used in the data, some are prefixed with the vocative marker *ya* and others are used without it. Table 5.1 lists the types of address terms used (in both English and Arabic), and the number of times they occur in the data.

A closer examination of the family's use of address terms reveals some distributional patterns. First of all, as table 5.1 shows, nearly all the address terms are in Arabic. The exceptions are the children's proper names (Adam and Hamid), baby (an English endearment), and Maama and Baaba, which could be either Arabic or English. Secondly, the most frequent address terms found in the data are Maama (Mum, 25 percent) and Baaba (Dad, 22 percent), together constituting 47 percent of the address terms used. The third most frequent address term is Habeebi (my beloved), used by the parents to address their sons. Third, the children never address their mother and father with the vocative *ya* but in contrast the parents frequently use the vocative when addressing the children. Fourth, on some occasions, reverse-role address terms are used by adults to address children (e.g., *ya maama* meaning "O my daughter/son"), which serve to mitigate the asymmetry between speaker and addressee. Although the outcome (of whether egalitarianism is achieved or not) is based on context and difficult to measure, the use of the reverse role usually makes the child feel obliged in some way to comply to the requests of the elder because of the deference they have been shown (see Yassin 1977 for extensive examples). Fifth, 'ya Hamid' and 'Hamid' constitute 11 percent of the address terms, while 'ya Adam' and 'Adam' occur at a rate of 5.4 percent across the data set. Finally, there are a number of Arabic endearment terms to be found in the data, including *ya habeebi* (O my beloved), *ya ouleedee* (O my little boy), *ya sagheer* (O little one), *ya awlaad* (O children), and *ya batal* (O hero).

As Braun (1988) points out, the primary function of address terms is to seek the attention of the addressee. As the above analysis of the distribution of address terms demonstrates, the family members indeed use proper names, kinship, endearment, and reverse-role address terms primarily for attention and other functions, as will be explained shortly. For example, the children frequently call out 'Baaba! Baaba!' or 'Maama!' when they want to ask for permission or simply begin a conversation. A close analysis is carried out below to examine how the address terms are used in the mealtime interactions among the family for strategic functions that go beyond the primary function of seeking attention.

Table 5.1. Use and distribution of address terms

Address term	Type/category	Number of times it occurs (165 in total)
Maama (mum)	Kinship term	42 (25%)
Baaba (dad)	Kinship term	36 (22%)
Adam	Proper name	6 (3.6%)
Hamid	Proper name	9 (5.5%)
Shaatir (clever boy)	Adjective (singular, masculine)	8 (4.9%)
Baby	Noun (singular, neutral)	1 (0.6%)
Habaaybee (my beloveds)	Personal pronoun (deictic) + plural masculine noun	1 (0.6%)
Habeebi (my beloved)	Personal pronoun (deictic) + singular masculine noun	19 (11.6%)
Khaltee (my sister's daughter)	Reverse role (bipolar) singular feminine noun + personal possessive pronoun (deictic)	1 (0.6%)
Khaltee (my maternal aunt)	Kinship term, singular feminine noun + personal possessive pronoun (deictic)	1 (0.6%)
Ya habeebi (O my beloved)	Vocative marker + singular masculine noun + personal possessive pronoun (deictic)	4 (2.4%)
Ya ouleedee (O my little boy)	Vocative marker + singular masculine noun + dimunitive marker + personal possessive pronoun (deictic)	3 (1.8%)
Baaba (my son)	Reverse role/bipolar, kinship term	2 (1.2%)
Ya Baaba (O my son)	Reverse role/bipolar, vocative marker + kinship term	2 (1.2%)
Ya Abee (O my father)	Vocative marker + classical Arabic kinship term (singular masculine)	1 (0.6%)
Ya sagheer (O little one)	Vocative marker + singular masculine adjective	1 (0.6%)
Ya awlaad (O children)	Vocative marker + classical Arabic plural masculine noun	1 (0.6%)
Ya Adam	Vocative marker + proper name	3 (1.8%)
Ya Hamid	Vocative marker + proper name	9 (5.5%)
Ya batal (O hero)	Vocative marker + singular masculine noun	1 (0.6%)
Ya 'iyaali (O my children)	Vocative marker + plural masculine noun	2 (1.2%)

Source: Said 2014

Power and Solidarity

Our analysis shows that first, when parents use address terms, they do so not only to reinforce their authority as parents, especially when the terms are followed by commands or reprimands, but also to connect with their children. Excerpt 1 is taken from a dinner episode in which the mother and the boys are present without the father (March 2009). The mother has set the table and is bringing the last dish over. The boys, however, are running around and show no intention of sitting down and getting ready to eat. So the mother calls out to them.

Excerpt 1 MD3.03.09:1-2

1.	**Mum**:	Stop.... *wagifuu*... *Ya 'iyaali*... Hamid , *Ya* Adam *Yalla* behave.... We are on camera... *yalla iglisuu*!
	%glo:	Stop.IMP.Pl.Msc.. O (VOC) kids.POSS...O (VOC) ..come on come on sit.IMP.Pl.MSc
	%tra:	Stop...stop... O my children...Hamid, O Adam come one behave we are on camera.... come on sit down
	%situ:	Very high pitched especially when using Arabic
2.	**Adam**:	Haha....okay.. haha...stop [Hamid ...no no
3.	**Mum**:	*Yalla* I'm not repeating myself [*Yalla al heen*!
	%glo:	Come on.IMP Come on.IMP the.DET Now.N
	%tra:	Come on I'm not repeating myself come on right now
4.	**Adam**:	Okay sorry Maama.... .Come on let's sit down.... no...no...now

In this episode, the mother follows up her direct command with three consecutive address terms. She uses the vocative marker *ya* twice in one utterance, first in "ya 'iyaali" (O my children) and second in "ya Adam" (O Adam). Three instances of address terms in one utterance not only serve to pin the troublemakers down, but also to convey a sense of urgency and reflect the multidimensional nature of the family relationship. The idea of the multidimensional nature of a relationship (i.e., the coexistence of power and solidarity) is closely examined by Tannen (2003, 2007). She argues that the unidirectional understanding of power in conversation (i.e., that a speaker can only express either power or solidarity and not both) cannot account for many communicative exchanges, especially in family interactions where emotion, love, allegiances, and conflicts are a significant part of the relationship. Instead, she suggests that both power and solidarity can be expressed in a single term of address, reflecting the multidimensional nature of the relationship. In line with this argument, we argue that address terms used by the parents to the children represent more than one dimension of their relationship and social hierarchy.

In the excerpt, the mother chooses an Arabic personal possessive address term (*ya 'iyaali*) to address her children. *'Iyaali* is formed of the plural noun *'iyaal* and suffixed with *yaa* (-y), which is a first-person possessive (connected) pronoun (together it means "my children"). Used in the context of the excerpt, this address term not only attracts the children's attention, but also serves as a reminder of their family bonds. In a single utterance she asserts her authority as a parent, while at the same time bringing them close by acknowledging that they are *her* children. As a result of the mother's pleading, in turns 2 and 4, Adam asks Hamid to stop running around and he also apologizes to his mother.

Deference, Resistance, and Agency

As discussed previously, the Arabic address system provides speakers with a number of options to address interlocutors. One of the options is the reverse-role address term, whereby the senior (in this case, parents) addresses the junior (children) using the same term the children would use to address them. This functions to bring the child closer, evoking an egalitarian relationship implicit in the degree of respect the elder has chosen to confer upon the junior. This use is supposed to have such an effect on the addressee that they are left feeling obliged to appease the speaker because of the deference shown to them.

The following excerpt is an example in which the father attempts to exploit the function of the reverse-role address term. The interaction takes place in July 2009 during a late lunch with all family members present. The father has been encouraging Hamid to finish eating his food (a recurring pattern in the data) before he can start dessert. It is a general rule in their household that food is not to be wasted (as is evident in the data collected) and dessert is only for those who finish their meal (the address terms under discussion are highlighted in bold).

Excerpt 2 JL4. 06.09:35-43

35. **Dad**: *Yalla Kul Ya* Hamid!
%glo: come on. IMP. Neut eat.IMP.Sing.Msc O.VOC
%trans: Come on eat Hamid!

36. **Hamid**: Ohh...but it's too much

37. **Dad**: Yalla, finish it **Baaba**!
%glo: come on.IMP.Neut Dad.N.Sing.Msc
%trans: Come on, finish it son!

38. **Hamid** ...No, I'm...umm ***Ya Abee***, I'm full
%glo: O.VOC father.N.Msc.Sing.POSS
%trans: ...No, I'm full...umm my father, I'm full

39. **Dad**: Already? Laa try ***Ya batal***!
%glo: No.NEG O.VOC hero.N.Sing.Msc
%trans: Already? No try [you] champion!
%situ: Hamid pulls face as if to cry looks at mum and dad and at Adam.

40. **Hamid**: ***Ya Abee***...mmmmm
%glo: O.VOC father.N.Msc.Sing.POSS
%trans: O my father...mmmmm

41. **Dad**: *Bass **Ya habibi***...eat as much as you can
%glo: suffice.N 0.VOC beloved.N.Sing.Msc.POSS
%trans: That's enough my darling....eat as much as you can

42. **Hamid**: Okay Baaba...oh oh it's hot
%glo: dad.N.Sing.Msc
%trans: Okay dad....oh oh it's hot

43. **Mum**: Oh is it? So be careful, don't blow that hard...come on, one more spoon

The father begins with an address term "ya Hamid" and asks Hamid to eat his food (turn 35). Hamid resists by responding that the food is too much (turn 36), which leads to repetition of the same request by the father (turn 37). The difference, however, is that he uses a reverse-role address term in his repeated request. By referring to Hamid as *baaba* (meaning "my son"), the father exploits the reverse-role address term to make his request more pressing and this obliges Hamid to comply, due to the sense of deference and respect as well as connection, bond, and solidarity evoked by the address term. Nonetheless, in turn 38, Hamid continues his refusal, declaring that he is full. What is remarkable, however, in his refusal is that he uses a formal Standard Arabic address term, *ya abee*. One of the consequences of its use (due to its formality) is that it creates distance between the addressee and the speaker because of its extremely high degree of deference for the addressee. Structurally, it is made up of the vocative marker *ya* and the noun *ab* meaning father, and the personal possessive pronoun *yaa* (-y) to signal belonging to the speaker (*ya* + *ab* + *yaa* = *ya abee*). This is the only time Hamid uses the *ya* vocative marker when addressing his father, and the use of *abee* rather than the usual *Baaba* reflects even greater politeness and is marked.

In particular, Hamid's choice of *abee* further magnifies the asymmetry between himself and his father, and this choice is similar in its effect to his father's use of the reverse-role address term. Where the father wishes to index closeness through the reverse role term, Hamid creates distance through the highly formal address term; and where the father wishes to reinforce his power subtly, Hamid challenges it openly through the distance created by the term *abee*. This is a clear example of the child showing astute awareness of the indexical values and symbolisms of their languages through the strategic selection of address terms in order to challenge or refute the parents' practices of socialization.

In turn 39 the father attempts to renegotiate power and solidarity with Hamid. This time, he uses an endearment term combining the vocative marker *ya* with the address term *batal* meaning "hero." He attempts to coax Hamid into finishing his food through praise, perhaps even using a term Hamid likes. Yet again in turn 40 Hamid protests and refuses through the repetition of his last tactic, using the grand and highly formal *ya abee*. This second attempt pushes the father to ease the pressure off Hamid and again he addresses Hamid with another endearment term, *ya habíbi*, meaning "my beloved." At this point it seems the father gives up as he tells Hamid calmly to "eat as much as" he can (turn 41). In the end, Hamid gives his plate to his mother with food on it and he gets to eat dessert. He has reproduced a family practice whereby one can still have dessert even if they have not eaten all their food. Hamid's awareness of the symbolisms of the Arabic language was a tool in his reproduction of an established family practice (Ochs 1990).

Socialization of Gender Roles

There are some instances in which address terms are used by parents to index masculinity and therefore serve as an indirect means of socializing gender roles. In the above excerpt, the father's choice of the address term *ya batal* meaning "O hero" is such an example. It reflects expectations about how boys should be or should behave that are prevalent in many cultures. Boys need to be strong, brave, and tough, just like heroes who are admired for their courage and achievements (see Cohen-Mor 2013). Socialization of the qualities of bravery and strength is echoed elsewhere in another interaction that takes place in May 2009, between the mother, her sister, the two boys, and their two cousins (May and Khalid). In this part of the excerpt Hamid has been crying because he wants more biscuits.

Excerpt 3 MT6.05.09: 26

21.	**Hamid**:	Mmmm…okay but I took a bad one and I wanted…
	%act:	Still sobbing and wiping his tears as he takes one. His aunt reaches over to wipe his tears and pat his head whilst making sympathetic sounds.
22.	**Mum**:	*Yalla bass khalaas ya ouleedee… yalla* Hala *madry* about this boy… I am worried he cries for the smallest thing! *Allah yastur*
	%glo:	not.NEG know.1st.PRS.Sing God protect.PRS.Sing.Msc
	%tra:	Come on that's enough, enough my little boy…come on, Hala I don't know about this boy… I am worried he cries for the smallest thing! May God protect [us]
	%situ:	Addresses her sister in a half whisper then moves to Hamid and gives him a kiss
23.	**Hala**:	*Bass ya habibi bass… ma'alaaay* mm? Sheikha *la tukkabiril maudhu'* it's fine, he'll get over it. Such a worrier!
	%glo:	Enough O.VOC beloved.POSS enough… no.NEG trouble… don't.PRO make big.PRS.Sing. Fem the.DEF subject.OBJ.ACC
	%tra:	Enough my beloved enough… don't worry mm? Sheikha don't make such a big deal [out of it] it's fine he'll get over it. Such a worrier!
	%act:	She turns to look at her sister and touches her shoulder.
24.	**Hamid**:	mmmmm
	%act:	Still sobbing and takes a sip of his drink
25.	**Mum**:	*Shaatir ya habibi*
	%glo:	Clever.ADJ.Msc O.VOC beloved.POSS
	%tra:	Clever boy O my dear

26. **Hala**: Aiwa *intal asad ya khaltee* now come on wipe your tears
%glo: Yes you.Msc.Sing lionMsc.Sing maternal aunt.POSS. N. Fem
%tra: Yes my beloved nephew you are a lion, now come on wipe your tears

The excerpt begins in turn 21 with Hamid crying, pleading with his mother and asking her for a biscuit. In turn 22, Mum reassures him through her use of the diminutive kinship address term *ya ouledee* (O my little boy). This pattern is repeated over the next few turns with different address terms brought in: *ya habibi* meaning "my beloved," by the aunt in turn 23 and *Shaatir ya habibi* meaning "clever boy O my dear" by the mother (turn 25). Elsewhere, we have reported how *shaatir* is a desirable family value that the parents try to socialize the boys into (Said and Hua, in press). It can mean, based on the context of use, "cleverness," "good behavior," or "maturity" in how one deals with things. The parents constantly use this cultural keyword to praise and encourage the children to aim for this value. In this excerpt, the mother uses that same keyword in turn 25 along with the diminutive and endearment address terms to comfort Hamid and position him as a little beloved child as she works to stop him crying. Importantly, it is the aunt in turn 26 who says "intal asad ya khaltee" (you are a lion my nephew). This is similar to the way Dad used "hero" in the previous excerpt: the choice of *asad* (lion) by the aunt brings to the fore the Arabic concept of bravery, especially in reference to boys. In Arab culture boys are socialized to be strong in both body and mind, and although crying for a boy is not frowned upon, they are taught not to be weak over trivial matters (Aboul-Fatouh 1969).

The gender socialization taking place in this family is similar to that reported in Luykx's work (2003) on Aymara-Spanish speaking families. She reports that girls were taught gender roles through their exclusive use of Aymara, whilst boys were encouraged to code-switch between Aymara and Spanish to reflect their position as men in the community. In all, the use of "hero" and "lion" as address terms evokes the desirable attributes of masculinity, reflects expectation of gender roles by the parents, and unearths the moments of indirect, subtle learning in everyday life.

Conclusion

Address terms have long been studied by sociolinguists through questionnaires (self-reporting) and observations. While these works have pointed to address terms as a socially driven phenomenon and a site for power negotiations, few studies have attempted to examine the multiple functions of address terms during interaction, their role in language socialization, and above all, their role in maintaining and negotiating shifts in family values in the overall transformative context of "diversification of diversity" (Vertovec 2007). By employing a methodology different to the conventional approach in studies of address terms and focusing on understanding how cultural values are negotiated, this chapter carried out a close, turn-by-turn analysis of address terms in mealtime conversations of a multilingual family. What has emerged from our analysis is an illustration of the family members' awareness of and ability to use address terms strategically. This strategic use serves to show how socialization takes place, how parents make efforts, and how children resist and transform the socialization in everyday interaction. The preference to use address terms of the home languages also provides some insights into the kind of cultural values and traditions immigrant families wish to preserve and pass onto the younger generations. Importantly, our analysis highlights that children are not passive recipients of socialization and, similar to their parents, they are able to use address terms strategically and to their advantage. Through such agentive uses and acts the children contribute toward their own socialization and are able to transform some of the cultural practices into new hybrid ones that suit the needs of this transnational family.

These findings contribute to our understanding of the role of multiple languages, the impact of migration and the changing power relations and cultural values in transnational families. Family members, despite their relaxed attitude toward the use of multiple languages and their flexible multilingual practices, use Arabic address terms (rather than English equivalents) almost exclusively when they are addressing one another. This raises the issue of why a language is preferred over another when it comes to a particular function. A limited number of available studies on language use among immigrant families who settle in English-speaking countries (see Song 2007; Zhu Hua 2010) suggest that the families in these studies, similar to the family under study here, seem to prefer address terms of their home languages over the language of the host society. Such a preference may be attributed to the fact that address terms are not just a means of seeking someone's attention or referring to someone, but are a means of reflecting the interrelationship between language use, social relations, and cultural values, as reviewed earlier in this chapter.

The Arabic language offers this family an address system that allows the members to strategically use terms of address not just as a means of communication but also as a way to reflect their positions. An example would be the option of addressing junior speakers through the reverse role-address term, allowing the senior to hierarchically bring the junior closer. Although such a move is outwardly egalitarian, it in fact serves to pressure the junior to adhere to the senior's request or advice, hence positioning the senior in a stronger place in the relationship. The multiplicity and myriad of address terms in the Arabic language gives speakers the option to use language as a means of achieving desired outcomes and building relationships. In order to strengthen the claims made here, more work needs to be carried out with regard to how other Arabic families use address terms. However, it is hoped that this chapter goes someway in understanding the roles and functions of Arabic address terms among multilingual transnational families.

Notes

We would like to thank Dr. Norbert Vanek and Professor Leah Roberts for their initial comments and constructive feedback on the first drafts of this chapter.

1. Further information on Arabic address terms can be found in Yassin (1977) on Kuwaiti Arabic, Mitchell (1986) on address terms in a rural Jordanian village, Parkinson (1985) on Egyptian Arabic address terms in Cairo, Abuamsha (2010) on Palestinian Arabic (Gazan dialect), and Holes (1983) on choice and use of address terms in Bahrani Arabic in Manama.

Transcription Conventions

Symbol	**Function**
Italicized	Arabic (spoken for both Yemeni and Algerian Arabic)
Bold	Standard Arabic
Normal script	English
%glo	Is the gloss of the original Arabic utterances and is the grammatical presentation of the word (nouns, imperatives, pronouns)
%situ (or **%act**)	Is a description of the extra-linguistic nonverbal actions that accompany the verbal exchanges of the conversation
Dots (...or......)	Show a pause, the longer the pause the more dots are placed
%tra	Translation of the original Arabic, where needed
xxxx	Inaudible or unintelligible speech
[	
[	Parallel square brackets in two different turns means an overlap or simultaneous speech
((	Mean that there was an absence of a pause between one speaker and the other, though it does not constitute an overlap
!	High tone in speech

References

Abuamsha, D. 2010. "Terms of Address in Palestinian Arabic." Abstract. MA thesis, Ball State University, Muncie, Indiana. Accessed May 30, 2015. https://cardinalscholar.bsu.edu/handle/123456789/193706.

Aboul-Fatouh, Hilmi M. 1969. *A Morphological Study of Egyptian Colloquial Arabic.* London: Walter de Gruyter GmbH & Co.

Ahearn, Laura M. 2001. "Language and Agency." *Annual Review of Anthropology* 30:109–37.

Alba, Richard, and Victor Nee. 2003. *Remaking the American Mainstream: Assimilation and Contemporary Immigration*. Cambridge, MA: Harvard University Press.

Auer, Peter, ed. 2002. *Code-Switching in Conversation: Language, Interaction and Identity.* London: Routledge.

Baquedáno-Lopez, Patricia, and Shlomy Kattan, ed. 2008. "Language Socialisation in Schools." In *Encyclopedia of Language and Education*, edited by Nancy Hornberger and Patricia Duff, 161–73. Dordrecht, Nld.: Springer / Kluwer Academic Publishers.

Bayley, Robert, and Sandra R. Schecter, ed. 2003. *Language Socialization in Bilingual and Multilingual Societies.* Clevedon, Eng.: Multilingual Matters.

Blum-Kulka, Shoshana. 1997. *Dinner Talk: Cultural Patterns of Sociability and Socialization in Family Discourse.* Mahwah, NJ: Erlbaum.

Bourdieu, Pierre. 1991. *Language and Symbolic Power.* Boston: Harvard University Press.

Braun, Friederike. 1988. *Terms of Address: Problems of Patterns and Usage in Various Languages and Cultures.* Berlin: Mouton de Gruyter.

Brown, Roger, and Albert Gilman. 1960. *The Pronouns of Power and Solidarity*. Indianapolis: Bobbs-Merrill.

Brown, Penelope, and Steven. C. Levinson. 1978. "Universals in Language Usage: Politeness Phenomena." In *Questions and Politeness: Strategies in Social Interaction*, edited by Esther N. Goody, 56–311. Cambridge: Cambridge University Press.

Bugge, Annechen B., and Reider Almås. 2005. "Domestic Dinner: Representations and Practices of a Proper Meal among Young Suburban Mothers." *Journal of Consumer Culture* 6:203–28.

Busch, Gillian. 2012. "Disputes in Everyday Life: Social and Moral Orders of Children and Young People." *Sociological Studies of Children and Youth* 15 (2): 27–56.

Cohen-Mor, Dalya. 2013. *Fathers and Sons in the Arab Middle East.* New York: Plagrave MacMillan.

De Leon, Lourdes. 2011. "Language Socialization and Multiparty Participation" In *The Handbook of Language Socialization*, edited by Alessandro Duranti, Elinor Ochs, and Bambi Schieffelin, 81–111. Malden, MA: Wiley-Blackwell.

Douglas, Mary. 1970. *Natural Symbols*. London: Random House.

———. 1972. "Deciphering a Meal." *Daedalus* 101:61–81.

Duranti, Alessandro, and Steven Black. 2011. "Socialization and Improvisation." In *The Handbook of Language Socialization*, edited by Alessandro Duranti, Elinor Ochs, and Bambi Schieffelin, 443–63. Malden, MA: Wiley-Blackwell.

Edwards, John. 1994. *Mutilingualism*. London: Routledge.

Farghal, Mohammed, and Abdullah Shakir. 1994. "Kin Terms and Titles of Address as Relational Social Honorifics in Jordanian Arabic." *Anthropological Linguistics* 36 (2): 240–53.

Garcia, Ricardo L., and Carlos. F. Diaz. 1992. "The Status and Use of Spanish and English among Hispanic Youth in Dade County (Miami) Florida: a Sociolinguistic Study." *Language and Education* 6:13–32.

Gomaa, Yasser. A. 2011. "Language Maintenance and Transmission: The Case of Egyptian Arabic in Durham, Eng.." *International Journal of English Linguistics* 1 (1). http://www.ccsenet.org/journal/index.php/ijel/article/viewFile/9295/7026.

Holes, Clive. 1983. "Bahraini Dialects: Sectarian Differences and the Sedentary/Nomadic Split." *Zeitschrift für Arabische Linguistik* 10:7–38.

King, Kendall, Lynn Fogle, and Aubery Logan-Terry. 2008. "Family Language Policy." *Language and Linguistics Compass* 2 (5): 907–22.

Li, Wei. 1994. *Three Generations, Two Languages, One Family: Language Choice and Language Shift in a Chinese Community in Britain*. Clevedon, Eng.: Multilingual Matters.

Luykx, Aurolyn. 2003. "Weaving Languages Together: Family Language Policy and Gender Socialization in Bilingual Aymara Households." In *Language Socialization in Bilingual and Multilingual Societies*, edited by Robert Bayley and Sandra R. Schecter, 25–43. Clevedon, Eng.: Multilingual Matters.

MacWhinney, Brian. 2000. *The CHILDES Project: Tools for Analysing Talk*. Mahwah, NJ: Lawrence Erlbaum Associates.

Meissner, Fran, and Steven Vertovec. 2015. "Comparing Super-Diversity." *Ethnic and Racial Studies* 38 (4): 541–55.

Mitchell, Terence F. 1986. "What Is Educated Spoken Arabic?" *International Journal of the Sociology of Language* 61: 7–32.

Mondada, Lorenza. 2009. "The Methodical Organisation of Talking and Eating: Assessments in Dinner Conversations." *Food Quality and Preference* 20 (8): 558–71.

Ochs, Elinor. 1990. "Indexicality and Socialization." In *Cultural Psychology: Essays on Comparative Human Development*, edited by James. W. Stigler, Gilbert Herdt, and Richard Shweder, 287–308. Cambridge: Cambridge University Press.

Ochs, Elinor, and Bambi Schieffelin. 1984. "Language Acquisition and Socialization: Three Developmental Stories." In *Culture Theory: Mind, Self, and Emotion*, edited by Richard Shweder and Robert A. LeVine, 276–320. Cambridge: Cambridge University Press.

———. 2011. "The Theory of Language Socialization." In *The Handbook of Language Socialization*, edited Alessandro Duranti, Elinor Ochs, and Bambi Schieffelin, 1–23. Malden, MA: Wiley-Blackwell.

Ochs, Elinor and Merav Shohet. 2006. "The Cultural Structuring of Mealtime Socialization." In *New Directions in Child and Adolescent Development*, edited by Reed W. Larson, Angela Wiley, and Kathryn Branscomb, 35–50. San Francisco: Jossey-Bass.

Okita, Toshie. 2001. *Invisible Work: Bilingualism, Language Choice and Childbearing in Intermarried Families*. Amsterdam: John Benjamins.

Parkinson, Dilworth B. 1985. *Constructing the Social Context of Communication: Terms of Address in Egyptian Arabic*. Berlin: Mouton de Gruyter.

Paulston, Christina B. 1994. *Linguistic Minorities in Multilingual Settings*. Amsterdam: Benjamins.

Paulston, Christina B., and Mary N. Bruder. 1976. *Teaching English as a Second Language: Techniques and Procedures*. Nova Scotia: Winthrop Publishers.

Peoples, James G., and Garrick A. Bailey. 2010. *Humanity: An Introduction to Cultural Anthropology*. Boston: Cengage Learning.

Rieschild, Verna R. 1998. "Lebanese Arabic Reverse Role Vocatives." *Anthropological Linguistics* 40 (4): 617–41.

Said, Fatma. 2014. "A Sociolinguistic Study of Multilingual Talk at Mealtimes: The Case of an Arab Family in London." PhD diss., University of London, Birkbeck, Eng..

Said, Fatma, and Zhu Hua. In press. ""No, no Maama! Say shaatir ya ouledee shaatir!": Children's Agency in Language Use and Socialisation." In *International Journal of Bilingualism. Special Issue: Family Language Policy and Transnationalism-Resistance and Transformation*, edited by Kendall A. King and Elizabeth Lanza, in press.

Schwimmer, Brian. 1996. "Kinship Terminology." Retrieved July 2015. http://www.umanitoba.ca/faculties/arts/anthropology/tutor/kinterms.

Smagulov, Juldyz. 2015. "Reviving a Native Language: Kazakh as a School Language." Paper presented at GURT 2015, Georgetown University, Washington, DC, March 13–15.

Snow, Catherine E., and Diane E. Beals. 2006. "Mealtime Talk that Supports Literacy Development." *New Directions for Child and Adolescent Development* 111 (03): 51–98.

Song, Juyoung. 2007. "Language Ideologies & Identity: Korean Children's Language Socialisation in Bilingual Settings." PhD diss., Ohio State University.

Tannen, Deborah. 2003. "Gender and Family Interaction." In *The Handbook of Language and Gender*, edited by Janet Holmes and Miriam Mayerhoff, 179–201. Malden, MA: Blackwell.

———. 2007. "Power Maneuvers and Connection Maneuvers in Family Interaction." In *Family Talk: Discourse and Identity in Four American Families*, edited by Deborah Tannen, Shari Kendall, and Cynthia Gordon, 27–48. Oxford: Oxford University Press.

Turrel, Maria, and Melissa Moyer. 2010. "Transcription." In *The Blackwell Guide to Research Methods in Bilingualism and Multilingualism*, edited by Li Wei and Melissa Moyer, 192–213. Malden, MA: Blackwell Publishing.

Vertovec, Steven. 2007. "Super-Diversity and its Implications." *Ethnic and Racial Studies* 30 (6): 1024–54.

Vidal, Mónica, and Agnes W. He. 2015. "Intergenerational Interaction through Heritages: A Comparative Study of Spanish and Mandarin Chinese." Paper presented at GURT 2015, Georgetown University, Washington, DC, March 13–15.

Williams, Ashley. 2005. "Fighting Words and Challenging Expectations: Language Alternation and Social Roles in a Family Dispute." *Journal of Pragmatics* 37:317–28.

Wood, Linda A., and Rolf O. Kroger. 1991. "Politeness and Forms of Address." *Journal of Language and Social Psychology* 10 (3): 145–68.

Yassin, Mahmoud A. F. 1977. "Bi-polar Terms of Address in Kuwaiti Arabic." *Bulletin of the School of Oriental and African Studies* 40 (2): 297–301.

Zhu Hua. 2008. "Duelling Languages, Duelling Values: Codeswitching in Bilingual Intergenerational Conflict Talk in Diasporic Families." *Journal of Pragmatics* 40:1799–1816.

———. 2010. "Language Socialization and Interculturality: Address Terms in Intergenerational Talk in Chinese Diasporic Families." *Language and Intercultural Communication* 10 (3): 189–205.

Chapter 6

Everyday Encounters in the Marketplace

Translanguaging in the Super-Diverse City

ADRIAN BLACKLEDGE, ANGELA CREESE, AND RACHEL HU

WESSENDORF (2014) CONCEPTUALIZES THE normalization of difference as "commonplace diversity" to describe ethnic, religious, linguistic, and socioeconomic diversity experienced and perceived as a normal part of social life (44). She argues that diversity becomes normalized over time and as a result of accumulated experiences of difference: "Because of these regularly occurring encounters with difference, diversity becomes commonplace" (45). This does not mean that difference is therefore neutralized. Commonplace diversity does not mean that people's national, ethnic, religious, and class backgrounds are unnoticed. While these differences are not seen as particularly unusual, they are at the same time commonly acknowledged. Difference is something that people live with, and acknowledgement of diversity can contribute to unity. This does not indicate an indifference to difference; rather, difference is acknowledged and people are aware of the manifold cultural variance around them, but they do not see this as unusual. Wessendorf (2014) argues that in order to navigate a public space characterized by a variety of languages and backgrounds, people need to master a code of practice and certain social skills (61). Padilla, Azevedo, and Olmos-Alcaraz (2015) explore the notions of sameness and difference in super-diverse settings, and find that "heterogeneity is common and experienced on a daily basis, such that 'difference / otherness' is internalized and may be transformed into a quotidian positive feature" (632). Watson (2006) argues for an understanding of encounters enacted in public space which is predicated on a commitment to the public acknowledgement of others who are different from ourselves, and to the social relations these encounters produce.

Wessendorf cites Lyn Lofland's (1998) notion of 'civility towards diversity,' and argues that in a super-diverse context, "civility towards people who look, speak or behave differently is learned through everyday contact and interaction in a multiplicity of day-to-day, social situations" (2014, 64). She refers to "cosmopolitan pragmatism" (2010, 20), where, in order to get around, buy things, get help to get on a bus, carry a buggy up the stairs, and so on, individuals cannot afford not to be interculturally competent. Wessendorf (2010) points out that the demographic nature of a super-diverse context also brings with it the emergence of numerous "zones of encounter" (Wood and Landry 2007). Lofland (1998) makes a distinction between private, public, and parochial realms in which encounters occur. She argues that a crucial dynamic of the public realm emerges from the fact that not only do many of its inhabitants not 'know' one another in the biographical sense, they often also do not know one another in the cultural sense. The public realm is populated not only by persons who have not met but often, as well, by persons who do not share symbolic worlds. For Lofland the public realm is constituted of those areas of urban settlements in which individuals in copresence tend to be personally unknown or only categorically known to one another. Put differently, the public realm is made up of those spaces in a city which tend to be inhabited by persons who are strangers to one another or who know one another only in terms of occupational or other nonpersonal identity categories (e.g., bus driver, customer). The public realm is a form of social space distinct from the private realm and its full-blown existence is what makes the city different from other settlement types. The public realm is the city's quintessential social territory (Lofland 1998, 9).

Wessendorf takes this up, proposing that while the private realm is characterized by relations with friends and kin, the parochial realm is characterized by more communal relations among neighbors, with colleagues in the workplace, or acquaintances through associations and informal networks. The public realm, in contrast, is the world in the streets where one meets strangers. However, the boundaries between these realms are fluid: a market can, for example, be experienced as the public realm by a person who goes there for the first time, but it can gradually turn into a parochial space for traders and their regular customers.

Wise and Velayutham (2009) propose the term "everyday multiculturalism" to describe the everyday practice and lived experience of diversity in specific situations and spaces of encounter (3). Wise and Velayutham (2009) explore how social actors experience and negotiate cultural differences on the ground and how their social relations and identities are shaped and reshaped in the process (6). They point out, however, that even where cross-cultural contact is civil and courteous, this does not necessarily translate to a respect for difference, or signal any shift in private attitudes to otherness. Wise (2009) turns to the notion of the 'contact zone' to describe the space in which people engage in cross-cultural encounters and negotiate through the deployment of improvised language resources. Wise (2009, 22) suggests the term "quotidian transversality" to describe how individuals in everyday spaces "use particular modes of sociality to produce or smooth interrelations across cultural difference, whether or not this difference is a cultural one" (23). The term highlights how cultural difference can be the basis for commonsensality and exchange, where identities are not left behind, but can be shifted and opened up in moments of nonhierarchical reciprocity, and are sometimes reconfigured in the process. Wise points out, however, that while everyday civil encounters are important, they do not ensure a culture of tolerance, and inequalities must be recognized and addressed.

Hall (2012) argues that individuals need to socially acquire repertoires to traverse and participate in different spaces of the city (18). Crossing boundaries between the familiar and the unfamiliar demands particular social and cultural skills. Hall refers to Amin's (2002) notion of "micro-publics," "the social spaces in which individuals regularly come into contact" (Hall 2012, 6). These are not simply spaces of encounter, but of participation, requiring a level of investment to sustain membership. Semi and colleagues (2009) found that one of the most relevant practices in the everyday use of difference was translation, as the everyday sphere emerges as a place where one adapts what one has to the specific demands of the context. It is an ongoing process of adjustment, repositioning and reattribution of meaning in which difference, its representations and related discourses, and the recipes for action which are available and deemed satisfactory for capitalizing on it or opposing it, are translated and adapted for concrete use in the specific contexts people find themselves operating in (Semi et al. 2009, 70).

Conviviality

Wessendorf (2014) proposes that the notion of *conviviality* is a useful heuristic to describe people living together or sharing the same life. Gilroy (2006a) points out that although public and political discourses often associate immigration with crime and conflict, other varieties of interaction have developed alongside these discourses. These patterns of interaction emerge "with an unruly, convivial mode of interaction in which differences have to be negotiated in real time" (39). He refers to the interaction of sameness and difference as "conviviality— just living together" (Gilroy 2006b, 7). Gilroy (2004) further defines conviviality as "the processes of cohabitation and interaction that have made multiculture an ordinary feature in Britain's urban areas and in postcolonial cities elsewhere" (xv). Gilroy argues that convivial social forms have come into being spontaneously and unappreciated, rather than as the outcome of government policy. Conviviality, he argues, is a social pattern "in which different metropolitan groups dwell in close proximity, but where their racial, linguistic and religious particularities do not—as the logic of ethnic absolutism suggests they must—add up to discontinuities of experience or insuperable problems of communication" (2006a, 40). In these conditions, he proposes, a degree of differentiation can be combined with a large measure of overlapping. Betsy Rymes (2014) takes up the notion of communicative overlapping in proposing that individuals communicate across difference by negotiating or seeking out common ground and then creating new shared terrain. She argues that the extent to which we can communicate is contingent on the degree to which our repertoires expand, change, and overlap with others. People form alignments not necessarily by speaking the same native language or categorizing each other demographically, but when they find some kind of common ground. Understanding 'the other' is not a matter of identifying difference, but of raising awareness of multiple repertoires and expanding points of communicative overlap.

Gilroy (2006b) argues that problems often assumed to be inevitable features of a clash of civilizations, cultures, and outlooks melt away in the face of a sense of human sameness. He points out that institutional, generational, educational, legal, and political commonalities intersect with dimensions of difference. These commonalities complicate the simple notions of 'cultural groups' or 'communities,' which might otherwise be held to be united by their apparent difference from others. He suggests that conviviality acknowledges this complexity and, though it cannot banish conflict, "can be shown to have equipped people with means of managing it in their own interests and in the interests of others with whom they can be induced heteropathically to identify" (2006a, 40). Gilroy argues that this is far from being a romantic notion, nor is it a panacea to solve tensions which continue to exist in society. Gilroy emphatically points out that "recognising conviviality should not signify the absence of racism" (40). Rather, in conditions of conviviality racial and ethnic differences have been rendered unremarkable and ordinary, as people discover that the things which really divide them are much more profound: taste, lifestyle, leisure preferences. Gilroy suggests that in such a scenario, difference is less of a threat to social cohesion because it is commonplace, everyday, and almost unnoticeable. Gilroy's view is that sustaining and valuing conviviality is a legitimate goal for bringing citizenship to life, and one which requires acts of creativity and imagination.

Varis and Blommaert (2014) propose that in the super-diversity that characterizes online-offline social worlds, it is too easy to focus on differences and downplay the level of social structuring that actually prevents these differences from turning into conflicts. They suggest that relationships of conviviality are characterized by largely "phatic" and "polite" engagement in interaction. Rampton (2014) adds a word of caution, counseling that we take care with the term 'convivial.' He argues that whether or not small talk can be characterized as convivial will very much depend on the contingencies of where, when, how, and by and to whom it is produced. Rampton points out that "there are no forms of communication that are inalienably convivial" (5), and this simply follows from the fact that although it is a very valuable part of the puzzle, you can never get at what people mean through language alone. Rampton emphasizes the importance of detailed description of the shared spaces and everyday routines which make ethnic and linguistic difference subsidiary to people getting on with their quotidian lives. It is to such a detailed description of the shared spaces and everyday routines of people in Birmingham Bullring Indoor Market that we now turn.

Methods

Three researchers, Adrian Blackledge, Angela Creese, and Rachel Hu, recognized Birmingham Bull Ring Indoor Market as an ideal site in which to investigate how people communicate in business settings when they bring different biographies, histories, and linguistic/semiotic proficiencies to the commercial encounter. The research team identified a Chinese-owned business: a butcher's stall inside the indoor market hall. We approached the proprietors, Kang Chen (KC) and Meiyen Chew (MYC), for permission to conduct ethnographic observations of communicative interactions in and around their stall. The couple were willing to be involved in the research as key participants and signed consent forms. The empirical research began on September 1, 2014, and ended on December 19, 2014. During that time Rachel visited the stall twice a week, and Adrian once a week (always while Rachel was also observing). We wrote thirty sets of field notes, running to more than 104,000 words. After five weeks of observation we fitted small digital audio-recording devices to the butchers and recorded their spoken interactions during our observational visits. In addition to KC and MYC, we also audio-recorded two of the assistant butchers on several occasions. One of the assistants, Yiran, was a Chinese student working part-time on the stall. The other, Bradley, was English, and a long-term member of the staff team. In all we audio-recorded thirty-five hours of workplace interactions. We also video-recorded one three-hour session at the stall. We interviewed the key participants, and Rachel audio-recorded other informal conversations with them. We interviewed eighteen of the other stallholders in the market. We took 300 photographs inside the market hall, and a further 120 in the surrounding neighborhood. We also asked KC and MYC to audio-record themselves at home in their domestic setting with their family. They had three very young children, and MYC's parents were visiting them from Malaysia at the time of our research. In all they audio-recorded forty-seven hours of family and domestic interactions. In addition we asked the couple to copy and send to us examples of their online and social media communications. KC audio-recorded some of his regular QQ conversations with his mother in Fujian.[1] The couple also sent us 550 WeChat messages from their mobile phones. We do not draw on either the home or social media data in this chapter. Subsequent to the data collection period Rachel transcribed the audio-recorded material, and the researchers met for two hours each week to discuss transcripts and field notes.

Communicative Repertoire in the Market

While conducting a field-site visit to the market, we noticed a group of customers approaching the butcher's stall. They looked like a family. MYC told Rachel that some customers "all come together in big groups, this way it's cheaper, I think they have many sons, kids." In this instance there are just three in the group. Adrian's field notes are followed by a transcript of the audio-recording of the same events:

> Two heavily overweight women in headscarves, long skirts, cardigans, and striped socks stop at the stall. They are perhaps Romanian (although I am guessing). They buy a large bag of chicken wings. They also want to buy a hen, and are unimpressed with the price. Bradley holds the hen up in two hands, stretching it from end to end. "Look at the size of that," he says. The women buy the hen. Now a young man appears and joins the women. He starts by (I think) asking Mr. C how to say 'good morning' in Chinese. Mr. C tells him and the man mimics him two or three times. The customers want to leave their purchase behind the stall to collect later. There are gestures here I don't quite understand. Mr. C mimes driving a car, and says "Car." The young man at this point bends forward with the upper half of his body, sticks out his bottom and extends his left arm and the forefinger of his left hand out behind him. They all laugh. I'm sure the mime means something, but at the same time it might be untranslatable. B picks up the tiny mantelpiece-style clock from its usual position next to the till and points to it, saying "Eleven o'clock." This seems to be the time arranged for the collection of the meat.

◆ Transcript 1
Female customer (FC); male customer (MC); Bradley (BJ); Meiyen Chew (MYC); Kang Chen (KC)

1. MC Good morning
2. KC Good morning
3. MC How do I greet good morning?
4. KC Eh?
5. MC Good morning
6. KC Good morning
7. MC No, in your language
8. KC 早上好
<zaoshang hao>
9. MC Zaoshang hao
10. KC 早上好
<zaoshang hao>
11. MC Zaoshang hao
12. KC Ah
13. MC Zaoshang hao
14. FC (xxxx)
15. BJ The tail? Are we waiting for delivery?
16. FC Yea (xxx)
17. BJ I gotta wait for delivery
18. KC Car coming later
19. MC Pork
20. BJ Yea
21. MC Delivery coming later
22. KC Driver
23. BJ Eleven, eleven o'clock
24. MC Eleven
25. FC Eleven
26. MC (xxxx)
27. BJ Yeah, walk around, come back, hahahaha
28. MC I leave it here everything
29. FC I buy, leave here (xxx)
30. BJ Okay, yep
31. MC How much?
32. BJ Twenty six so far
33. FC That's too, that's too much
34. KC 这个是她妈，这个肯定是她妈，跟她一样一样的！
<This must be her mum, this must be her mum, a spitting image of her!>
Your wife's mum? (xxx) Yea, no sister?
35. MC Not sister
36. BJ My brother, this one my brother, he's my brother, yea, hahaha, four pounds, thank you

The field note describes what was in many ways a typical and everyday interaction between the butcher, KC, his wife, MYC, his assistant, BJ, and three customers looking to buy chicken wings, a hen, and pigs' tails. The customers complain about the price of the hen, and the butcher's assistant responds with good humor but refuses to drop the price. Adrian, stationed relatively unobtrusively four or five yards away from the action with his notebook, is not able to hear everything that is going on. Moreover, if he were able to hear everything he still might struggle to interpret the fine grain of rapid-fire interaction in the marketplace. This was the kind of interaction observed repeatedly during the four months of observations of the butcher's stall. However, two aspects of the interaction mark it as less than typical. First, one of the customers asks KC to teach him how to say good morning "in your language." This was not a unique instance of this kind of request, but neither was it typical. In turn 1 of the transcript the customer initiates contact with the butcher as he approaches the stall, saying, in accented English, "Good morning." KC responds in kind, also saying, in differently accented English, "Good morning." However, the customer has not quite made clear his intention that he would like KC to teach him how to say good morning in Chinese. Turns 3 to 7 negotiate this request. In making the request for KC to teach him how to pronounce the Chinese greeting, the customer acknowledges difference (Watson 2006), as it is clear that at the very least the communicative repertoires of the customer and the butcher are different. The customer's request is a (metasemantic) *metacommentary* on that difference (Rymes 2014, 20). Paradoxically, in acknowledging and commenting on difference the customer creates "a point of communicative overlap" between the two protagonists, as he opens up a space for interaction (Rymes 2014, 6). The metacommentary also implies common ground, as both customer and butcher are speakers of languages other than English, and speak English with heavy accents.

In her research in Hackney, London, Suzanne Wessendorf (2015) was told by a migrant from Chile, "all the people speak bad English, so I feel very comfortable, so that's nice because all the people have an accent and a lot of people don't speak English so I feel like phew, it's not strange to speak bad English" (10). Wessendorf found that in the context of commonplace diversity, various accents as well as limited proficiency in English had become commonplace, and local residents were used to dealing with such linguistic varieties. In cosmopolitan settings, foreign language accents could be described as commonplace. They could even become a form of capital, as accent did not straightforwardly index social class. Another of Wessendorf's informants told her that you cannot treat people differently according to their backgrounds because almost everybody comes from elsewhere. In the example in Birmingham Bull Ring market, both the butcher and the customer speak a form of English with foreign accents. This seems to unite rather than divide them, as the customer hands the role of expert to the butcher, who becomes teacher to his new pupil. In this instance acknowledging difference creates the potential to limit difference, and opens up a space for communication. The customer's convivial request holds up 'difference' for scrutiny, and difference becomes a resource for exchange and interaction. As soon as KC understands what it is the customer is requesting, he is more than willing to engage in the linguistic game of teaching the customer how to say "Zaoshang hao." In turn 12, KC makes a sound that seems to indicate his approval of the customer's pronunciation, and the customer has one more iteration of the greeting before leaving the activity aside.

More unusual than this was the customer's subsequent mime. We had become used to customers pointing to the cut of meat they wished to purchase. We had also noticed customers using other physical gestures to order their meat—a man touched his own tongue when he wanted ox tongue; a man pointed to his own head when he wanted to buy pig's head. As we will see, another man widened and narrowed his arms repeatedly, as if pulling a piece of elastic, as he asked for pig's small intestine. The mime described in the field note here, however, goes beyond these examples, in that it was of the order of *performance* rather than merely communication. As the field note describes, the man "bends forward with the upper half of his body, sticks out his bottom and extends his left arm and the forefinger of his left hand out behind him." Neither of the researchers observing the performance and writing field notes understood the meaning (if any) of the mime. As the field note reports, although it was assumed that the physical performance probably meant something, it "might be untranslatable." Only later, when the audio-recording of the same incident was listened to repeatedly and transcribed, did it become clear that the young man's wife (or mother-in-law—it was not clear which) had asked the butcher's assistant for "tail." Then it was clear that the man was making a physical representation of a pig, or possibly an ox, as the stall also sold ox tail—but the fact that the man's sole utterance during the performance was "Pork" suggests he was 'being' a pig in order to support his wife's request. The mime was probably unnecessary, as the butcher's assistant, BJ, understands the woman's question immediately (turn 15). The mime is convivial (Gilroy 2004), and part of the entertainment for an audience comprising the market traders and the man's wife and her mother, two researchers, and any passers-by. During our four months in the indoor meat and fish market we frequently heard and saw traders shouting their wares and putting on larger-than-life performances to attract customers to their stall. As such, performance and conviviality were part of the everyday fabric of the market. That is, they were a feature of the "spatial repertoire" of the market (Pennycook and Otsuji 2015). It was certainly less usual for customers to put on a performance for traders than vice versa, but the performative aspect of this customer's repertoire was permitted, and was deployed, because in the market hall clowning around is commonplace and acceptable. Also, the particular type of performance presented on this occasion was not inappropriate because, as we have noted, gesture was a common feature of the discourse (the orders of discourse), and therefore of the spatial repertoire of the market hall.

The corporeal dimension of the interactants' repertoires is further evidenced when KC mimes driving a car, presenting his hands to the customers as if he were holding a steering wheel. While acting out this mime KC says "Car coming later" (18) and "Driver" (22). Whether the mime clarifies anything for the customers is not clear. Again the mime may be more to create a convivial space than merely to communicate. In the field note we find evidence of more visual cues, this time for a more explicit communicative purpose, as BJ "picks up the tiny mantelpiece-style clock from its usual position next to the till and points to it." At the same time BJ says "Eleven, eleven o'clock," indicating with both words and his pointing gesture that the delivery of pigs' tail will not arrive before eleven, and that they should return at that time. The male customer says something which we were not able to hear clearly enough for transcription, and BJ says "Yeah, walk around, come back, hahahaha" (turn 27). At this point the male customer says "I leave it here everything," asking whether it is all right for him to leave his purchases at the stall and return later to pick them up. His wife adds her voice, saying "I buy, leave here." Before he leaves the scene the male customer asks how much his purchase of meat has cost so far, and when BJ replies "Twenty-six so far," the female customer says "That's too much." She appears to want to argue about the price, and perhaps to negotiate down the cost of the meat. We saw many customers attempt to do this during our time in the market. We spoke to market traders who were happy enough to engage in this kind of haggling, and were prepared to do a favor for some of their customers. Others were less enthusiastic about the practice. In any event it was clear that haggling was an aspect of the spatial repertoire of the market, linking the repertoires formed through individual life trajectories to the particular places in which these linguistic resources were deployed (Pennycook and Otsuji 2015). On this occasion, however, the female customer did not push the point.

It was not uncommon for the couple, KC and MYC, to comment to each other on their customers, creating a private moment in the parochial space of the market. Here we perhaps have an overlap between Wessendorf's (2014) public, parochial, and private realms, as KC looks at the two women customers and says to his wife, in Mandarin, "This must be her mum, this must be her mum, a spitting image of her." The moment is private in that it is a metapragmatic comment between husband and wife, and is spoken in Mandarin in the hearing only of interlocutors who have no comprehension of that language. It is parochial in that it leads to a moment of conviviality, as KC offers the older woman a (teasing) compliment—'No sister?'—extending communal relations in a way that transcends the mere economic transaction of the sale of meat. The metacomment on the appearance of the older woman, good-natured and good-humored, again creates a point of communicative overlap between the protagonists in the interaction. The several good-humored activities between the traders and these customers in the short time they are in contact may be ephemeral, but they are more sustained than many interactions between market traders and their customers. The moment is clearly also in the public realm, conducted in a place where, on the whole, strangers encounter each other in the process of buying and selling meat and fish.

BJ joins in with KC's joke, picking up his cue and contributing his own version, pointing to KC and telling the customers: "My brother, this one my brother, he's my brother, yea, hahaha." Everyone present laughs at the joke. When BJ says (three times) that KC is his brother it is funny because it is a comment on visible difference—KC is ethnically Chinese, while BJ is not, so the idea that they are brothers is humorous (see figure 6.1).

The metacomment on difference again has the potential to limit difference, as BJ validates and rewards KC's joke by repeating his own version of the same. BJ's joke limits difference while commenting on difference because it aligns BJ with KC, and

Figure 6.1. "My brother, this one my brother."

also aligns the traders (whether Chinese or otherwise) with the customers (whether Romanian or otherwise) through shared laughter. Here we see what Wessendorf (2014) terms "commonplace diversity." This does not mean that people's national, ethnic, religious, and class backgrounds are unnoticed. While differences here are not seen as particularly unusual, they are at the same time acknowledged. Difference is something that people live with, and at times like this diversity can have a unifying effect. Wessendorf (2014) argues that in order to navigate a public space characterized by a variety of languages and backgrounds, people need to master a code of practice and certain social skills (61). In this context the social skills to be mastered are not principally a 'full' proficiency in English. Rather, they are constituted in, and constitute, the spatial repertoire of the market.

In another example of customer and trader deploying a communicative repertoire that did not depend on shared proficiency in a single language, a customer approached BJ with the intention of buying a pig's small intestine.

Transcript 2
Bradley (BJ); first male customer (MC1); second male customer (MC2); female customer (FC)

1. BJ Hello boss
2. MC1 Is this er pork?
3. BJ Pork, yea
4. MC1 (xxxx) Is it this erm

5.	BJ	No no no you want the in- the small intestine don't you, no no, you want that one but the small one
6.	MC1	Goes long
7.	BJ	Yea, that goes long but not that one, not that one, no
8.	MC1	Tomorrow?
9.	BJ	No we don't we can't get it no more, no more, finished
10.	MC1	Finished
11.	BJ	Goya? No
12.	MC2	(xxxx)
13.	BJ	This one?
14.	MC2	(xxxx)
15.	BJ	How much? All of it?
16.	MC2	Give me one
17.	FC	(xxxx)
18.	BJ	Nice one, yea
19.	MC2	Yea nice
20.	BJ	Just one? Or one more?
21.	MC2	No just one
22.	BJ	Are you sure? Oh you want one as well, one each
23.	MC1	Five kilos
24.	BJ	Five kilos

Here a customer approaches the stall and Bradley, the butcher's assistant, realizes that the customer wants to buy pig's small intestine. Bradley explains to the customer that although the stall once sold this item, they are no longer able to do so. Bradley and the customer negotiate mainly by means of graphic gestures that represent the large and small intestine. The customer initiates the interaction by representing the small intestine with a sign made by opening his arms wide (figure 6.2), bringing his hands together in making the same sign, and opening his arms wide again.

Figure 6.2. Customer requests 'small intestine' with a hand/arm gesture

In response, Bradley points to his own stomach to represent the intestine (figure 6.3), and then points to the pig's large intestine (figure 6.4), which is displayed on the counter. With reference to the large intestine, Bradley makes a sign to represent "smaller" with his finger and thumb (figure 6.5), and repeats the sign of pointing to his own stomach to represent the intestine. He then makes a sign with his hands clasped to represent "the small one" (figure 6.6). Next Bradley mimics the customer's original gesture with arms apart to represent the small intestine, and points to the large intestine, saying 'Not that one" (figure 6.7). Finally he makes a shrug with his hands and arms as he says "No more." Although the customer was not successful in achieving his aim of purchasing the pig's small intestine (in fact the stall had recently been told it was no longer allowed to sell it except as dog food), this is not

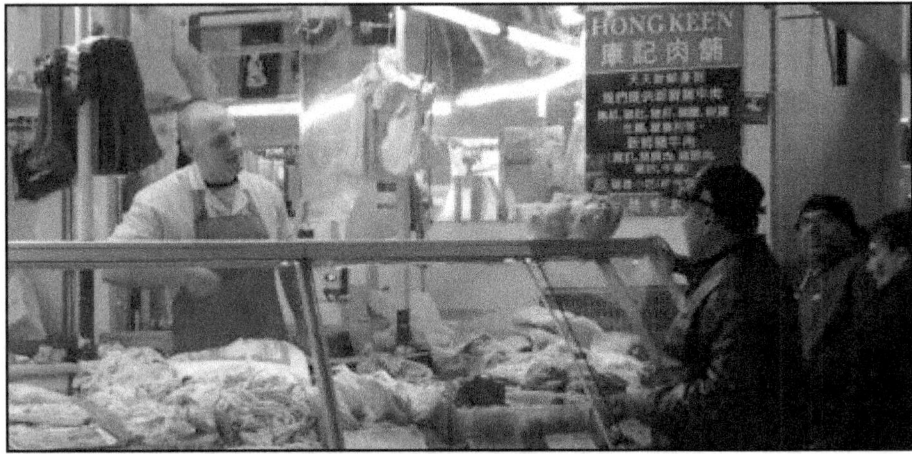

Figure 6.3. Bradley points to own stomach to signify small intestine

Figure 6.4. Bradley makes alternative sign for small intestine

Figure 6.5. Bradley makes third sign for small intestine

Figure 6.6. Bradley mirrors customer's gesture

Figure 6.7. Bradley points to large intestine

because the customer and the butcher do not share proficiency in a single language. In fact they are able to communicate quite well with their hands, making gestures which represent the objects about which they communicate. Sigrid Norris (2004) points out that commonly a participant in an interaction employs hand/arm gestures when speaking, and gesturing starts slightly earlier than the words expressing the same idea. Norris suggests that it is probably not useful to separate these kinds of gestures from the language with which they co-occur. Four types of gesture are typically distinguished (McNeill 1992): iconic, metaphoric, deictic, and beat gestures. Iconic gestures depict pictorial content and mimic what the individual wants to communicate verbally. In the example above the customer makes an iconic gesture to depict the long (although called, in English, "small") intestine. Metaphoric gestures may also depict pictorial content, but they portray abstract ideas or categories. An example of this is Bradley using his finger and thumb to represent small, without making an iconic portrayal of the intestine. Deictic gestures often point to objects in the physical world, but they can also point to events in the past of the future, or point to ideas and notions as if they had a physical location in the world. In the last photograph here we are firmly in the realm of the physical, as Bradley points to the large intestine on the counter. Beat gestures refer to the movement of hands/arms up and down, or back and forth. In the next three photographs a customer indicates with a repeated beat gesture that he wants his pork cut in a particular way (figures 6.8, 6.9, and 6.10).

Figure 6.8. Up beat

Figure 6.9. Down beat

Figure 6.10. Up beat

Gesture was a very common feature of what we observed in the market-hall. Customers and traders pointed to produce, they held up fingers to refer to the number of pork chops required or the amount in pounds a purchase would cost, they pointed to their own tongue if they referred to ox-tongue, and they raised a thumb to signify consensus or agreement. These were all frequent dimensions of the communicative repertoires in play in everyday encounters across the counter. Most gestures in the market refer to that which is evident on the stall, or at least close by. In this example the interaction refers on both sides to a piece of offal which is notable by its absence. It is for this reason that the customer and the trader are pressed into the creative deployment of "a continuum of iconic and metaphoric gestures" (Jaworski and Thurlow 2009, 254).

In these interactions the participants reach an understanding through consensus which is achieved at least partly (and perhaps mainly) by "extra verbal means" (Habermas 1984, 86). We saw repeatedly that gesture was a key means of communication in the market. Rymes (2014) points out that communicative repertoire goes beyond the linguistic to include the collection of ways individuals use not only language but other means of communication (gestures, dress, posture, accessories) to function in the multiple communities in which they participate. She asks, "Why not build relationships on the basis of shared non-linguistic cues?" (20). We saw that in the market commercial transactions were based on precisely such means.

It is noticeable here that Bradley asks the second pair of customers "Goya?" (turn 11). We heard this word deployed by the butchers in the stall on many occasions. When we asked MYC what it meant, she said it was a word she had learned from her East European customers. She said it means pig's intestine. She told us that East European customers particularly like the product, as they can stuff it with minced pork for deep frying. She said she didn't know how to spell the word, but she shared it with BJ and KC and all of them used it, "just like those English or foreigners saying nihao, zaijian in Chinese, we just use it so the customers know we have that product."

Pennycook and Otsuji found, in their research in markets and restaurants in Sydney, that while people engaged in "metrolinguistic practices" as they went about their daily business, getting things done with whatever resources were available, there was also a strong current of conviviality, "of people celebrating the diverse environments in which they work" (2015, 90). Pennycook and Otsuji point out that although the interactions they observed were often characterized by convivial multilingualism, a more-or-less harmonious getting along together, such conviviality was often double-edged, "leading back to forms of exclusion and discrimination" (90). Pennycook and Otsuji (2015) point out that their discussion of the everyday does not assume that "everydayness is free of discrimination, contestation or rubbing together that causes friction" (97). They acknowledge that it is precisely the everydayness of discriminatory discourse, and discriminatory practice, that makes it so pernicious. In Birmingham indoor market, the same everyday practice may be either convivial or discriminatory, subject to its accent. We saw that the deployment of the greeting, 'nihao,' was done with a range of tones and accents. Whereas at times it was a cheery greeting from a customer to open communication, at other times it appeared to have discriminatory overtones. Here the greeting is shouted not by a customer, but by a young passer-by (PB) who does not stop at the stall.

Transcript 3

1.	PB	Nihao! Nihao!
2.	KC	Nihao! [to BJ:] Your brother coming, hehe

KC does not ignore the sarcastic greeting, but throws it back at the young man. He then says to BJ "your brother coming." It may be that the perpetrator of the faux-Chinese greeting resembled BJ physically. On another occasion when Yiran (YG), the Chinese student who was working part-time in the stall, greeted a customer (MC) with "Nihao," he engaged in a brief discussion of the customer's proficiency in Chinese.

Transcript 4

1.	YG	Hello boss you all right (.) Nihao nihao nihao
2.	MC	Nihao nihao
3.	YG	Nihao nihao nihao (.) One second
4.	MC	(xxxx) Spanish? Español?
5.	YG	Why not speak Chinese man?
6.	MC	I can speak Chinese
7.	YG	Haha that's only one word man

In response to Yiran's repeated Chinese greeting the customer responds with the same greeting, but then asks Yiran why he doesn't speak Spanish, with an utterance in both English and Spanish. Yiran retorts with "Why not speak Chinese man?" and the customer says he can speak Chinese. Yiran, unconvinced, makes fun of the customer's Chinese proficiency. The discussion of languages acknowledges difference, and that difference once more becomes a site for convivial communication, and the shared conversation offers a moment of unity, if a contested unity. In our field notes we recorded further examples of contested instantiations of the greeting. In a first example, from Rachel's field notes, the deployment of the Chinese greeting appears to be for the amusement of the speaker's friends more than as phatic communication: "Nihao! Nihao! A group of five well-built Asian guys shouting greetings sounded like funny-toned Chinese walking past the stall without stopping. Brutal laughter exploded among them as they passed by."

In another example, this time from Adrian's field notes, MYC responds differently from her partner to the Chinese greeting: "A couple of men of Asian appearance in black leather jackets appear. 'Nihao,' says one. 'Nihao,' replies KC, mimicking the man's accent. The men examine the meat on offer. One of them now says 'Nihao' to MYC. She replies in kind, although with tolerance rather than the irony of her husband."

Holly Link, Sarah Gallo, and Stanton Wortham (2014) conducted ethnographic research in school settings on the United States-Mexico border, and found that

English-speaking African American students sometimes engaged in (what the researchers called) *faux-Spanish*—that is, deploying words which sounded like Spanish. The researchers found that the students' imitation of their Spanish-speaking peers were instances of them "making sense of difference" in their school and community (Link, Gallo, and Wortham 2014, 255). At first sight, the deployment of 'nihao' as an opening gambit by customers who are not Chinese-speaking (and, often, appear not to be English-speaking) indexes conviviality and willingness to open up a space for communication. At times this appeared to be what was happening. At other times, however, the deployment of the Chinese greeting seemed to carry a more sinister, stylized, and mocking connotation. At times, in the markets, there were conflicts and contestations, arguments, and even fights. As we have seen, discrimination was not unknown. But the day-to-day practices of buying and selling in the Birmingham indoor market were, as far as we could see during four months of observation, normally characterized by good humor, conviviality, generosity of spirit, and people's willingness to get on with other people. The place was certainly super-diverse, with people of myriad national, educational, and socioeconomic backgrounds, with different legal statuses and biographical trajectories, coming together in zones of encounter where social relations were rapidly formed, and just as rapidly moved on from.

Conclusion

During our time observing in the market we took brief glimpses of many people in the often-crowded hall. Some of them we saw from week to week as they visited the Chinese butcher to buy chicken feet, blood curd, or pigs' hearts. Most of them, however, we would never see again. We were fortunate that we were allowed to observe the traders at the Chinese butchers' stall repeatedly and frequently. We observed speech events that were connected on pathways and trajectories that allowed us to make visible how they travelled from one to another and shaped not only subsequent events, but also ways of being. We were able to analyze discourse beyond the individual speech event and "capture the heterogeneity of relevant resources and study the contingent emergence of social actions" (Wortham and Reyes 2015, 182). We saw and heard in the butchers' interactions in the market their humor, teasing, sales patter, clowning around, complaining, mocking, and much more. We saw and heard them engage in complex language exchanges with people who brought different histories and backgrounds to the interaction. We saw and heard communication that went beyond 'languages,' as people made meaning by whatever means possible.

Many of the interactions we observed included movement across languages, but languages were by no means the most significant dimension of the translanguaging event. The translanguaging repertoire in play was a repertoire which incorporated biographies and learning trajectories; it included aspects of communication not always thought of as 'language,' including performance, humor, mock flirtation, wolf-whistling, and so on. The translanguaging event was a record of mobility and experience; it was responsive to the marketplace in which, and the people with whom, it occurred. In all of these examples of translanguaging events, and in many more we observed in Birmingham Bull Ring Indoor Market, spaces for communication were opened up, and people made meanings in whatever way possible. The market was a place where this could happen. This was a place where communicative resources could be tried out in translanguaging spaces and events. It was a place where people made fun of each other, teased each other, and sometimes became irritated with each other. Fundamentally it was a place for buying and selling, and translanguaging was a means by which this was successfully and convivially managed.

Transcription Conventions

Symbol	**Function**
(xxxx)	unclear speech
!	animated tone or exclamation
(.)	a brief interval within an utterance
(2)	a brief interval within an utterance, in seconds
[word]	paralinguistic features and situational descriptions
< >	English translation of speech

Note

1. QQ is a free multilanguage chat program. See http://qqchat.qq.com/.

References

Amin, Ash. 2002. "Ethnicity and the Multicultural City: Living with Diversity." *Environment and Planning* 34 (6): 959–80.

Gilroy, Paul. 2004. *Postcolonial Melancholia.* New York: Columbia University Press.

———. 2006a. "Multiculture in Times of War: An Inaugural Lecture Given at the London School of Economics." *Critical Quarterly* 8 (4): 27–45.

———. 2006b. "Colonial Crimes and Convivial Cultures." A transcript of a video letter made by Paul Gilroy in London and screened at the Public Hearing "Debating Independence: Autonomy or Voluntary Colonialism?" in Nuuk, Greenland, on April 22.

Habermas, Jurgen. 1984. *The Theory of Communicative Action.* Vol. 1, *Reason and the Rationalisation of Society.* Boston: Beacon Press.

Hall, Suzanne. 2012. *City, Street and Citizen. The Measure of the Ordinary.* London: Routledge.

Jaworski, Adam, and Crispin Thurlow. 2009. "Gesture and Movement in Tourist Spaces." In *The Routledge Handbook of Multimodal Analysis*, edited by Carey Jewitt, 253–62. New York: Routledge.

Link, Holly, Sarah Gallo, and Stanton Wortham. 2014. "Gusame Ka' Lata!: Faux Spanish in the New Latino Diaspora." In *Heteroglossia as Practice and Pedagogy*, edited by Adrian Blackledge and Angela Creese, 255–74. Dordrecht, Nld.: Springer Science and Springer Media.

Lofland, Lyn H. 1998. *The Public Realm: Exploring the City's Quintessential Social Territory.* Hawthorne, NY: Aldine de Gruyter.

McNeill, David. 1992. *Hand and Mind: What Gestures Reveal about Thought.* Chicago: University of Chicago Press.

Norris, Sigrid. 2004. *Analyzing Multimodal Interaction. A Methodological Framework.* London/New York: Routledge.

Padilla, Beatriz, Joana Azevedo, and Antonia Olmos-Alcaraz. 2015. "Superdiversity and Conviviality: Exploring Frameworks for Doing Ethnography in Southern European Intercultural Cities." *Ethnic and Racial Studies* 38 (4): 621–35.

Pennycook, Alastair, and Emi Otsuji. 2015. *Metrolingualism. Language in the City.* London: Routledge.

Rampton, Ben. 2014. "Dissecting Heteroglossia: Interaction Ritual or Performance in Crossing and Stylization?" In *Heteroglossia as Practice and Pedagogy*, edited by Adrian Blackledge and Angela Creese, 275–300. Dordrecht, Nld.: Springer Science and Springer Media.

———. 2015. "Conviviality and Phatic Communion?" *Multilingual Margins* 2 (1): 83–90.

Rymes, Betsy. 2014. *Communicating beyond Language. Everyday Encounters with Diversity*. London: Routledge.

Semi, Giovanni. 2008. "The Flow of Words and the Flow of Value: Illegal Behaviour, Social Identity, and the Marketplace. Experiences in Turin, Italy." In *Lived Experiences of Public Consumption. Encounters with Value in Marketplaces on Five Continents*, edited by Daniel T. Cook, 137–55. London: Palgrave MacMillan.

Semi, Giovanni, Enzo Colombo, Ilenya Camozzi, and Annalisa Frisina. 2009. "Practices of Difference: Analysing Multiculturalism in Everyday Life." In Wise and Velayutham, *Everyday Multiculturalism*, 66–86.

Varis, Pia, and Jan Blommaert. 2014. "'Enough is Enough.' The Heuristics of Authenticity in Superdiversity." In *Linguistic Superdiversity in Urban Areas: Research Approaches*, edited by Joana Duarte and Ingrid Gogolin, 143–60. Amsterdam: John Benjamins.

Watson, Sophie. 2006. *City Publics. The (Dis)enchantments of Urban Encounters*. London: Routledge.

———. 2009a. "Brief Encounters of an Unpredictable Kind: Everyday Multiculturalism in Two London Street Markets." In Wise and Velayutham, *Everyday Multiculturalism*, 125–40.

Wessendorf, Susanne. 2010. "Commonplace Diversity: Social Interactions in a Superdiverse Context." *Max Planck Working Paper*, WP 10–11.

———. 2014. *Commonplace Diversity. Social Relations in a Super-diverse Context.* Basingstoke, Eng.: Palgrave Macmillan.

———. 2015. "'All the People Speak Bad English': Coping with Language Differences in a Super-diverse Context." *Institute for Research into Superdiversity Working Paper Series* 9/2015. Edgbaston, Eng.: University of Birmingham.

Wise, Amanda. 2009. "Everyday Multiculturalism: Transversal Crossings and Working Class Cosmopolitanisms." In Wise and Velayutham, *Everyday Multiculturalism*, 21–45.

Wise, Amanda, and Selvaraj Velayutham. 2009a. *Everyday Multiculturalism*. London: Palgrave.

———. 2009b. "Introduction: Multiculturalism and Everyday Life." In Wise and Velayutham, *Everyday Multiculturalism*, 1–20.

Wood, Phil, and Charles Landry. 2007. *The Intercultural City: Planning for Diversity Advantage.* London: Earthscan.

Wortham, Stanton, and Angela Reyes 2015. *Discourse Analysis beyond the Speech Event.* London: Routledge.

Chapter 7

(In)convenient Fictions

Ideologies of Multilingual Competence as Resource for Recognizability

ELIZABETH R. MILLER

IN THIS CHAPTER, I explore how adult immigrants to the United States, in producing accounts of their multilingual workplace discursive practices and their complex linguistic repertoires, frequently reconstituted traditional or high-modern ideological categories of language (as autonomous systems), conflated language-ethnicity-culture-nation as "natural" linkages, and oriented to lingua-cultural authenticity as objectively real. In exploring the performative effects of these interview accounts, I draw on Makoni and Pennycook's (2007) notion of (in)convenient fictions. They view traditional ideologies of language as "inconvenient fictions to the extent that they produce particular and limiting views on how language operates in the world" (27). But they add that the same perspectives can be "convenient fictions to the extent that they provide a useful means for understanding the world and shaping language users" (27). The inconvenient fictions that Makoni and Pennycook reject include commonplace understandings or ideologies of languages as autonomous systems that can be demarcated, counted, sometimes mixed (as in code-switching), and sometimes pluralized (as in multilingual practices).

The analysis in this chapter does not consider the actual interactions in which my participants engaged in multilingual talk but rather it investigates how they characterized such interactions. I thus explore how traditional linguistic and ethnic/cultural identity categories are taken up and reproduced in interview accounts. More importantly, I consider how these linguistic and identity categories serve as an "epistemological frame" (Butler 2001, 23) for gaining recognizability as a particular kind of subject in the world and simultaneously as "vectors of power" (Butler 1993, 187) by which the terms of recognition often reconstitute hierarchies of power, privileging some people more than others.

Complexity, Not Multiplicity

Our late-modern era has been characterized as multicultural, multilingual, hybrid, and diverse—a social world that is continually refashioned due to global flows of people, ideas, and cultural forms. This contemporary era is often understood to have replaced, or at least developed out of, a high-modern era of essentialized identities, cultures, and languages that are tied to place, ethnicity, and nationality. Likewise, late-modern views of language treat it as performed through a range of complex discursive practices rather than as an autonomous object or system that can be pluralized. For this reason, a growing number of applied linguistic and sociolinguistic researchers have advocated that we need to abandon the nomenclature of multiplicity or plurality altogether as suggested in terms such as *multi*lingualism, *pluri*lingualism, *multi*vocality, and/or *inter*lingualism. In turn, new labels have been proposed for identifying "multi" language practice with the goal of promoting more accurate conceptualizations of diverse or hybrid discursive practice. These new labels include "translanguaging" (García 2009), "translingual practice" (Canagarajah 2014), and "metrolingualism" (Otsuji and Pennycook 2010), among others.

In investigating how these theoretical conceptualizations apply to actual practice, Pennycook and Otsuji (2014) analyzed workplace interactions among restaurant employees in the large urban centers of Sydney and Tokyo. They observed interlocutors moving rapidly across languages in attending to the tasks at hand, language activity that they call "metrolingual multitasking" (161). They thus contend that as individuals such as these research participants engage in their everyday work tasks in these urban centers they "may find it unimportant in what language interactions occur," because "it is not so much about 'which' language but 'getting things done' with language that matters here" (171). Likewise, Canagarajah's (2014, and this volume) interview-based study among skilled-professional migrants from Africa who are now working in English-dominant contexts led him to argue that "what language" is used is of less concern than the "social value" of the interaction in which negotiation is expected of all participants (94). In discussing migrant neighborhoods in Belgium, Blommaert (2010) points to the "extreme mixedness" of languages and culture which makes the notion of a dominant language "hard to identify" if not often irrelevant (11).

Recognizability and Categories of Language and Identity

Of course, despite the efforts of this growing but still rather small cadre of scholars who adopt a complexity perspective on language, traditional labels for languages, ethnicities, and cultures, and for the multiplicity of these categories remain in wide circulation. Not only are such high-modern labels still ubiquitous, but, as Blommaert (2010) reminds us, "'sedentary' or 'territorialized' patterns of language use" have not disappeared in late-modern contexts either (4). Rather these high-modern forms of language practice are understood to be complemented by "'translocal' or 'deterritorialized' forms of language use" (4). Relatedly, Blommaert, Leppänen, and Spotti (2012) have noted that even as our understanding of language complexity holds true for much of contemporary on-the-ground discursive activity, high-modern ideological and institutional perceptions of identities, languages, and cultures, as tied to geographical location and ethnicity, continue to thrive and be reproduced. They write, "The challenge for contemporary sociolinguistics is not simply to reject or dismiss these modernist reflexes and responses, but to understand them as real forces in our field and as features of any sociolinguistic reality we intend to address in the age of late modernity" (18). Not only are the labels and categories that we assign to the social world commonplace, they serve as the material—however constructed and ideological—by which we establish recognizability and by which we make sense of our place in the world, of our experiences, and those of others.

As such, these ideological categories are often our best resource for understanding fluidity, diversity, and multilingualism (see Otsuji and Pennycook 2010). One could rightly argue that (re)constituting normative categories of nation, people, and language is objectively wrong and highly reductive. For example, if one conflates "American" identity with the "English" language, one clearly ignores the enormous complexity of language use within this national context, including within English itself. But more important, such ideological perspectives can lead to normalizing discriminatory views of people, language, and culture (i.e., the English language is "naturally" dominant and more desirable in the American context), resulting in highly inconvenient fictions. And yet, from a performativity perspective, such constraining norms—what Butler (1997) refers to as terms of "foreclosure" and "limitation" (47)—still serve as resources by which individuals gain recognizability.

Butler (1997, 2001) views the need to be recognized as a particular type of person as fundamental to gaining subjectivity and notes that it is through re-citing or reiterating cultural norms that our subjectivity becomes interpretable and visible. As she puts it, "It is by being interpellated within the terms of language that a certain social existence of the body first becomes possible" (1997, 5). Butler then adds that "One 'exists' not only by virtue of being recognized, but, in a prior sense, by being *recognizable*. The terms that facilitate recognition are themselves conventional, the effects and instruments of a social ritual that decide, often through exclusion and violence, the linguistic conditions of survivable subjects" (Butler 1997, 5). Gee (2014) also refers to "recognition work" as a means for constituting subjectivity (54). He describes such work as the efforts people undertake when "they try to make visible to others (and to themselves as well) *who* they are and *what* they are doing. People engage in such work when they try to recognize others for *who* they are and *what* they are doing" (54, italics in original).

Not only are our identities and/or subjectivity constituted, in part, through reiterated performative acts, those same acts recreate the social order(ing) by which normative recognition is enabled. This is not to say that there is uniformity of experience, of belief, or of identity, but rather that the norms that have been produced elsewhere become the material by which we and others assign meaning and order to our own experiences. Though some have taken the performativity approach to be inescapably deterministic, Butler insists that one's ability to act agentively depends first on being recognized as someone who can or should act and that such actions are enabled as we reiterate and sometimes transform normative conventions.

In the analysis below of the language and identity categories invoked by the research participants in my study, I consider how their discursive activity most typically served to renew high-modern categories of language and identity. While it is possible that these individuals voice alternative categories in other situations and with other interlocutors, I can only explore how the reiterated categories in their interview accounts (re)produce a social order of recognizable identities—a necessary effect as Butler (2001) would likely argue, but one that must be problematized.

Interview Accounts of Language and Identity

The data analyzed here come from an interview study with immigrant small business owners in the United States. I interviewed eighteen individuals who fit the following criteria: they immigrated to the United States after childhood, they learned English after childhood, and they opened their own businesses in the United States as adults. I met these research participants at their places of business and conducted the interviews in their restaurants, nail/hair salons, and dry cleaning pick-up stores, among other sites. The interviews were audio-recorded and transcribed, resulting in 430 minutes of interview talk and 280 pages of transcribed text (see Miller 2014 for more comprehensive exploration of this data corpus).

Reflexive approaches to research have demonstrated that interviewees do not simply relay information, they co-construct particular identities in the process of responding to interview questions (De Fina 2011; Roulston 2010; Talmy and Richards 2011). Bucholtz and Hall (2005) describe such identity work as the "relationality phenomenon" and contend that identities are never "autonomous or independent" but become recognizable or socially meaningful in "relation to other available identity positions and other social actors" (598). That is, particular kinds of identities only make sense when positioned in relation to particular kinds of configurations of actors and situations. The relationality phenomenon is not peculiar to interview talk; it is an inevitable aspect of producing narrative accounts of self. Butler (2001), for example, insists that "my account of myself is never fully mine" because it depends on what is recognizable—norms that have been created external to us, that precede us—and also that giving an account of self can only occur in relation to an addressee even when the addressee "remains implicit and unnamed, anonymous and unspecified" (26). I see these relational processes as mechanisms for constituting recognizability, as performativity at work.

In the analysis sections below, I consider how interviewees positioned themselves and others and the language activities that comprise their workplace practices according to Bucholtz and Hall's (2005) three types of relational processes: (1) authentication and denaturalization, (2) authorization and illegitimation, and (3) adequation and distinction (599). These "tactics of intersubjectivity" (599) provide recognized methods and familiar discursive "material" for producing recognizability. They also serve as heuristics for my own attempts to assign order to and derive meaning from these interview accounts.

Authentication and Denaturalization

Bucholtz and Hall (2005) indicate that the relational processes of *authentication* and *denaturalization* refer to discursive work whereby we make "claims to realness and artifice" (601). A commonplace and utterly mundane ideological mechanism for authenticating a language identity (i.e., "I am an English speaker" or "She is a Vietnamese speaker") comes from claiming or ascribing native-speaker status to someone as well as by discursively linking ethnic and/or national origins to a particular language, and treating them as natural, essential ties. Blommaert, Leppänen, and Spotti (2012) refer to this linkage as the "ethnolinguistic assumption" which, they note, is based on an ideological understanding that a "'normal' person belongs to only one language and culture unit" (3). Further, in referring to languages as self-evident categories that can be presupposed rather than interrogated and treated as provisional, the interviewees and I demonstrate our implicit orientation to languages as commonsensically unitary, bounded entities that can be named and discussed as real objects in the world.

We see this kind of mundane ideological work enacted in my interview interaction with Don, a Vietnamese man who owns a restaurant supply store. In talking about the languages he uses in his store, he indicated that his use of English is "half and half." When I asked what other languages he uses, he named Chinese, Vietnamese, and Spanish. Don then explained that he knows Chinese because his family is Chinese, and I treated this conflation of a national/ethnic identity with a linguistic identity as normative in commenting, "Well that explains that." Don added that he was born in Vietnam, thereby supplying an easily interpretable explanation for his competence in Vietnamese. Don's knowledge of Spanish could likewise be understood given his explanation that he learned it from his employees, a situation that is "sensible" in an urban context with a large population of Spanish-speaking immigrants. Our mutual orientation to birthplace and ethnic heritage and language contact as straightforward, causal explanations for Don's language competence demonstrates ratification of the "ethnolinguistic assumption" (Blommaert, Leppänen, and Spotti 2012, 3). Though Don's identity of linguistic diversity requires some discursive work to create order out of "abnormal" multiplicity, the ideological perspective in which a natural linkage exists among these place-identity-language characteristics also provides a resource whereby Don can be recognized as someone who has an interpretable link to particular places and cultures. He is thus able to provide a "plausible, positive account of recognition" (McQueen 2015, 49). I interpellated Don as a particular kind of social and linguistic being through my questions, and as Giles and Vintimilla (2007) put it, the "desire for recognition demands not only coherence and self-identity but also to be part of a conventionality and a normativity that will allow me to be recognized by the other" (37).

By contrast, another interviewee did not claim a native-language identity that I ascribed to her. When I asked Donna, who owns a dressmaking shop, what languages she knows, she replied, "Uh just Thai and English" (see interview excerpt below, turns 1–2). I followed up with a further question regarding whether she uses mostly English in her shop or mostly Thai. She then indicated that her customers are Thai and Lao (turn 6), and I followed this response by asking whether she can also speak Lao (turn 9). Donna replied with a lengthened production of the word "Yeah" (turn 10). This kind of stretched verbal production of a word can be used to mark potential interactional trouble (Schegloff, Jefferson, and Sacks 1977) even though Donna did so when producing a discourse marker that signaled agreement with my prior utterance. She then constructed a multiturn explanation that seems to be a justification for why she did not claim to speak Lao even though she apparently can. She indicated that Lao is the language of her part of the country (turns 10–14) but that Thai is the official language and the one learned at school (turns 16–18) whereas Lao is the language spoken at home (turn 20). When she ended her explanation, I summarized it by saying, "Well so you know three languages" (turn 23). Perhaps she did not want to attempt yet another long explanation regarding her connection to the language; this time she simply replied "yeah" (turn 24).

Interview excerpt with Donna

1. INT How many languages do you know?
2. DON Uh just only Thai and English
3. INT Thai and English
4. DON Yeah
5. INT Do you um do you use mostly English here or are many of your customers Thai?
6. DON No my customer is Thai and Lao.
7. INT Thai and Lao.
8. DON Yeah
9. INT And so do you know some Lao. Can you speak Lao?
10. DON Yeah::: yeah. I speak Lao because the part of the country where I live, we use Lao.
11. INT Yeah okay
12. DON Because we in the borderline.
13. INT Uh huh
14. DON Borderline with Lao. So whoever live in the part of country where I live they speak both.
15. INT Yes
16. DON Yeah you speak Lao but it's not a official language you know.
17. INT Yeah
18. DON But you talk you know. And then official language is still you know like you go to school you learn Thai word.
19. INT Mhm
20. DON And you come home you speak Laos.
21. INT Right.
22. DON Uh huh
23. INT Right. Okay. Well so you know three languages.
24. DON Yeah.

I do not fully understand why Donna did not include Lao as one of her languages in response to my initial question. Perhaps because Lao is regarded as a "home language" rather than the "official language" in the borderland area between Laos and

Thailand, a situation saturated with political conflict and marked by economic disparities, there can be a loss of status associated with claiming Lao as one's language. My desire to get the facts straight by determining how many discretely namable languages Donna knows, in part because of wanting to give her credit for knowing more languages than she had claimed, shows my orientation to an ideology of languages as autonomous, and thus countable systems. Further, in treating Lao as an objective entity, separate from institutional reification or social status, I orient to an ideology of languages as neutral symbolic systems that can be used and learned with no need to account for differential regimes of power. However, Donna treats my question of whether she speaks Lao as requiring a complex response thereby challenging my "commonsensical" perspective in treating language identity as a neutral fact. That said, even when attempting to problematize my attribution of an authentic Lao (language) identity to her, Donna oriented to the features that comprise authenticity: the "natural" connections of language to geographical location, the political recognition of languages, and typical domains of use. As such, these ideological notions provide her with familiar terms of recognition by which she can attempt to deflect my attribution of "speaker of Lao" to her.

It seems that for the interviewees in this study, references to ethnolinguistic identities can serve as a mundane resource for creating "order" out of identities marked by multiplicity, such as Don's. Such ordering activity is not neutral activity, however, as was illustrated in my problematic attribution of a "naturally" authentic language identity to Donna. Though these terms of recognition are highly reductive (inconvenient fictions), these are at the same time resources (convenient fictions) for providing plausible accounts of self and experience because they align with familiar (i.e., ideological) methods for making sense of language and diverse language identities. There are likely many highly nuanced accounts of in-between-ness (suggested in Donna's account) that could have been told, and yet as Butler (2010) has noted, it just as important "to ask how a banality becomes established as such" (148).

Authorization and Illegitimation

The relational process of *authorization* refers to how identities are sanctioned or authorized through institutional and ideological discourses, whereas *illegitimation* is the process by which identities are "dismissed, censored, or simply ignored by these same structures" (Bucholtz and Hall 2005, 603). In this section, I examine accounts in which interviewees' native languages are treated as "naturally" illegitimate in their own business spaces, depending on the identities of their customers. In these cases, English was authorized as the commonsensical default language. All of the interviewees oriented to the normative view that English is the language that should be used in their business spaces when there are English-speaking customers present. Of course, it is true that they produced these accounts when interacting with me, a Caucasian native speaker of English who directly asked them about their use and learning of English. However, given that many of them also gave positive accounts of using non-English languages (see following section), it seems that their English-affirming responses cannot be attributed solely to a desire not to incriminate themselves with me. Their orientation to a "natural" authorization of English was demonstrated in several accounts of managing and suppressing non-English languages in their business spaces. In one such case, Lois, a Vietnamese owner of a nail salon, described her difficulty ("it very hard") in getting her Vietnamese employees not to talk together in Vietnamese "too much" in the presence of their clients. She said, "I just tell them, 'Don't talk too much.'" She then added, "Sometime...when we talk- they talk [in Vietnamese] and stuff, I always tell customer, 'We don't talk about you.' We we explain what we talk to each customer. We said, 'Sometime we do like sleepy, so sometime we just talk...[to] wake up.' So we explain to customer. They understand. So they come back. They very friendly."

In this account, it seems that the potential for offense in Lois's shop arises when English-speaking clients are unable to understand what the Vietnamese-speaking salon employees say to each other. Such implicit authorization of English and overt illegitimation of Vietnamese is perhaps "sensible" in a business climate where a widely accepted ideal is that "the customer is always right." But it seems that the lack of mutual understanding is only consequential when the dominant-language speakers are the ones who are unable to understand the language in use. The possibility that the Vietnamese employees may not understand everything their English-speaking clients say or talk about is not treated as relevant or within "the domain of the sayable" (Butler 1997, 133).

Interviewees also frequently produced accounts of how they were able to learn bits of English through interacting with "Americans," sometimes by just "picking it up" and sometimes by directly asking customers to correct their English, demonstrated in another Vietnamese nail salon owner's report of what she tells her clients: "I say, if you think it [her English] not right, you please correct me." Interviewees typically cast these English-learning interactions as friendly and mostly unproblematic exchanges. But what is notable is the unidirectionality of the teaching (English-speaking native Americans) to learning (immigrant nonnative users of English) activity rather than mutual learning and teaching. The social order in which English speakers do not seek usage tips from these multilingual business owners on their languages is treated as commonsensical, not even meriting comment.

There was only one account of institutional authorization of an immigrant language in an English-dominant context. In the same interview with Lois, the nail salon owner who reported on her efforts to suppress the use of Vietnamese among her employees, she commented on her son's ability to speak Vietnamese by noting that "he speak *our* language," thereby constituting language ownership and a normative ethnolinguistic identity for her son. Lois then described how competence in Vietnamese is advantageous for her son in his job with an investment company. She indicated that when Vietnamese people "call in," her son is always called up to speak to them regarding "how to invest their money." It seems that in this relatively high-status context, her son's competence in Vietnamese is authorized as a value-added competence, an identity feature that lends him cultural (and economic) capital as it simultaneously allows the investment company to expand its customer base. Of course, the authorization of Vietnamese in such a context is only possible because Lois's son is also fully proficient in English; English is not displaced as the default language for this business context, it is merely supplemented.

In reiterating the inconvenient fiction of "Vietnamese" as an objectively real category, Lois can claim a causal connection between her son's ownership of his/their language and the advantage it brings him in a situation where its usage is authorized by privileged Others. More significantly, this kind of simplified identity category allows Lois and others to assume recognizable positions in a broader social order. Without knowing the details of their life histories, we already "know" something about them if we know what language(s) they speak and what culturally and politically defined space they grew up in. There are many terms of recognition that might be possible for these individuals. In this situation, in which they are interpellated as immigrants and as nonnative users of English through my interview questions, the terms of recognition upon which we draw long preceded our interview encounter. They also serve as structures of intelligibility for this particular interview context. And an effect of such familiarity is that particular kinds of accounts of language use and learning come to be regarded as plausible and desirable.

It is likely true that interviewees' apparent acceptance of the status quo in using English contributes to the success of their businesses in the urban context where their businesses operate, but of course this success is grounded in an ideology regarding who "naturally" adopts the language practices of the Other. When interviewees could show themselves to be responsive to ideologies of responsibility (i.e., immigrants are "commonsensically" responsible to learn and use the dominant language, at least in public spaces and when English speakers are present; Miller 2014), they align with an aspirational—and desirable and sanctioned—immigrant identity. In these scenarios, utterly mundane in their familiarity, interviewees are cast as deficit users of English who are also users of other, sometimes problematic, languages.

Adequation and Distinction

The relational processes of *adequation* and *distinction* refer to the methods by which we construe ourselves as sufficiently similar to or different from others. The many, many ways in which individuals or social groups differ from one another must be downplayed in order for similarity to be foregrounded and adequation established. Likewise a seemingly minor difference can be used to construct identities of distinction.

At the time I interviewed my study participants, I was focusing primarily on their experiences with learning and using English, but I also asked them to identify all of the languages that they knew and whether they used languages other than English in their workplaces. All of them were able to identify more than one language, and usually a minimum of three, in their repertoires, but only seven of the eighteen interviewees indicated that they use non-English languages to conduct some aspect of their business. Suggestive of Canagarajah's (2014) and Pennycook and Otsuji's (2014) studies, and contrary to the accounts discussed in the previous section, these seven interviewees described scenarios in which "what language" (Canagarajah 2014, 94) is used seems to matter less than establishing intersubjectivity with their interlocutors who, in all cases, were other multilingual immigrants.

The possibility for achieving such intersubjectivity was attributed in some cases to their similar cultural identities (i.e., adequation). For example, Donna, the Laotian dressmaker, contended that even though she and her Asian customers come "from many different countries," such as "Cambodia, Lao[s], or Vietnam" and speak to each other in "broken English," they still "understand each other." She added that in conversations with these individuals she "know[s] exactly what they mean" and that they all "figure [it] out" because they are all "about the same." Likewise, Keith, a Chinese owner of a Chinese pastry shop, indicated that his "Laos, Thai, Vietnamese...[and] Chinese" customers, who are "all the Asian people," have no difficulty understanding each other. He added, "So when they come here most you will know you will know what is [going on]" Similarly, Soo, a Korean owner of a dry-cleaning pick-up store, said that "most Korean people and Asian people go for the cooperation"; hence, as she explained, she doesn't "have a problem" in interacting with and understanding them. Language and national differences are still recognized in these accounts, and, in fact, it seems that it is these individuals' ability to establish intersubjectivity despite these differences that is treated as notable and desirable. More important than being able to tap into the "same" language system, it seems that it was these interlocutors' similarity in "being Asian" that allowed them to interact meaningfully. "Being Asian" thus becomes a discursive resource for creating an interpretable explanation for their workplace interactions and for domesticating their discursive complexities.

A somewhat different case of adequation is demonstrated in Ivan's depiction of how he, a French owner of a bakery, is able to get along so well with his Latino employees. He indicated that at one point he had "seven nationalities" represented on his bakery staff (though he listed only six countries of origin: Mexico, El Salvador, Chile, Germany, Russia, and Switzerland). Ivan then added that "it was almost too much. It was like the Babylon tower that nobody could understand each other." However, he followed this comment with "but I do very well with the Latinos, being French." He explained his ability to establish solidarity with these employees as based in their shared "Latin root." This case of adequation was used to explain how he was able to "understand their type of humor, what they like to joke about." Ivan continued, "I know that if I go along with them in the joke I'm not going to be sued for sexual harassment." In this case, the radical differences among his staff ("nobody could understand each other") are treated as surmountable when he and a subset of his employees share a "Latin root" (and possibly the same gender).

In other descriptions of workplace talk with fellow immigrant customers or employees, interviewees described cases of easy, brief, unplanned language teaching-learning exchanges in the process of conducting routine service transactions. Unlike the English-learning interactions noted earlier, in these accounts the *mutuality* of teaching and learning is treated as natural, pleasurable, and as consequential for establishing friendly relations in their workplace milieu. For example, Tony commented that the Lao, Thai, and Hmong customers at his Vietnamese sandwich shop will teach him "a little bit" of their languages and that he "teach[es] them a little bit" of Vietnamese. He and the other interviewees described themselves as "not having a problem" when interacting with customers from different language backgrounds. At the same time, they uniformly treated such exchanges as trivial in terms of language competence, indicating that, like Tony, they knew only "a little bit" of their customers' or employees' languages.

It seems that *implicit adequation* is achieved in these accounts of shared "truncated repertoires" (Blommaert 2010, 103), their knowing "a little bit" of other immigrants' languages. Blommaert (2010) points out that super-diverse contexts are always stratified in terms of how differing language resources are treated (11). What matters in such spaces is "what counts as language in particular contexts: what is ratified and recognized as a valid code for making oneself understood" (12). In interviewees' metatalk about contexts of interaction with fellow multilingual immigrants, their mixed, truncated, incomplete language repertoires seem to be treated as "valid enough." None of them reported on any efforts to suppress a particular language (though that may have occurred); rather, their mutual efforts seem to be invested in establishing intersubjectivity through engaging in brief interactions that contribute to low-key "conviviality" (Blommaert 2013, 112).

The cases of adequation produced in the interview talk allowed interviewees to assign sense to the complex practices that emerged in their places of business and to position themselves and others in an interpretable social order. Their ability to establish intersubjectivity with their clients and employees is rendered interpretable, in part, through the shared cultural or linguistic identities that they posit, even though such recognition is enabled through what might be regarded as highly reductive ("Asian") and highly suspect ("Latin root") categories. Blommaert (2013) notes that "popular views" of "polycentric, multifiliar, dynamic" situations typically lead to a "reduction of complexity in [their] interpretations" (108). Such flattened interpretations distort what actually takes place (inconvenient fictions) in these complexly diverse contexts and pose great risks when one seeks for descriptive and analytic fidelity. However, if we take these simplifying categories as (mostly unreflective) shorthand methods for representing events so that they become interpretable, they seem quite "convenient." In contrast to the immigrant selves who "naturally" orient to English usage and who suppress the "non-local" languages in their workspaces, here we recognize a *multi*lingual self who is capable of managing the complex interactional contingencies he or she encounters.

At the same time, even as interviewees were able to establish recognizable selves through invoking desirable multilingual identities, they simultaneously constituted sometimes explicit and often implicit orientations to identities of inadequacy. The language teaching-learning exchanges among fellow immigrants are treated as trivial in terms of the quality of the emergent language knowledge ("just a little bit"). When commenting on how they manage to communicate with their customers or employees despite their language differences, the language in play is typically cast as relatively limited (i.e., "broken English"). Interviewees oriented to the potential for social disorder to emerge because of language difference. In some cases it is expressed overtly ("it was like the Babylon tower that nobody could understand each other"), but most often interviewees' comments that they "do not have a problem" implicitly suggest that communicative problems could be expected in such interactions. In this way, discursive interactions that are marked by full fluency and ease of expression are cast as valued and normative (Blommaert and Rampton 2011); they serve as the implicit comparative standard and point to an ideology in which only full competence counts as real or good language knowledge (Canagarajah, this volume). Further, when "ties between language and identity" are essentialized as stable and natural, then "acts of appropriation" of a language become "more vulnerable to accusations of...incompetence in the Other's language" (Park and Wee 2009, 397). Thus, the convivial encounters with fellow multilingual immigrants are not simple cases of happy hybridity, of triumph over difference. We find instead low-grade "scale-sensitivity" (Blommaert and Rampton 2011, 10) demonstrated in these accounts through interviewees' talk about the limitations and inadequacy of their linguistic competences.

In orienting to the authorization/illegitimation and authenticity/inauthenticity of their ethnolinguistic identities, as well as to features of adequation/distinction, interviewees made themselves interpretable to me. But this interpretability does not occur merely on the merits of interviewees' narrative skills or through establishing "local" comprehensibility between them and me. Butler contends that "the 'I' cannot tell the story of its own emergence and the conditions of its own possibility" for it must, in fact, make use of "norms that govern the humanly recognizable" (2001, 26). Norms emerge as ideological resources, serving as mechanisms for domesticating complex assemblages of meanings. For this reason, in a late-modern world marked by linguistic complexity, the process of gaining recognizability as "multilingual" individuals often develops through the inconvenient fictions of high-modern ideologies that constrain how language and identity are made meaningful.

Conclusion

When considering the effects of interviewees' metatalk from the perspective of recognizability, I see their reliance on static categories of language and ethnolinguistic identity as productive material for gaining visibility, for establishing themselves as particular kinds of persons, even when the terms for doing so are not of their own making or choosing. The inconvenient fictions of multiple, separate languages and of inherent, essential linkages between ethnicity-nation-culture-language provide material for establishing an identity and for "doing being ordinary" (see Miller 2009). In contrast to some of the studies that have drawn on performativity theory when examining interactions among multilingual individuals, these interviewees do not supply accounts of engaging in parody of traditional identities or of playfully inventing new ones (see Harissi, Otsuji, and Pennycook 2012), though that may certainly happen in encounters that they did not recount to me. The performative effects of these interviewees' metatalk are far more conservative in relation to high-modern categories of the world. It seems that without categories of "trans-" or "metro-" in their repertoires, they necessarily flatten the interesting complexity of their workplace discursive practices. However, gaining desirable recognizability is not about using better, more accurate labels or words that reflect who one *really* is, but rather, it is about participating in the ongoing flow of "language whose historicity exceeds in all directions the history of the speaking subject" (Butler 1997, 28).

Kramsch (2012) frames researchers' efforts to describe, with greater fidelity, the "multiplicity of identities" true of multilingual individuals and the desire to "change people's [biased] representations of reality by offering an alternative representation and hav[ing] it collectively recognized and accepted" as a modernist perspective (494). By contrast, a post-structural perspective focuses on understanding the sense-making or normative discourses that make particular identities possible. This post-structural stance leads to problematizing the taken-for-granted by asking questions regarding the terms of recognition that are drawn on in these interactions, questions such as: Why is it "sensible" to attempt to silence Vietnamese in a workplace staffed by Vietnamese-speaking employees? Why is Lois's son's use of Vietnamese a source of pride for her while her employees' use of Vietnamese is a source of worry? Why does it seem normal and desirable for the immigrant business owners to take advantage of informal opportunities to learn English but unthinkable that the English-speaking clients should seek to learn bits of the languages of the business owners? Why, by contrast, is mutuality of language teaching and learning among fellow immigrants regarded as pleasurable and desirable, even if somewhat trivial? Who gets to determine authenticity, or its opposite? What benefits do claimed or attributed authentic identities provide? Under what circumstances can denaturalization lead to charges of betrayal or mere peculiarity?

Though I cannot supply definitive answers, the questions themselves help to raise awareness of who benefits more clearly from some of the normative resources we use in gaining recognizability and thereby (re)creating social order. We also need to consider the selves that are not recognized. That is, we need to ask what the terms of unsayability and unintelligibility might be. My confusion with Donna's apparent refusal to claim Lao as one of "her" languages points to my inability to make sense of the identity she projected. In a small way and for a few moments, it was rendered unintelligible according to my understanding of normative ethnolinguistic identities.

Most importantly, if we understand that sayability resides in *norms* rather than *essential* entities, that it undergoes continual renewal and as such is also susceptible to negotiation, resistance, and transformation, then we can, as Kramsch (2012) contends, "interrogate the larger flows of people, knowledge and capital and their own vulnerability in playing the paradoxical roles that are required of them" (499). Ameliorating unfair identity attributions is not simply a matter of calling out dominant groups or of modifying dominant ideologies, let alone of changing labels—though none of these is a simple change, of course. When we consider social "reality" in relation to recognizability, we can begin to see how modes of exclusion operate—not monolithically and not at all times or in all places.

As noted earlier, Judith Butler has identified the normative terms by which we gain recognizability as "epistemological frames" (2001, 23) (as opposed to essential entities) but also as "vectors of power" (1993, 187). We know that durative norms benefit some people more than others and thus contribute to inequality. For this reason, Butler also asserts that "becoming visible, becoming sayable is [not] the end of politics" (in Olson and Worsham 2000, 743). It is more important, she adds, to ask, "What are the conditions of sayability, of speakability, of visibility? Does one want a place within them?" (in Olson and Worsham 2000, 744).

Recognizability need not confine us to a closed world of endless repetition of norms, for if we treat normative categories of language or ethnic or cultural identities as inconvenient fictions, one can then undertake a "double movement," by which Butler (1993) means we "invoke the category and, hence, provisionally...institute an identity and at the same time...open the category as a site of permanent political contest" (222).

References

Blommaert, Jan. 2010. *The Sociolinguistics of Globalization*. Cambridge: Cambridge University Press.

———. 2013. *Ethnography, Superdiversity and Linguistic Landscapes: Chronicles of Complexity*. Bristol, Eng.: Multilingual Matters.

Blommaert, Jan, Sirpa Leppänen, and Massimiliano Spotti. 2012. "Endangering Multilingualism." In *Dangerous Multilingualism. Northern Perspectives on Order, Purity and Normality*, edited by Jan Blommaert, Sirpa Leppänen, Päivi Pahta, and Tiina Räisänan, 1–21. New York: Palgrave Macmillan.

Blommaert, Jan, and Ben Rampton. 2011. "Language and Superdiversity." *Diversities* 13:1–21.

Bucholtz, Mary, and Kira Hall. 2005. "Identity and Interaction: A Sociocultural Linguistic Approach." *Discourse Studies* 7:585–614.

Butler, Judith. 1993. *Bodies that Matter: On the Discourse Limits of "Sex."* New York: Routledge.

———. 1997. *Excitable Speech: A Politics of the Performative*. New York: Routledge.

———. 2001. "Giving an Account of Oneself." *Diacritics* 31:22–40.

———. 2010. "Performative Agency." *Journal of Cultural Economy* 3:147–61.

Canagarajah, Suresh. 2014. "Theorizing a Competence for Translingual Practice at the Contact Zone." In *The Multilingual Turn: Implications for SLA, TESOL and Bilingual Education*, edited by Stephen May, 78–102. New York: Routledge.

De Fina, Anna. 2011. "Researcher and Informant Roles in Narrative Interactions: Constructions of Belonging and Foreign-ness." *Language in Society* 40:27–38.

García, Ofelia. 2009. *Bilingual Education in the 21st Century: A Global Perspective.* With contributions by Hugo B. Beardsmore. Malden, MA: Wiley-Blackwell Publishers.

Gee, James P. 2014. *An Introduction to Discourse Analysis: Theory and Method*. 4th ed. New York: Routledge.

Giles, Graham, and Christina Delgado Vintimilla. 2007. "The Opacity of the Self, Sovereignty and Freedom: In Conversation with Arendt, Butler and Derrida." *Paideusis* 16: 35–44.

Harissi, Maria, Emi Otsuji, and Alistair Pennycook. 2012. "The Performative Fixing and Unfixing of Subjectivities." *Applied Linguistics* 33:524–43.

Kramsch, Claire. 2012. "Imposture: A Late Modern Notion in Poststructuralist SLA Research." *Applied Linguistics* 33:483–502.

Makoni, Sinfree, and Alistair Pennycook. 2007. "Disinventing and Resconstituting Languages." In *Disinventing and Resconstituting Languages*, edited by Sinfree Makoni and Alistair Pennycook, 1–41. Clevedon, UK: Multilingual Matters.

McQueen, Paddy. 2015. "Honneth, Butler and the Ambivalent Effects of Recognition." *Res Publica* 2: 43–60.

Miller, Elizabeth R. 2009. "Orienting to "Being Ordinary": The (Re)construction of Hegemonic Ideologies among Adult Immigrant Learners of English." *Critical Inquiry in Language Studies* 6:315–44.

———. 2014. *The Language of Adult Immigrants: Agency in the Making.* Bristol: Multilingual Matters.

Olson, Gary A., and Lynn Worsham. 2000. "Changing the Subject: Judith Butler's Politics of Radical Resignification." *Journal of Advanced Composition* 20:727–65.

Otsuji, Emi, and Alistair Pennycook. 2010. "Metrolingualism: Fixity, Fluidity and Language in Flux." *International Journal of Multilingualism* 7:240–54.

Park, Joseph Sung-Yul, and Lionel Wee. 2009. "The Three Circles Redux: A Market-Theoretic Perspective on World Englishes." *Applied Linguistics* 30:389–406.

Pennycook, Alistair, and Emi Otsuji. 2014. "Metrolingual Multitasking and Spatial Repertoires: 'Pizza mo two minutes coming.'" *Journal of Sociolinguistics* 18:161–84.

Roulston, Kathryn. 2010. *Reflective Interviewing: A Guide to Theory and Practice*. Thousand Oaks, CA: Sage Publications.

Schegloff, Emanuel A., Gail Jefferson, and Harvey Sacks. 1977. "The Preference for Self-Correction in the Organization of Repair in Conversation." *Language* 53:361–82.

Talmy, Steven, and Keith Richards. 2011. "Theorizing Qualitative Research Interviews in Applied Linguistics." *Applied Linguistics* 32:1–5.

Chapter 8

Constructed Dialogue, Stance, and Ideological Diversity in Metalinguistic Discourse

ANASTASIA NYLUND

THIS CHAPTER INVESTIGATES STANCETAKING toward language among African American residents of Washington, DC. I argue that taking stances toward language and its role in their community, which Jaffe (2009a) terms *metasociolinguistic stancetaking*, allows speakers to negotiate their own and others' roles with respect to the complex, circulating discourses surrounding race, place, and identity in a city that is undergoing rapid social change. In their responses to language-related prompts from an interviewer, speakers are able to recruit the notion of *language* to do fine-grained, complex discursive negotiation of social issues in the city. Speakers pinpoint misunderstandings about language in their community—ideas about who talks like Washingtonians and what Washingtonians' language reveals about them as people—and attribute erroneous stances and ideas to imagined interlocutors through the use of constructed dialogue, as they simultaneously attribute contrasting stances to themselves and other Washingtonians, stances which more accurately describe the links between Washingtonian identity and linguistic practice in the speakers' minds.

The relationship between the notions of language, stance, and ideology is a particularly interesting one to analyze in the context of Washington, DC. Washington, DC, is the capital city of the United States and, as such, occupies a peculiar position in the imagination of the American public. Since its founding as the seat of the federal government in 1790, Washington, DC, has symbolized an a-regional, cosmopolitan, and political place.

Washington, DC, is situated on the border between Maryland and Virginia, and therefore occupies a boundary space between the cultural North and South of the United States. The city is also situated in a boundary space between the Mid-Atlantic and Southern dialect regions (Labov, Ash, and Boberg 2006; Nylund 2013). Speaking to the city's identity as a border city and as an a-regional space, a well-known quote, attributed to President John F. Kennedy, suggests that Washington is "a city of Southern efficiency and Northern charm" (highlighting, of course, the contrasting stereotyped discourses of Southerners as charming but lazy, and Northerners as rude but efficient). In effect, this image portrays Washington, DC, as a "placeless" place, neither here nor there.

A related circulating discourse, borne out of the heavy and steady influx of in-migrants to the area over the decades, plays up the scarcity and exoticism of the native Washingtonian. During my fieldwork in the DC area, I interviewed Walter, the owner of a local business in the close-in suburb of Takoma Park, Maryland, which lies directly adjacent to the District of Columbia. When I explained to my interviewee that I was interested in talking to lifelong residents of Washington, DC, he told me that he was born and raised on Capitol Hill ("in the shade of the Capitol"), after which he extended his arm toward me and exclaimed: "I'm a real Washingtonian; go ahead and touch!" Such statements by lifelong Washingtonians, relaying the perceived surprise of outsiders that there are, in fact, native Washingtonians, are common.

Washington, DC, has also become associated in the public's imagination, through media portrayals, with primarily white-collar labor (i.e., government work), and eventually with a transient population of political appointees and cabinet members. The Washington, DC, area is ethnoracially diverse (see, e.g., Manning 1998; Nylund 2013) and home to a variety of industries, but the widely circulating image of a Washington area residents as affluent, white, highly educated persons who commute from the suburbs into the city for their government job is ingrained in the discourses circulating about the city. Political dramas and other media products portray Washington, DC, as a city full of white-collar transplants working in federal and international politics, with the exception of the occasional local character, as in the case of *House of Cards,* whose sole DC-resident character is a cook who supplies authentic barbecue to the president. In news media, pundits frequently comment on how out of touch "Washington" is with the "real" needs of Americans in legislators' constituencies.

In addition to discourses of "placelessness," white-collar employment, and social and geographic mobility, an enduring discourse of Washington, DC—and one championed by the city's long-term residents—is that of an African American city with deep roots. Manning (1998) provides a historical perspective on DC's demography dating back to the nineteenth century, and finds that Washington, DC, has always been characterized by its large and diverse African American community, originating in the city's significant population of enslaved African Americans. By the 1970s, Washington, DC's population was over 70 percent African American, earning the city the moniker "Chocolate City" by funk band Parliament, an affectionate nickname that has remained popular despite the gentrification-driven decline in the African American population in recent years. At the time of the US Census in 2010, Washington, DC was 51 percent African American, a majority that has surely been lost since that time (Nylund 2013).

One of the participants in the study from which data for this chapter originates, Zara, a twenty-one-year-old student at Howard University and racial justice activist, sums up the centrality of ethnoracial identity to Washingtonian identity when answering a question about the general character of Washington, DC, residents: "DC people are nice, but they're not nice to white people." In suggesting mutual exclusivity between DC people and white people, Zara suggests that authentic Washingtonians are not white, and thus that authentic Washingtonian identities are those of the people of color (in particular, black Washingtonians) who reside in the city. The city's African American community is its largest and oldest, further strengthening the link between African American practice and local practice.

In this chapter, I investigate how the notion of *language* figures into African American Washingtonians' imaginations and ideologies, and into the making of authentic Washingtonian selves in interaction. I argue that stancetaking toward language, particularly through the use of constructed dialogue, is a powerful mechanism for identity construction in this community.

Metalinguistic Discourse in the Sociolinguistic Interview

In this chapter, I focus on metalinguistic commentary, or utterances in which speakers directly address and comment on language as a cultural and social object in the community. Metalinguistic commentary in the sociolinguistic interview, although a key part of the interview protocol (cf. Labov 1972), has often been overlooked as a site for research on language awareness, ideology, and performance, perhaps due in part to two assumptions: that language produced in metalinguistic commentary reflects a high degree of awareness to speech (Labov 1972) and is therefore less authentically vernacular, and also that the interview as a speech event is constrained and engineered, thus occasioning edited speech. Interactional sociolinguists, meanwhile, have argued that interview speech is indeed a fruitful site for the investigation of situated speaker identity (Johnstone 1996; Schiffrin 1996) and its interactional enactment and negotiation (De Fina 2011; De Fina and Perrino 2011; Mishler 1986), given that the interview itself is an authentic speech event whose power exceeds the gathering of information. In the interview, interviewees are asked topical questions, and in the same instance "also position themselves interactionally and evaluate aspects of the social world through the same discourse that they use to refer to and predicate about the topic" (Wortham et al. 2011, 49).

My approach to analyzing the stylistic and ideological potential of metalinguistic commentary in the sociolinguistic interview is further guided by the *speaker design* approach to style, which foregrounds the agentive and interactional motivations for shifting between more and less vernacular ways of speaking (Coupland 2007; Schilling 2013). Speakers style shift both 'up' and 'down' in performing aspects of local language in order to project facets of self, real or imagined, for strategic purposes within the interview (Schilling-Estes 1998). By talking about language and its users, speakers are able to perform and evaluate different kinds of people, whether themselves or others they agree or disagree with. Speakers are also able, through discussing language use, to construct narrative portrayals of social and linguistic intimacy or distance, and to create storyworlds within which language plays an ideologically important role. Metalanguage is therefore an important component of identity work in interaction, and the metalinguistic commentary in the sociolinguistic interview presents a rich opportunity to witness the links between linguistic and social realities in Washington, DC.

The case for studying metalanguage as a window on speakers' and communities' social realities, awareness, and ideologies is perhaps even greater in the case of African American communities and African American English (henceforth AAE). African American speakers' language is policed and subject to scrutiny given the pervasive Standard Language ideology (Lippi-Green 1997) in the United States, and African American speakers constantly juggle the demands of a "linguistic push-pull" (see, e.g., Smitherman 2006; Rickford and Rickford 2000), positioning themselves in relation to the linguistic identities of self and community while also walking the fine line of the demands of a professional world where AAE is stigmatized. Rahman's (2008) participants highlight linguistic virtuosity as a key to success. In short, African Americans' language awareness is inherently political and necessitates delicate maneuvering in discourse, through acts of stancetaking and positioning. One powerful discourse strategy for the positioning of self and other vis-à-vis social issues is constructed dialogue (Tannen 1986, 2007).

Constructed Dialogue

Tannen (1986, 2007) describes constructed dialogue as a reformulation of the phenomenon commonly known as reported speech (i.e., the narrative reenactment of speech from a prior speech event). Tannen argues:

> First, much of what appears in discourse as dialogue, or "reported speech," was never uttered by anyone else in any form. Second, if dialogue is used to represent utterances that were spoken by someone else, when an utterance is repeated by a current speaker, it exists primarily, if not only, as an element of the reporting context, although its meaning resonates with association with its reported context [...] the words have ceased to be those of the speaker to whom they are attributed, having been appropriated by the speaker who is repeating them. (2007, 112–13)

Constructed dialogue is thus not the recounting of words spoken by somebody at some previous point in time. Rather, dialogue is recruited, by the speaker, as a strategy for affecting some outcome in the reporting context, or the interaction in which they are recounting somebody else's speech. The speech itself is not literally quotation of a prior speech event, and is instead emblematic of what someone *might* have said, what someone *could* say, what people *frequently* or *habitually* say, and so on.

The use of constructed dialogue in interactionally constructed narratives—both canonical Labovian narratives (see, e.g., Labov and Waletzky 1967) and small/fragmented/hypothetical or otherwise noncanonical narratives (see, e.g., Bamberg and Georgakopoulou 2008)—thus allows speakers to create immediacy and to vividly portray a scenario that typifies their experiences and allows them to align with or distance themselves from a proposition, opinion, or belief. For example, Hamilton's (1998) study of constructed dialogue (referred to as 'reported speech') in doctor-patient narratives shows the construction of doctors' "verbatim" and frequently face-threatening instructions contribute to patients' oppositional stancetaking to the medical establishment and the discursive construction of a solidary, 'survivor' identity in interaction. These identities, Hamilton argues, constitute an important dimension of socialization into the community.

In a discussion of metalinguistic commentary in Pittsburgh, Johnstone (2006) suggests that particular narrative forms become conventionalized in communities where questions of language are often foregrounded in discussion of community identity. In so-called *language encounter narratives,* Pittsburghers make use of a limited set of narrative devices to contrast their knowledge of 'Pittsburghese' with the lack of understanding they perceive among outsiders. Johnstone shows that speakers construct narratives in which a character from Pittsburgh (often the speaker themselves) either leaves the area or encounters a non-Pittsburgher at home. To show that outsiders have erroneous assumptions and stereotypes of Pittsburgh speech, speakers attribute statements about the dialect, with which they do not agree, to the outsider character. These statements are frequently in the form of constructed dialogue, especially performance of stereotypical local forms. Given that the speakers attribute erroneous statements to others, they are able to contrast their own knowledge of Pittsburghese from these inaccurate ideas and thus create oppositional stances against the stereotypes of Pittsburgh speech.

Thus constructed dialogue is a powerful tool for interactional stancetaking, which forms part of the construction, reconfiguration, and maintenance of more enduring social identities and community norms. In turn, interactional stancetaking is a powerful mechanism for individual and community positioning. Understanding stance in the context of community history and tension can help disambiguate the ways in which members of diverse communities conceive of and comment on both linguistic and social ideologies circulating in their everyday lives.

Stance

In a formulation of the nature and functions of interactional stancetaking and its mechanisms, Du Bois (2007) suggests that "stance can be approached as a linguistically articulated form of social action whose meaning is to be construed within the broader scope of language, interaction, and sociocultural value" (139). Stance is a form of social action in the sense that it communicates, to an interactional partner, something about a speaker's ideation and evaluation of some social object. Taking a stance toward some stance object—a proposition, event, or person, for instance—showcases a speaker's *subjectivity*, or their individual experience and evaluation of said stance object (Du Bois 2007). Stancetaking is also highly *intersubjective* (Kärkkäinen 2006); since it takes place in an interactional context, stancetaking not only reflects a person's subjective experience but also serves functions for the immediate interaction and its interpersonal dimensions. As Kärkkäinen (2003, 2006) shows, *epistemic* stance acts—which reflect a speaker's degree of certainty of or commitment to a stance object—are frequently not only proactive (i.e., the speaker wants their interactional partner to know their stance toward an object), but also co-constructed within the interaction, for example through being given in response to some condition in the immediate interaction context. In short, speakers frequently take stances in response to questions or prompts, reacting to their interactional partner. In turn, stancetaking in interaction can also set up expectations and norms for the current speech event (Kärkkäinen 2006; Damari 2010) or future events of the same type (Jaffe 2009b). Jaffe's (2009b) analysis of teacher stancetaking toward minority language and national pride shows that everyday stancetaking within an institutional context leads to the formation and maintenance of institutional and broader social ideologies, and to the creation of students' future sociolinguistic subjectivities.

Given that much of the community-oriented discourse that sociolinguists gather comes from sociolinguistic interviews, analyzing stance as it happens in this type of speech event is a fruitful way to approach an understanding of how links between language, community, and social life are enacted and evaluated among community members. Stancetaking addresses not only the stance object itself, but the structures and ideologies that surround it as well. As Jaffe (2009a) points out, "the linguistic systems indexed by stance are all embedded in political, social, ideological, and cultural fields of action" (13). A speaker's choice of stance object, and the ways in which they enact their stances toward said objects, all speak to evaluation, both epistemic and affective, of social life at a broader scale.

Metasociolinguistic Stance

Given the importance of language (as a concept and practice) in the everyday experience of African American speakers, as discussed above, stancetaking toward language as an object should present an interesting and fruitful site for the study of ideological engagement and awareness in the diverse community of Washington, DC. In the examples discussed in this chapter, I address three speakers' interactional enactments of what Jaffe (2009a, 2009b) calls *metasociolinguistic stance*, or stance with language itself and its social context(s) as the stance object. Jaffe defines metasociolinguistic stance as follows:

> Stancetaking can also have as its object the underlying assumptions, processes, and motivations behind those sociolinguistic correlations. That is, speakers can use sociolinguistically salient forms in such a way as to call into question—or leave unchallenged—specific language hierarchies: convictions that particular variables are inherently more or less prestigious, intimate, authoritative, and so on. At an even more basic level, people can take up stances toward the assumed connections between language and identity, from the individual to the collective level. We might call this display of an attitude or position with respect to language hierarchies and ideologies a *metasociolinguistic* stance. (2009a, 17)

In Jaffe's formulation and based on the observations about the dynamic and intersubjective nature of interactional stancetaking, metasociolinguistic stance very explicitly links ideas of language and its social context and contributes to the construction of metalinguistic awareness and ideology at several levels of social engagement at once. A metasociolinguistic stance is at once individual (i.e., it showcases a speaker's affective or epistemic evaluation of the aspect of language that is the object of their stance), interpersonal (i.e., it can either *lead* a following stance in a particular direction or *follow* a prior stance with alignment or disalignment [Du Bois 2007, 161–62], as well as creating norms and possibilities for stancetaking within the interaction at hand), and ideological (i.e., metasociolinguistic stancetaking allows speakers to engage directly with the circulating discourses and stereotypes that underlie ideas of language and social life in their community). The multidimensionality and multifunctionality of metasociolinguistic stance makes it a powerful mechanism for individual- and community-level identity construction and negotiation in interaction.

Constructed Dialogue as a Metasociolinguistic Stance Mechanism

In the remainder of this chapter, I analyze instances of constructed dialogue in interactionally embedded metalinguistic discourse as examples of metasociolinguistic stancetaking, and argue that metasociolinguistic stancetaking through the mechanism of constructed dialogue allows speakers in a diverse and contested linguistic community to evaluate and analyze language in its social context—a context that is often associated with assumptions and sociolinguistic stereotypes of African American speakers—in a way that is less epistemically certain than would be unambiguous and potentially politically and emotionally charged statements. Using such a tactic allows speakers to attribute erroneous stances regarding the speech of Washington, DC, and therefore African American speech, to others, and to develop and maintain their own subject positions and interpersonal capital as knowledgeable about the local variety/ies and about their own individual linguistic biographies. The analysis suggests that metasociolinguistic stancetaking in the sociolinguistic interview is a powerful mechanism for ideological engagement in interaction.

Data

In this chapter, I analyze metalinguistic discourse in three sociolinguistic interviews with African American Washingtonians. The interviews form a subset of data from a larger study (Nylund 2013) in which I investigated phonological variation and identity construction among African American (N = 11) and European American (N = 10) Washingtonians. The sample included six African American men, five African American women, five European American men, and five European American women. The interviews were conducted between 2007 and 2012 by me and by graduate students in the Department of Linguistics at Georgetown University. The speakers ranged in age from twenty-one to fifty-nine years of age, represented a variety of occupational categories (including a security guard, a college student, a youth pastor, an antiques dealer, and a dog walker), and also reflected the high level of educational attainment in the region, with only two speakers (a fifty-four-year-old European American woman and a fifty-nine-year-old African American man) having completed less than a college education.

Guided by inquiry about regional and ethnoracial variation in this cultural and geographic boundary community, I analyzed twenty-one sociolinguistic interviews with native Washingtonians. Table 8.1 shows the demographic profiles of the three speakers I focus on in this analysis. Each of the three speakers is a lifelong Washingtonian, meaning that they have resided in Washington, DC, for the majority of their life, from childhood to adulthood. Some speakers went away for university, graduate school, or work, but all have moved back to the DC area. They all currently live in Washington, DC, or the immediately adjacent suburbs, and all orient to the city as their home.

The speakers participated in semistructured, sociolinguistic interviews, conducted in their homes (Phil and Mona) and place of employment (Azza). Interviews were around one hour in length and included a variety of topics, including speakers' individual biographies, family history, childhood neighborhood and activities, professional development, reflections on their communities and DC in general, social change, and language.

In the following three sections, I analyze several instances of constructed dialogue in metalinguistic discourse and argue that speakers employ constructed dialogue as a strategy for metasociolinguistic stancetaking. I follow with a discussion of the findings in the context of community diversity and positioning, and propose some further avenues for research.

Constructed Dialogue as Stancetaking to Regional Misidentification

Azza is a fifty-five year old African American woman who was interviewed at her place of employment, a mosque and Islamic community center in Washington, DC. Azza grew up in Anacostia, an old and well-established majority–African American community in the southeast quadrant of the city. Anacostia has in recent decades been at the center of public discourse about urban, African American poverty, social services, and crime in the DC area. Washington, DC's Ward 8, of which Anacostia is part, also represents a culturally authentic African American and Washingtonian identity, standing in contrast to other parts of the city which have gentrified and become majority white. This connection highlights the inextricable sociocultural link between African American life, history, and culture, and the city of Washington, DC.

At the time of the interview, Azza lived in the Capitol Hill neighborhood of Southeast DC. She discusses in the interview that she has remained in a majority–African American neighborhood but that her community has changed a lot over the years, particularly since the height of the widespread abuse of crack cocaine and

Table 8.1. The speakers' demographic profiles

Speaker	Sex	Age	Education	Occupation	Neighborhood (childhood neighborhood)
Azza	F	55	College	Speech pathologist/ Islamic school aide	Capitol Hill SE (Anacostia SE)
Mona	F	40	Graduate degree	Nonprofit sector	Takoma Park, MD (Takoma NW)
Phil	M	34	Graduate degree	Architect	Trinidad NE (Bloomingdale NW)

violent crime that plagued her neighborhood in the mid-1990s. At one point, Azza tells a story about how she discovered that an infamous drug kingpin lived on her block, and his arrest and eventual conviction.

Prior to the extract below, the interviewer and Azza had been discussing the importance of education and eloquence for a successful life. The interviewer introduces the topic of Azza's own language use by asking her if she has 'ever tried to change' something about her speech at some point in her life.

Extract 1 Interview with Azza

1.	Interviewer	Um, have you ever tried to change something about the way that *you*
2.		speak? During your life course?
3.	Azza	You in a linguistics class or something? Oh, okay! I was, I was uh-
4.		my degree is in speech path and audiology, yeah, so I'm saying, why
5.		would she ask? Um, actually, have I ever- No. I- I, many people- people
6.		have asked me if I'm from the South. They seem to hear a Southern drawl
7.		or something and it's probably there cause both of my parents are from
8.		South Carolina. So maybe I try to, um, not sound so... Southern, like, even
9.		though I love the South! I love the South and I don't see anything wrong
10.		with that. No, I don't think, no, I just think this is how I've spoken most of
11.		life, really. That- that may be a question more suited for someone
12.		who's- who comes from another, who has maybe, yeah, from some other
13.		country maybe.
14.	Interviewer	When you said that sometimes people, can tell, people can tell that maybe
15.		you have-
16.	Azza	They ask me where I'm from.
17.	Interviewer	Do you think it- that happens in DC?
18.	Azza	Oh, most definitely! "Where are you from? Georgia, Tennessee,
19.		Kentucky, Virginia, where did you get that accent?"
20.	Interviewer	And you're from here!
21.	Azza	And I'm from DC! Raised! Reared! DC! I'm a Washingtonian.[1]

In this example, the interviewer opens the floor for Azza's metalinguistic discourse by introducing the idea that Azza may have attempted to alter her speech at some point of her life (lines 1–2). Azza initially appears to take issue with the question itself by inquiring after the interviewer's field of study (line 3). She then underscores her own educational background in speech pathology and audiology—fields adjacent to linguistics—perhaps as a way to showcase her understanding of the interviewer's interest in the topic of language (lines 3–5), after which she returns to the question at hand, initiating a reply with "have I ever-" (line 5) followed by a quick assertion that no, she has not tried to change anything about the way she speaks. Others appear to hear a "Southern drawl or something" which is "probably" present in her speech due to her parents' South Carolina roots (lines 6–8), and "maybe" she tries to avoid sounding Southern despite her overall positive appraisal of the South (lines 8–10).

Through her use of adverbials like "probably," "maybe," and global characterizations of perceived accent like "Southern drawl or something," Azza appears to suggest that she does not entirely agree with the characterization of her speech as Southern. In lines 14–15, the interviewer follows up on her talk about being perceived as Southern by restating that "people can tell that maybe you have-," which Azza very quickly affirms with her assertion that "[t]hey ask me where I'm from" (line 16). The interviewer seeks more information with a follow-up question: do these questions come from outsiders or from people in DC (line 17)? Azza exclaims, again very quickly, that this "most definitely" happens in DC (line 18).

Following the establishment of the orientation of this scenario—what can be called a small story given its fragmented and habitual nature (Bamberg and Georgakopoulou 2008)—Azza employs constructed dialogue as a tool for showing what people's questions about her accent actually look like, on the ground. The contextualization cues (Gumperz 1982) that alert us to the presence of constructed dialogue in this extract are phonetic: Rather than using a quotative (e.g., *go, say, be like*, etc.) to introduce speech, Azza's pitch range widens considerably when she says, "Where are you from? Georgia, Tennessee, Kentucky, Virginia, where did you get that accent from?" (lines 18–19). Additionally, Azza appears to perform Southern features in the speech of the people who think that she herself sounds Southern. For example, Azza's pronunciation of "Georgia" and "Virginia" in lines 18–19 is /r/-less, evoking a genteel brand of Southernness, while her talk as a whole is relatively /r/-ful, showing that /r/-lessness is not a feature of her own speech.

Coupland (2007) and Schilling-Estes (1998) discuss dialect performance in interaction as a tool for self-styling and ideological engagement. The phonetic contrast between the constructed dialogue and Azza's own speech heightens the distinction between her own voice and that of the performed speaker and highlights the performative nature of it, contributing to Azza's attribution of and taking of stances toward the notion that her speech (and thus DC speech) is Southern. Azza attributes a stance to the constructed speaker, who evaluates her speech as Southern, but she does not align herself with it. The interviewer, in line 20, appears to pick up on the contrast created by Azza: she laughs and exclaims "And you're from here!" in effect communicating to Azza that she has interpreted the narrative exchange as it was intended. Stancetaking in interaction is co-constructed and functions, as discussed above, at individual and interpersonal levels simultaneously, setting up parameters for interpretation by the speaker's interactional partner. Having attributed a particular stance to the constructed speaker, who erroneously identifies Azza's speech as Southern, and having been understood by her interviewer, Azza is then able to contrastively take her own stance toward the idea. In line 21, she very directly and somewhat forcefully states her own regional (and, given the topic of conversation, linguistic) belonging as "I'm from DC! Raised! Reared! DC! I'm a Washingtonian."

In this example, constructed dialogue creates a character that misidentifies the speech of a lifelong, African American resident of Washington, DC, as Southern. Through attributing this stance, with which the speaker does not agree, to a fictional third party, Azza is able to distance herself from the incorrect assumption she is negotiating, and in effect "correct" this stance by taking an oppositional stance of her own. This maneuver in talk-in-interaction allows Azza to engage with ideas of misunderstanding and erasure of DC life—which is inherently African American life—without implicating herself as someone who harbors those thoughts.

In the next example, Mona, a middle-class woman, uses constructed dialogue to tackle racist ideologies in the community.

Constructed Dialogue as Stancetaking against Racist Ideologies

This extract is from a sociolinguistic interview with Mona, a forty-year-old African American woman and lifelong Washingtonian. Mona grew up in the neighborhood of Takoma in northernmost Northwest DC. Unlike Azza's childhood neighborhood of Anacostia, Takoma was, and still is, a quiet, lower-middle-class neighborhood. At the time of the interview, Mona lived with her husband and young child in Takoma Park, a Maryland suburb directly adjacent to Takoma, DC. In the interview, Mona talks at length about the big cultural differences between DC and Maryland, although her current home is only about a mile and a half from where she grew up. Mona holds a master's degree and works in the nonprofit sector.

In the following extract, the interviewer introduces metalinguistic discourse by asking Mona to describe the social differences between DC and Maryland. When she replies that there is "simply a difference in the thinking," despite how close the two are to one another, the interviewer prompts Mona further on how the difference impacts her own life.

Extract 2 Interview with Mona

Interviewer So then, and- and- then, um, so are you-
Would you say that you're <clicks tongue> other than the purpose of this
interview, are you- are you conscious of liv- that you're living on one side
or the other? Do you think that way, or?
Mona I do, but only when I tell someone where I'm from?
Interviewer Okay.
Mona And they tell me, and I hate this: "You're so well spoken to be from
DC!"
And I *hate* that!
Interviewer That's shocking <laughs>
Mona Because<laughs> <baby crying> *But,* I started off going to college at
Howard University, and I would tell people that, and that's what they
would say. I'm thinking, "Okay, well I'm in college. What would you
expect?" I can put my verbs together and that sorta thing, but...
But I mean just surprisingly, people are surprised because...
I-I-I- guess it doesn't fit with the television stories on the news that you
see of people in DC and-and- that sort of thing.

In lines 1–4, the interviewer elicits personal experiences of difference, asking whether Mona is, in her daily life, conscious of living in Maryland. Mona's reply, that she does experience the contrast, but only "when I tell someone where I'm from" (line 5) suggests that her encounters with ideologies surrounding DC happen even as close to home as the immediately adjacent suburbs. Her next statement elaborates on why telling people where she is from produces responses that foreground difference and distinction in her mind: "And they tell me, and I hate this: 'You're so well spoken to be from DC!' And I *hate* that!" (lines 7–9).

Just like Azza encounters people who can't place her accent but round her up to Southern, Mona encounters people who are surprised to hear that she—an articulate person—is from Washington, DC, or, alternatively, that a Washingtonian is as articulate as Mona. Mona chooses to use constructed dialogue, cued by the quotative verb "tell," to attribute the statement directly to people who ask her where she is from. The experience that Mona relays, of being viewed as well-spoken in contrast to an implied perception of Washingtonians as inarticulate, is well-documented in research on everyday racist discourse (Hill 2008; Alim and Smitherman 2012), particularly against African Americans. Mona uses this narrative format, creating an encounter that typifies her experience of telling outsiders where she is from, as a powerful way to convey pervasive racist attitudes toward Washingtonians, as is evident from the following discourse.

In lines 11–13, Mona continues to describe the situation, and gives the interviewer more insight into the production of these benign slurs: "I started off going to college at Howard University, and I would tell people that, and that's what they would say." Now Mona is attributing the stance—positively evaluating Mona's articulateness but in the same breath denigrating the articulateness of other Washingtonians—not simply to "people," but to those who either know that she is/was a university graduate or those with whom she interacted while studying at Howard University, a premier institution among Historically Black Colleges and Universities (HBCUs) in Washington, DC.

While Mona directly evaluates the racist discourse through affective stancetaking in lines 7 and 9 ("I *hate* that!"), she also recruits constructed dialogue attributed to herself as a way to further distance herself from the statements, in effect taking an oppositional stance to the one attributed to "people": "I'm thinking, 'Okay, well I'm in college. What would you expect?'" (lines 13–14). In effect, Mona is talking back to the racist assumptions about Washingtonians' speech—despite her high level of education—by making explicit her thoughts when faced with such statements. Through creating this narrative encounter, Mona is able to voice the tension between non-Washingtonians who hold habitual assumptions about (African American) Washingtonians, and those Washingtonians, like herself, who are on the receiving end. Constructed dialogue contributes to a somewhat indirect, and contextually embedded, act of stancetaking toward the ideological relationship between language, race, and education, a complex discourse in frequent circulation in public and private negotiations of Washingtonian identity, black excellence, racialized gentrification, the overall highly educated and prestigiously employed population of the city, and so on. In sum, constructed dialogue contributes to the interactional creation of Mona's Washingtonian authenticity as an educated, savvy person who encounters racist stances in her daily life, and who has rebuttals to the outsiders who hold them.

In the third and final example of constructed dialogue in this chapter, another speaker negotiates what language in the community means to him, and points out contrasts not only between groups but also within the broader, diverse African American community.

Constructed Dialogue as Stancetaking Against Linguistic Essentialism

Phil is a thirty-four-year old African American man who grew up in the Bloomingdale neighborhood of Northwest DC, which has undergone rapid gentrification over the past decade. When Phil was growing up, Bloomingdale was still majority African American, established, and relatively well-to-do. After leaving DC to get his degrees and train as an architect, Phil has returned to Washington. At the time of the interview, he and his wife, who is European American, had recently bought a home in the Northeast DC neighborhood of Trinidad. Trinidad, unlike Bloomingdale, still has a somewhat stigmatized reputation and has not undergone the same process of commercialization and redevelopment as Bloomingdale. It remains a largely African American, residential neighborhood. Phil, in this sense, represents an intersection between local identity and upward mobility: He is a native, African American Washingtonian who has brought his considerable social capital (education, white-collar employment, and wealth) back home. Discourses of the so-called 'black gentrifier' have circulated in DC for some time, foregrounding the complexities of race and class in this diverse community. Phil's perspective on language in DC also offers commentary on community diversity and ideologies.

In the following extract, the interviewer introduces the notion of local language norms by asking Phil to discuss an earlier comment about the DC accent; that it exists, but that he does not have it. The interviewer elicits a language encounter narrative from Phil by asking if people have told him that he sounds different from other native Washingtonians.

Extract 3 Interview with Phil

Interviewer <laughs>Okay, so you mentioned that… people in DC kind of have an
accent that *you* don't necessarily have, so how would you say… I mean
have people told you that you sound different from most native
Washingtonians?
Phil For sure, I would say people from DC, I mean people who are from-
not from the area, they say I have a DC accent at times, but people who
are here… especially more so black folk- Basically, if you- if you're- if
you're black and you talk a certain way that's not urban or <pitch drops>
"yeah man, what's going on [*wit*] [*dis*] and [*dat*]," you know, use
a lot of urba- urban colloquialisms or what have you, then, you may not be
down or you're talking white or you're talking proper, or- or whatever,
and you're not in touch with culture. Um, I think that, uh… yeah, people
say that.

The narrative resulting from the prompt about differences between Phil's own speech and the speech of "most native Washingtonians" (lines 3–4) showcases Phil's experience not with outsiders who make assumptions about African American Washingtonians (as we saw with Mona), but rather, with other members of his own community. Phil begins by suggesting that outsiders say he has a DC accent "at times" (line 6), but quickly follows with his assessment of metalinguistic commentary from Washingtonians, and in particular of "black folk" (line 7). He introduces these reported thoughts of black Washingtonians with the discourse marker "basically" (line 7), suggesting a fundamental or habitual quality to the statement that follows.

Just like Azza and Mona comment on outsiders' assumptions that DC speech is Southern or inarticulate, Phil performs the stances that black Washingtonians "basically" take to his speech in part through constructed dialogue. He suggests that the basic assumption within the community is that black Washingtonians whose language use does not conform to "urban" (lines 8, 10) and "colloquial" (line 10) expectations are seen as somehow out of touch with local culture, and are viewed as "talking white [or] proper" (line 11). Phil thus points out an opposition from within the community to encroaching "white" speech norms, which takes the shape of rejection of a particular kind of less-vernacular speech. In line 9, Phil employs constructed dialogue to showcase the urban, colloquial variety, and he does so through phonetic stylization (Coupland 2007) of an imagined urban, colloquial speaker. The example sentence, "yeah man, what's going on with this and that," is performed with significantly lowered pitch from the surrounding discourse, as well as with stopped /th/ and /dh/. In this utterance, Phil pronounces *with* as *wit*, *this* as *dis* and *that* as *dat*. This utterance stands in contrast to Phil's own speech, as he does not regularly use the stopped variants of /th/ and /dh/, and works to distance himself from the idea that vernacular forms like stopping are part of authentic Washingtonian speech.

Phil's assessment of how other black Washingtonians perceive his speech, along with the performance of a highly vernacular speech style that stands in contrast to his own, suggests that he sees a language ideological tension in the African American community in Washington, DC. The negatively evaluative stance that less-vernacular speakers of AAE in DC are "out of touch with culture" is attributed to "black folk." Phil is able to explicitly contrast his own speech from the apparently prestigious vernacular speech by switching into a vernacular style in the context of constructed dialogue, and switch out of it when he resumes speaking as himself. Constructed dialogue, in this example, works to stylize the speech of people whose stances Phil rejects.

Metasociolinguistic Stance and Ideological Diversity in Washington, DC

In the examples in this chapter, the speakers are asked to comment on the status and evaluation of language in their community. How they interpret these questions, and how they use metalinguistic discourse to explore and explain the role of language in their lives, varies.

Each of the three speakers—although they orient to different dimensions of metalinguistic stancetaking in their discourse, including Southernness, education, and vernacularity—addresses some form of linguistic essentialism on the part of "others," and corrects these erroneous stances and assumptions through taking oppositional stances, all in the context of narrative encounters. In these instances of metalinguistic commentary, speakers do not simply exemplify and take stances toward linguistic stereotypes and ideologies, possibly in part because enregisterment of Washington, DC, language (Agha 2003) is at a less advanced stage than it is for many other urban varieties, for example Pittsburghese (Johnstone 2006; Johnstone and Kiesling 2008). Instead, speakers recruit the idea of language to negotiate other issues in the social life of Washingtonians, and specifically of African American Washingtonians. Language ideologies are necessarily also social ideologies, and the speakers in this study discuss evaluation and misunderstandings about language as a means of unveiling underlying ideologies of race, region, and education that are found at the heart of evaluations of language.

Azza orients to language in relation to region, and uses constructed dialogue to take a metasociolinguistic stance against the assumption that (African American) DC speech is Southern and not distinctively DC. Mona describes habitual experience of racist remarks about her language use, and uses constructed dialogue to attribute such metasociolinguistic stances to outsiders and to take an oppositional stance herself. Phil reflects on a different kind of language ideology, namely that some members of DC's African American community associate less-vernacular speech with whiteness, 'properness,' and lack of engagement with local African American culture, all concepts which stand in stark contrast to authentic Washingtonianness. By using constructed dialogue to voice a highly vernacular style that does not belong to him, Phil is able to exemplify his understanding of stylistic difference and, at the same time, take a stance against it.

The metalinguistic discourse, and the metasociolinguistic stancetaking, in Jaffe's (2009a) formulation, in interviews with lifelong Washingtonians reveals the wide array of associations and ideologies that speakers perceive, recruit, and interpret when asked about language use. Language plays an important role in Washington, DC, as part of the tapestry of intersecting experiences and ideologies that make up local identities. The diversity of tactics for construction of authentic local identities in interaction also presumably reveals the possibilities and options for more enduring local identities; when speakers reveal *habitual* experiences—like things they are 'always' told about their language—their stancetaking transcends the storyworld and the immediate interaction, and reveals habitual and more global orientation to the social issues with which language is inextricably linked, such as the sociopolitics of region, racist ideologies, and intracommunity differences.

If talking about language is ultimately a way of talking about social life, metasociolinguistic stancetaking through specific discourse maneuvers, such as constructed dialogue, can be an important asset in the analytical toolkit for sociolinguists interested in the links between discourse practice and broader language ideologies. In a community such as Washington, DC, whose major hallmarks are not internal cohesion and dialect enregisterment but diversity and contestation and a state of change and negotiation, metasociolinguistic stance forms part of speakers' means of self-expression and assertion of authentic identities even in the face of stigma and erasure by the social forces. Thus, metasociolinguistic stance and the linguistic means by which it is accomplished is a key site of investigation for furthering our understanding of language in diverse communities.

Transcription Conventions

Symbol	Function
.	declarative contour
,	intonation unit-final indicates slight rising intonation
!	animated speech, exclamations
?	rising intonational contour
italics	emphatic stress
<angle brackets>	non- or paralinguistic action (e.g., laughter)
underline	stretch of talk of analytical interest
[*bracketed italics*]	vernacular phonetic realization of a word (e.g., *dis* for *this*)
[ ]	overlapping speech
-	self- or other-interruption
...	pause longer than 0.5 seconds

References

Agha, Asif. 2003. "The Social Life of Cultural Value." *Language and Communication* 23:231–73.

Alim, H. Samy, and Geneva Smitherman. 2012. *Articulate While Black: Barack Obama, Language and Race in the U.S.* New York: Oxford University Press.

Bamberg, Michael, and Alexandra Georgakopoulou. 2008. "Small Stories as a New Perspective in Narrative and Identity Analysis." *Text & Talk* 28:377–96.

Coupland, Nikolas. 2007. *Style: Language Variation and Identity*. Cambridge: Cambridge University Press.

Damari, Rebecca Rubin. 2010. "Intertextual Stancetaking and the Local Negotiation of Cultural Identities by a Binational Couple." *Journal of Sociolinguistics* 14:609–29.

De Fina, Anna. 2011. "Researcher and Informant Roles in Narrative Interactions: Constructions of Belonging and Foreignness." *Language in Society* 40:27–38.

De Fina, Anna, and Sabina Perrino. 2011. "Introduction: Interviews vs. 'Natural' Contexts: A False Dilemma." *Language in Society* 40:1–11.

Du Bois, John W. 2007. "The Stance Triangle." In *Stancetaking in Discourse: Subjectivity, Evaluation, Interaction*, edited by Robert Englebretson, 139–82. Amsterdam: John Benjamins.

Gumperz, John J. 1982. *Discourse Strategies*. Cambridge: Cambridge University Press.

Hamilton, Heidi E. 1998. "Reported Speech and Survivor Identity in On-line Bone Marrow Transplantation Narratives." *Journal of Sociolinguistics* 2:53–67.

Hill, Jane H. 2008. *The Everyday Language of White Racism*. Malden, MA: Wiley-Blackwell.

Jaffe, Alexandra M., ed. 2009a. "Introduction." In *Stance: Sociolinguistic Perspectives*, edited by Alexandra Jaffe, 3–28. Oxford: Oxford University Press.

———. 2009b. "Stance in a Corsican School: Institutional and Ideological Orders and the Production of Bilingual Subjects." In *Stance: Sociolinguistic Perspectives*, edited by Alexandra Jaffe, 119–45. Oxford: Oxford University Press.

Johnstone, Barbara. 1996. *The Linguistic Individual: Self-Expression in Language and Linguistics*. New York: Oxford University Press.

———. 2006. "A New Role for Narrative in Variationist Sociolinguistics." *Narrative Inquiry* 16:46–55.

Johnstone, Barbara, and Scott Kiesling. 2008. "Indexicality and Experience: Exploring the Meanings of /aw/-monophthongization in Pittsburgh." *Journal of Sociolinguistics* 12:5–33.

Kärkkäinen, Elise. 2003. *Epistemic Stance in English Conversation: A Description of its Interactional Functions, with a Focus on 'I think'.* Amsterdam: John Benjamins.

———. 2006. "Stance Taking in Conversation: From Subjectivity to Intersubjectivity." *Text & Talk* 26:699–731.

Labov, William. 1972. "Some Principles of Linguistic Methodology." *Language in Society* 1:97–120.

Labov, William, Sharon Ash, and Charles Boberg, eds. 2006. *The Atlas of North American English: Phonetics, Phonology and Sound Change.* Berlin: Mouton de Gruyter.

Labov, William, and Joshua Waletzky. 1967. "Narrative Analysis: Oral Versions of Personal Experience." *Journal of Narrative and Life History* 7:3–38.

Lippi-Green, Rosina. 1997. *English with an Accent: Language, Ideology and Discrimination in the United States.* New York: Routledge.

Manning, Robert D. 1998. "Multicultural Washington, DC: The Changing Social and Economic Landscape of a Post-industrial Metropolis." *Ethnic and Racial Studies* 21:328–55.

Mishler, Elliot G. 1986. *Research Interviewing: Context and Narrative.* Cambridge, MA: Harvard University Press.

Nylund, Anastasia. 2013. "Phonological Variation at the Intersection of Ethnoracial Identity, Place, and Style in Washington, D.C." PhD diss., Georgetown University.

Rahman, Jacquelyn. 2008. "Reactions and Attitudes toward African American English." *American Speech* 83:141–77.

Rickford, John R., and Russell J. Rickford. 2000. *Spoken Soul: The Story of Black English.* New York: Wiley.

Schiffrin, Deborah. 1996. "Narrative as Self-Portrait: Sociolinguistic Constructions of Identity." *Language in Society* 25:167–203.

Schilling, Natalie. 2013. "Investigating Stylistic Variation." In *The Handbook of Language Variation and Change, 2nd Edition,* edited by Natalie Schilling and J. K. Chambers, 327–49. Malden, MA: Wiley-Blackwell.

Schilling-Estes, Natalie. 1998. "Investigating 'self-conscious' Speech: The Performance Register in Ocracoke English." *Language in Society* 27:53–83.

Smitherman, Geneva. 2006. *Word from the Mother: Language and African Americans.* New York: Routledge.

Tannen, Deborah. 1986. "Introducing Constructed Dialogue in Greek and American Conversational and Literary Narrative." In *Direct and Indirect Speech,* edited by Florian Coulmas, 311–32. Berlin: Mouton De Gruyter.

———.2007. *Talking Voices: Repetition, Dialogue, and Imagery in Conversational Discourse.* 2nd ed. Cambridge: Cambridge University Press.

Wortham, Stanton, Katherine Mortimer, Kathleen Lee, and Elaine Allard. 2011. "Interviews as Interactional Data." *Language in Society* 40:39–50.

Chapter 9

Citizen Sociolinguistics

A New Media Methodology for Understanding Language and Social Life

BETSY RYMES, GEETA ANEJA, ANDREA LEONE-PIZZIGHELLA, MARK LEWIS, AND ROBERT MOORE

SOCIOLINGUISTICS, CONVERSATION ANALYSIS, AND Linguistic Anthropology are increasingly overlapping fields broadly concerned with how language and communication are intertwined with social relations. While each of these perspectives has illuminated elements of language in use, or sociocultural linguistics, the sophistication of the research subjects and their own detailed understandings of their language practices has often been overlooked in favor of the interpretations of their researchers.

This chapter introduces a *citizen sociolinguistic* approach to mitigate this problem (Rymes and Leone 2014), offering a new sociocultural linguistic methodology that also accounts for and partakes of the social demands and affordances of massive mobility and connectivity in today's world. Drawing from the decades-old tradition of citizen science, citizen sociolinguistics traces the ways that citizens (everyday language users), more so than trained sociolinguists or other language professionals, understand the world of language around them. This chapter introduces the rationale for such an approach, as well as its potential to illuminate our contemporary communicative environment.

We use YouTube and other Web 2.0 (Jenkins et al. 2009) resources to explore how language and social life are thoroughly intertwined with one another in a citizen sociolinguistic approach. We focus in particular on YouTube videos and their uptake because YouTube is not merely a repository, but a site of participatory culture (Burgess and Green 2009), where language and other repertoire elements are constantly recontextualized and circulated in both the YouTube ecology and the material world (Rymes 2012). We pay particular attention to citizen sociolinguistic *metacommentary*, which we define as comments on a language performance, either self-referentially, by the performer, or by others, often in online comment sections, or as collectively expressed in these comment threads via shares, likes, and follows (Rymes and Leone 2014).

Citizen sociolinguistics relies precisely on what traditional sociolinguistic methodology has tried to avoid: speakers' own awareness of their language and their conscious attempts to manipulate it. The examples below illustrate the power of this metalinguistic awareness and its related commentary to illuminate the social value people themselves put on their own language use (Rymes 2014). Our chapter includes three topics, or flashpoints of metacommentary: the Roman dialect, the concept of the "native speaker" accent, and the highly institutionalized genre of the five-paragraph essay. We conclude by theoretically situating citizen sociolinguistics within a history of sociocultural linguistics.

In the first research example, Leone-Pizzighella illustrates how a look at citizen sociolinguistic metacommentary on "Roman dialect" by Italian social media users illuminates the sociocultural features of the regional language not traditionally captured in sociolinguistic research on Italian dialects. By looking at online metacommentary on one widely circulated video, Leone-Pizzighella shows how nonlinguistic features of context, as well as viewers' personal linguistic histories, appear to be far more relevant to a categorization of dialect than any systematic linguistic difference with the standard language.

In the next research example, Geeta Aneja illustrates how the term "nonnative speaker" (NNS) just like the category of "Roman dialect" is also a highly contextualized social construct. A "nonnative speaker" does not exist as an empirical identity that might be described by a professional linguist, any more than Roman dialect does.[1] Instead, Aneja illustrates how the concept of a "nonnative speaker" is generated through citizen sociolinguistic metacommentary, which is highly attentive to the nuances of context and participants. Even in YouTube videos that are self-defined as "How to Speak Like a Native Speaker," commenters take issue with this categorization and debate about it in comment sections. In one case, for example, comments slight the authenticity of one "native speaker" exemplar, citing that, perhaps, the person sounds "Canadian," in effect constituting that "Canadian speaker" as a nonnative speaker of English. For users of English concerned with "nativeness," what counts as an NNS is contextually emergent and thus, ungeneralizable as a linguistic feature.

In the third research exemplar, Mark Lewis illustrates how citizen sociolinguists co-construct the literary genre of the five-paragraph essay. In the case of the five-paragraph essay, commenters consistently point to institutional authority as the rightful source of ideas about the genre. Still, no comments cite literacy research or literary studies of genre that have for years leveled critiques against the five-paragraph essay, or more generally, pointed out that "genres" are infinite and variety is a good thing. In this way, Lewis's study illustrates, like Aneja's study of NNSs, how voluminous citizen sociolinguistic metacommentary constructs rigid distinctions, but how these distinctions are highly dependent on social context, not on linguistic or literary research. As Aneja and Lewis each demonstrate, the value of the five-paragraph essay or the native speaker is not supported by academic research, but from troves of metacommentary defining and upholding these categories.

In all these cases—speaking Roman dialect, being a "nonnative" speaker, or writing a "good" essay—linguistic or literacy researchers' descriptions of forms or genres are largely unimportant to people using and commenting on those same forms and genres every day. Everyday individuals, judging by their online contributions and participation, do seem to care deeply about defining and categorizing varieties of speech. These definitions and categories aren't created by consulting professional researchers for validation; rather, they emerge via citizen sociolinguistic metacommentary. In this way, citizen sociolinguists generate criteria and categories for language from the bottom up—their own usage and judgments of usage becoming definitive in any given context. Tracking the voices of these citizen sociolinguists is the basis of a citizen sociolinguistic methodology, as we are using those voices to understand the layers of sociocultural value heaped on distinctive communicative elements. While these citizen perspectives are not "generalizable" or even necessarily accurate descriptions of language, they are self-fulfilling, and as such, are the perspectives that matter to real speakers.

In the final section of this chapter, Robert Moore reveals that these tensions—between the seeming "objectivity" of scientific findings, and the facts of variation that matter to speakers—have been on the minds of sociolinguists ever since Labov's first studies and the genesis of sociolinguistics as a distinct subdiscipline of linguistics.

Each of these sections will illustrate and discuss a methodology for sociocultural linguistics that does not attempt to isolate language as separated from subjects' awareness, but focuses on individuals' detailed understandings of their own and others' online linguistic performances as important data. Now, we turn to these instances of contemporary citizen sociolinguistic research.

Citizen Definitions of the "Roman Dialect"

Andrea Leone-Pizzighella

During one of the hottest weeks of the year in July 2010, an Italian journalist and a camera crew at Ostia Beach (outside of Rome, Italy) were sent out to do a fluff piece for the news station SkyTG24. The journalist approached a bikini-clad teenage girl, asking "Fa caldo?" (Is it hot?),[2] and proceeded to do a fifty-two-second interview with Debora (right, figure 9.1) and Romina (left, figure 9.1) about how one tolerates the heat at the beach (nicves1992 2010). They told him that they keep cool and comfortable with beer and push-pops, as well as the occasional shower in order to keep from getting itchy from the salt water. The interview was broadcast on the station's news channel with exaggeratedly "correct" subtitles, and quickly went viral on YouTube. The subtitles, applied only to Romina and Debora's speech, are so hypercorrect as to be comical. For example, they use the expressions "epidermis" instead of "skin" and "kind regards" instead of "see you later," but they appear wholly unnecessary in terms of helping audiences comprehend the video. As described in greater depth in Leone (2014), Romina and Debora's decision to do the interview in an informal youth register of Italian peppered with Roman regionalisms elicited abundant metacommentary even before it began to circulate around YouTube: the news station claimed that it was Romina

Figure 9.1. Screenshot from SkyTG24 Interview with Romina and Debora

and Debora's "Roman accent" (no doubt highlighted by the news station's addition of the hypercorrect subtitles) that "immediately made them stars" (SkyTg24 2010), but their speech garnered a much wider range of metacommentary once it was released into Web 2.0.

Shortly after it aired, mixed reactions to the interview began to appear on Facebook and YouTube, and in blogs and local newspapers throughout Italy. One Facebook user finds Romina and Debora refreshing and spontaneous, commenting that everyone has it out for the Romans while the Milanese are never judged so harshly, while another user laments their use of Roman (as opposed to "Italian") in the interview, correlating it to their likelihood of having dim career prospects. Even the mayor of Ostia spoke out in an attempt to defend his city's reputation, saying "The coast isn't characterized only by the young lowlifes in the video, ours are beaches open to everyone; but enough with this redneck image of Ostia, we have an image to defend, too" (Nota dell'Associazione Culturale Severiana 2010).

Participants' reactions to Romina and Debora's language use all revolve around the way that linguistic elements are seen as second-order indices (Silverstein 2003) of particular types of Romanness. The well-known and very recognizable regional variety of Italian spoken in and around Rome is known under several names as *dialetto romano*, *romanesco*, and *romanaccio*, all of which are mentioned in the comments section on Romina and Debora's original interview on YouTube. Here, I briefly describe 1) the ways that dialetto romano, romanesco, and romanaccio get defined by YouTube users, and 2) what emerges from the citizen sociolinguistic metacommentary (Rymes 2014) as being emblematic of these Roman varieties and of Romanness more generally.

Citizen Definitions of Dialetto Romano, Romanesco, and Romanaccio

YouTube comments for this video provide various citizen definitions and uses of the terms romanesco, romanaccio, and dialetto romano, all of which have different social and historical connotations. Dialetto romano would be translated into English as "Roman dialect," which identifies this variety as being taxonomically inferior to standard Italian, but not being good or bad in itself. The suffix *-esco* in romanesco is likewise a neutral descriptive suffix, such as the English *-ish,* but it gives the regional variety a name rather than labeling it as a dialect. In romanaccio, the suffix *-accio* (or *-accia* in the feminine form) has a pejorative connotation that can either add or enhance the negative aspect of a word (e.g., *parola* is 'word' and *parolaccia* is 'curse word'). Accordingly, it would seem that those who use the term romanaccio are referring to either a bad type of the Roman variety or to the Roman variety being bad per se. The following provides a small sample of definitions and uses of each term drawn from the comments section of the YouTube video (nicves1992 2010) and translated into English:

The Roman Dialect (il dialetto romano)

- "Everyone says the same thing, 'What a stupid way to talk.' Meh, it's just the Roman dialect and it's not stupid."
- "This is the ROMAN dialect, it's not the dialect of low-class neighborhoods, or of lowlifes, or the slang of the outskirts."
- "Don't confuse the Roman way of speaking with the lowlife way of speaking, please...the Roman dialect is a completely different thing."
- "The Roman dialect is so beautiful...but like this...from two girls who are just two trashy [people]."
- "If you want to hear the Roman dialect read *Trilussa* and watch the videos by Gigi Proietti."

Romanesco

- "The real romanesco is a true and proper dialect of the "pure" Romans that I think a good part of the romanacci and of other Italians wouldn't understand (including me)."
- "Ancient romanesco more than Italian is scientifically part of the Tuscan dialect group, it's loved by almost all of Italy for its immediacy and its friendliness."
- "Unfortunately, romanesco isn't spoken by anyone anymore, maybe some old ladies in Trastevere or Testaccio."[3]
- "[The video] is NOT romanesco. If you want to do a comparison listen to how Alberto Sordi talked...that was romanesco. I've never understood why speaking Roman (romanesco) is synonymous with ignorance."
- "I dare you to find one sentence said by these two girls that is not part of the romanesco dialect."

Romanaccio

- "Romanaccio is the vulgar version of romanesco...romanaccio derives from romanesco but it has lost its musicality."
- "It's not dialect, guys...it's romanaccio which is different from romanesco (spoken by 700 thousand people in Lazio)...it's not enough to say "nnamo" [let's go] to speak dialect..."
- "Real romanaccio is spoken by real Romans, not by these [girls] who are surely from lower-class neighborhoods and therefore what they call Roman is just low-class talk, which has little to do with real Roman!"
- "Romanaccio doesn't exist, it's offensive to say it does, they're just juvenile variables of a dialect that's in continuous evolution just like Italian is."
- "To say romanaccio is already a moral mistake, it's called Roman. This is simply the new dialect that evolves in our time whether you want it or not. As a Roman you should never say romanaccio, it's a sad mistake."

In short, these citizen definitions indicate that there are many conflicting ideologies around these Roman varieties and what they index. The definitions of the three varieties described above seem almost entirely dependent on the context in which they are used and who uses them, rather than on their lexical or grammatical structures. The term "the Roman dialect" (il dialetto romano), for instance, is used when linking the variety to historical prestige, rather than to what it indexes about the people who speak it. Two of the above comments specifically state that the Roman dialect is beautiful and that Romina and Debora are the problem, separating the variety itself from those who speak it. Meanwhile, romanesco emerges as being considered a language of the past, an endangered variety that exists only in classic films and among the elderly Romans who live in well-established and somewhat isolated neighborhoods in Rome. These comments depict romanesco as having only positive or neutral connotations, similar to the previous set of comments about "the Roman dialect," but one user has a conflicting opinion: "I dare you to find one sentence by these two girls that is not part of the romanesco dialect." Finally, the term romanaccio apparently indexes several characteristics of the Roman variety, with the definitions above claiming that romanaccio is either a) a degraded version of romanesco, b) a way of speaking that is particular to "real Romans," or c) an offensive term used to describe "evolving" Roman varieties as being incorrect.

Closing Comments on Citizen Sociolinguistics and Dialectology

Many attempts have been made to categorize the social and situational dimensions of language use in Italy (Sanga 1985; Berruto 1989), but what seems to have resulted is that the term *dialetto* (dialect) remains fairly nebulous and continues to defy technical classification. What counts as dialetto varies immensely across individuals, social classes, and regions, and it is often linked to other aspects of an individual's communicative repertoire (Rymes 2010). A citizen sociolinguistic approach to analyzing dialetto in contemporary Italy emphasizes the circulating popular discourses about it, even if (and especially when) they do not match up with linguists' descriptions.

Careful exploration of the experiences of situated social actors themselves as they are expressed through social media is one way to begin addressing some of these ambiguities.

(Non)Native Speakers: Figments of the Citizen Sociolinguistic Imagination?

Geeta Aneja

The notion of an idealized native speaker who speaks one's language perfectly in all situations (Chomsky 1965) permeates applied linguistics, from theoretical frames like *fossilization* (Selinker 1972), *ideal language input* (Long 1981), and *target language norms* (Ellis 1994), to practical concerns like hiring teachers (Selvi 2010) and evaluating students' proficiency (see, e.g., ACTFL 2012). While such approaches have been critiqued for obscuring the deeply contextualized nature of language use and development (Selvi 2014), the native-nonnative dichotomy remains the dominant paradigm for understanding language and language users. Developing a comprehensive list of criteria defining native and nonnative speakers is further complicated because the social perception of an individual's (non)nativeness often depends on nonlinguistic factors like race, accent, or nationality, rather than proficiency (Amin 1997; Kubota 2002; Shuck 2006).

As a result, many researchers now conceptualize (non)native speakers as ideological constructs rather than objective entities—they are "undeniably 'there'...if very hard to pin down with any degree of empirical certainty" (Moore 2011, 44). These constructs are dynamic, constantly reinvented and reified through metacommentary in a process that I term *(non)native speakering* (Aneja, in press). I use this term for two reasons: 1) to encode the social invention of (non)native speakers as a dynamic process, and 2) to emphasize the mutually constitutive nature of native and nonnative ideologies—that is, the fact that a "native speaker" can be best defined as "not a nonnative speaker" and vice versa. Thus, (non)native speakers are not merely figments of linguists' imaginations as Paikeday (1985) suggests, but also of *citizen sociolinguists'* imaginations.

The theoretical reconceptualization of (non)nativeness as a social construct calls for a methodology that looks beyond so-called "native speaker effects" (Doerr 2009) on participants in physical classrooms, to consider how discourses of (non) nativeness are circulated and negotiated in the real world. I turned to YouTube not only because of its rich repository of citizen sociolinguistic data, but also because teachers and students frequently and increasingly utilize YouTube as a resource for language teaching and learning (Mullen and Wedwick 2008). My inquiry focuses on how citizen sociolinguists on YouTube negotiate and define (non)native speakers through metacommentary, and how they connect (non)nativeness to other ideologies.

"How to Sound Like a Native Speaker"

The data presented below consist of several excerpts taken from the video and comment threads of "3 tips for sounding like a native speaker" (Adam 2012), the top hit for the search "how to sound like a native speaker." This video, produced by a web-based English teaching organization called *EngVid*, is a virtual classroom in which Adam presents three pronunciation tips to help student-viewers sound more like American English speakers. Both Adam and the commenters connect (non)nativeness to a number of extralinguistic ideologies, such as nationality and accent, that collectively define (non)native speakers and reify their social position. In the video's introduction, Adam connects native accent to living in an English-speaking country.

Excerpt 1

Adam — The best way [to sound like a native speaker] is to live in an English-speaking country, of course, but of course you can do it anywhere, but it takes time; be patient, practice, practice, practice.... We're going to start with connecting words. Now think about your language. Whether you're speaking Spanish or Polish or Chinese, you do this in your language as well. [0:17–1:06]

While which countries "count" as English-speaking has been debated in academic circles for decades (see, e.g., Kachru 1985; Rampton 1990), Adam seems to assume that he and his viewers are drawing on a shared understanding of what constitutes an English-speaking country. At the same time, he constructs native-like pronunciation as a worthy goal to which students should aspire, regardless of how challenging it may be, though he later acknowledges that "native speakers" themselves "speak naturally" and "don't think about doing these things; it just rolls off the tongue" [6:55–7:00]. Finally, he cites discourses of linguistic ownership (Widdowson 1994) by asking viewers to think about *their* language, suggesting that even though the viewers understand English well enough to watch and understand the video, English is somehow not *their* language.

In the comments many YouTubers reinforce the connection between nationality and accent:

Excerpt 2

Akram Alabade — ...may I ask you what is the native speaker you talked about ? I mean , is it British accent as a native or American accent , please help , got confused , greeting from Iraq , Akram

JuiceBox — +Akram Alabade American accent :)

While Akram explicitly expresses uncertainty about what a native speaker is, he connects nativeness to British and American nationalities, suggesting alignment with Adam's association between nationality and language. JuiceBox's arguably tongue-in-cheek reply still imbues the American accent with value, particularly in the context of a video that presents American English pronunciation tips to help students sound more native. Other commenters reinforce the value of native-like pronunciation, even going so far as asking how they can "lose" their own accents:

Excerpt 3

jb youngfr	Can you give me specific advice to *lose my French accent* when I speak in English? What are the *main mistakes* a French speaker do in English in terms of pronunciation? [emphases added]

Thus, jb youngfr sees accent as a liability to be discarded and an error to be corrected rather than as an asset, indicating bilingualism, international experience, or intercultural familiarity (Park 2012).

Negotiating Adam's (Non)Nativeness

Adam positions himself as a native English speaker not only implicitly by virtue of being the teacher-presenter, but also explicitly by modeling the 'natural' pronunciation of a native speaker:

Excerpt 4

Adam	"Wha de ye do?" That's how a native speaker would say it *naturally* [2:26]
Adam	"Intresting," "in-tre-sting." "In-ter-est-ing," I have four syllables, when I actually say it *naturally*, it becomes three syllables. [5:09–5:14]

However, some commenters question Adam's nativeness because of his perceived accent:

Excerpt 5

buncari	But you aren't a native speaker, are you? Because you do have a slight accent plus your pronunciation isn't consistent, it mixes British and American pronunciation.
Sterling Archer	It Sounds like he's from Alberta or something, so I think he is a native speaker, just a different accent than you.

By citing accent as an indication of nonnative status, buncari constructs native speakers as accentless, in opposition to accented nonnative speakers. He also maintains nationalistic paradigms for accent, into neither of which Adam neatly fits. Sterling Archer presents an alternative possibility, reasserting Adam's native speaker status by citing geographic location (Alberta) and by extension nationality (Canadian).

Leveraging (Non)Nativeness in Comments

Commenters also leverage their native speaker status in order to legitimize their critiques of Adam's model of native-like pronunciation.

Excerpt 6

Aa M	I am a native english speaker and I disagree with his pronunciation of "comfortable". The "r" sound is not lost in the way that it is in his explanation... It's usually said more like "comf-ter-bl". Also I and many others don't make the "j" sound with "did you". I pronounce it with the proper "d" sound.

Christian-Rhen Stefani As a native English speaker, I do not say "coun chre" for the word "country." In fact, I say what you claim is not native pronunciation "coun tree". That said, I'm not saying that your dialect of English is wrong in any way. In fact, having studied linguistics, I know that some native English speakers do speak like you - but, not all do...

By reasserting the value of a native speaker's linguistic judgment, the commenters reinforce the notion that native speakers are linguistic and grammatical authorities (Chomsky 1965). Aa M also invokes discourses of usualness and properness. On the other hand, Christian-Rhen Stefani leverages her linguist's insight not in correcting Adam's speech but rather in demonstrating awareness of diverse forms of language use. While in academic circles the insights of an expert are expected and welcome, in this setting, they comes across as overly pedantic.

Closing Comments on (Non)Native-Speakering

In the video and comments above, YouTube citizen sociolinguists construct (non) native speakers through metacommentary, bundling ideologies that together constitute (non)nativeness in the citizen sociolinguistic imagination. A citizen sociolinguistic methodology offers two main contributions to studies of (non)native speakering. First, it forces researchers to focus on social use and description of "native speaker" and related terms as well as the negotiation of (non)native speaker status as an instance of social positionality, what Silverstein (2003) calls *higher order descriptions*, and simultaneously deemphasizes (non)nativeness as an abstract indication of linguistic characteristics. Second, it encourages researchers to look beyond the teacher education classroom when seeking to understand "native speaker effects" (Doerr 2009) on language teachers and students; no matter how carefully teacher educators regulate the discourses to which their students are exposed within the classroom, they cannot eliminate the native speaker concept as a production of the citizen sociolinguistic imagination.

'Follow the Procedure': Online Typification of the Five-Paragraph Essay

Mark Lewis

The *five-paragraph essay* (5PE) is familiar to many high- and middle-school students in the United States because it is often included in the teaching of literary analysis and argumentation (Johnson et al. 2003). As with any other recognized form of language, learners of the 5PE produce and respond to descriptions of its essential characteristics—what we can also call typifications or metapragmatic commentary. In this paper, I describe a small sample of online commentary on the 5PE. The enormous volume of metapragmatic online material about the 5PE necessitated actionable criteria for data collection. I mainly approached the problem as if I were a student looking for help writing my own 5PE. While ultimately I can only study a very small portion of the total amount of metapragmatic commentary about the 5PE, I did view a large portion of the most viewed and talked about commentary that is available to simple searches online in English from a United States IP address.

I undertook this study to ask: What kinds of metapragmatic commentary on the 5PE might a student writer encounter online if they were searching for help on their homework, perhaps the night before it is due? What typifications recur across commentaries from many sources?

Theoretical Frames for Approaching the 5PE

Bakhtin's (1986) notion of *speech genres* would regard the 5PE as one kind of language use among "boundless" and "inexhaustible" others (60). To see the 5PE as only one of many circulating *speech genres* implies a more democratic vision of schooling, keeping within our gaze the many other kinds of meaning-making activities in, across, and beyond language in which students participate (Rymes 2014). Like anything people do with language, the 5PE belongs to a particular time, space, and social domain, both in its production and reception. Contrary to professional metapragmatic discourse of schooling, which naturalizes the existence of any language form that is part of the curriculum, the 5PE is a product of social action, not an intrinsically meaningful form of language. Note that the word *genre* alone is a term of art within professional metapragmatic discourse of schooling, and the patterns of its use by school actors would necessarily be part of larger study of that discourse. Bakhtin's distinct analytic term *speech genre* draws attention to fundamental sociolinguistic aspects of any recognized use of language, but is insufficient by itself to explain how processes of naturalization of academic forms result in a particular language practice becoming recognizable to many people. Agha's (2007) model of *enregisterment* allows for a more direct account of how typifications like the 5PE spread and survive.

Agha most concisely defines enregisterment as roughly meaning the process by which "semiotic registers," also called "cultural models of action" are "formulated and disseminated through semiotic activities that evaluate specific behavioral signs as appropriate to particular scenarios of social-interpersonal conduct" (2007, 81). This means that to call the 5PE a register is to say that within a certain social domain (a group of people), there are regularities of metapragmatic stereotypes and typifications about the 5PE. These regularities include how a text comes to be recognized as a 5PE, how the 5PE is valorized and in what contexts, and what kinds of people the 5PE is associated with. Processes of enregisterment can be examined by paying attention to instances of citizen sociolinguistic metacommentary where linguistic practices themselves are discussed, typified, and debated. Agha stresses that to point to a register is to point to a particular phase of a wider sociohistorical process that is continuously unfolding. The small samples of metapragmatic commentary on the 5PE presented here all originate in a contemporary moment, though I see them as part of a longer history of metapragmatics backed by people linked to roles of authority in schools.

Analysis

In online metapragmatic commentary on the 5PE I surveyed, teachers and others who position themselves (and who might be institutionally positioned) as authorities on the practice have license to describe the genre unreflexively, in neutral terms. Students and others positioned as or who position themselves as victims of the 5PE take absurdist or otherwise totally oppositional stances against the 5PE, placing themselves outside the bounds of hegemonic writing practices, perhaps implicitly accepting these bounds rather than breaking or challenging them themselves. Or if they do not take oppositional stances, they take receptive ones, seeking a person in a teacher role who will tell them how the 5PE works so that they can successfully meet this aspect of the idealized model of the good student. Commentary from other critics is firm but closed off from any effort to imagine new models of students learning to do things with language. In sum, commentary was not only aligned in describing formal features of the 5PE, but also in consistently presupposing institutional authority as the rightful source of typification.

As illustrative examples of a broader study (Lewis 2014), I discuss two of the videos found on YouTube as top results for search terms related to the 5PE. The first search result on YouTube for "how to write a five paragraph essay" is titled "The Five-Paragraph Essay: Three Formulas for Writing the Basic Academic Essay." It is produced and narrated by David Taylor, who identifies himself on his YouTube profile page as a "University teacher of writing and communications." If Taylor's video were not the first search result, I would still want to include it in this analysis because of its special style of presentation. The video is very dry, but it does accomplish what it sets out to do—describe rules of a particular genre and establish itself as an authority. A still image from Taylor's video is shown in figure 9.2.

In his presentation, Taylor makes frequent use of *unmodalized* typifications (i.e., descriptions of the 5PE that are statements of fact, presented as if from no perspective), like "the number three has an important place in our culture" and "Follow these three formulas and you'll be producing a good, tight, organized essay." The dominant concern in this video is explaining the rules of the format so that listeners can learn

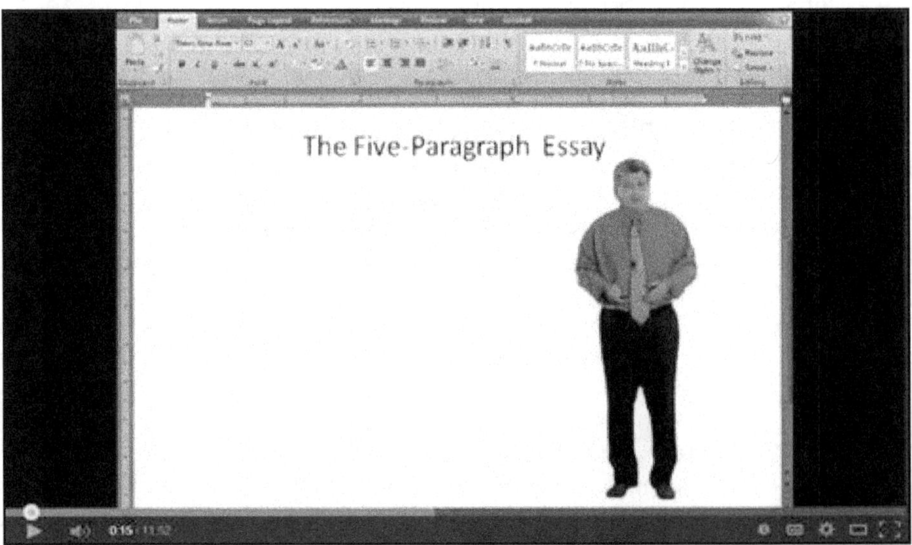

Figure 9.2. A still image from Taylor's video

to follow them. At several points, Taylor connects his directives to purposes like clarity, intelligence, or succeeding in college. As an example, he says at one point, "You come up with a position, because you've got to have a position, that's what being in college is all about. You're able to take a position, state an opinion, and then support it in a logical, acceptable way." Taylor is encouraging, but his instructions about the 5PE center on students doing what they are told to do (Taylor 2012).

Taylor's video does not motivate much interaction or exchange about the metapragmatics of the 5PE or academic writing in general. Almost every viewer comment (of the total of over 250 as of May 3, 2014) is thankful, and almost all of these are paired with acknowledgements and variations on the "you're welcome" theme from Taylor. The comments that explicitly thank Taylor for explaining or revealing the rules of production of the 5PE reinforce the poetic structure of a rules-giving video: as a response, "thank you" is evidence from the co-text that Taylor's video is intended and taken up for consumption, not discussion (Goffman 1976).

The "How to Write an Essay Rap" (Bloom 2013) has a deliberately much more youth-oriented presentation. Bloom's video, which he describes as a "rap slideshow," gives the essential rules of the 5PE format, as well as other directives about proper language use in an essay (e.g., "no need for 'I think' or 'I believe,' just state it"). A still image from Bloom's video can be seen in figure 9.3. The instrumental track is pulled from the 1999 single "Still D.R.E." by Dr. Dre, featuring Snoop Dogg. The lyrics, while spoken by Bloom, are displayed mostly verbatim over a series of colorful images related to schools or writing. Though quite distinct from Taylor's, Bloom's video is still centered on a determination of whether a written product meets the rules of the 5PE. These repeated lyrics are the best example of this ideology:

You want to write an essay?
You want to earn the best grade?
Gotta follow the procedure
And let the pen lead you

Figure 9.3. A still image from Blooms's video

These four simple lines summarize the entire video, which is all nomic and didactic in the same style as Taylor's video. Bloom operates from the same interactional position of someone who knows more about essays than his audience does. In both videos, the authors position themselves as information givers and position their audiences as information receivers. Both videos describe writing standards as nomic truths and exhibit a larger regularity of videos working to socialize students into comparing their products to idealized writing standards.

Closing Comments on the 5PE

The 5PE is so embedded in US schools and the lives of US students that considerable amounts of material have been created to serve interested students who resort to the internet for help writing their essay. Through its intense connection to schooling, the 5PE is a politically consequential genre. This study indicated that typification of the 5PE presupposed and reanimated social positions of teacher and student. Examining only YouTube videos and comments can't tell us everything about how the 5PE is situated among other genres, practices, and ideologies of schooling in the United States and beyond. However, such data might indeed offer insights unlocatable elsewhere, as well as unique corroborations of other studies.

Any researcher of language and education is presented with a number of perspectives on which to base a study of an activity like the writing of a 5PE. When we theorize the 5PE as one register among many others, continuously in flux as it is typified and retypified, we necessarily denaturalize it to an extent that users apparently rarely do. But the denaturalization of the "analyst" need not come with an abstraction away from concerns of the "practitioner." A strength of the citizen sociolinguistic approach is its ability to easily show the profoundly consistent and "everyday" quality of encounters with language and struggles around its typification. In the case of the 5PE, no matter the institutionally ratified source of our curiosity about it, a citizen sociolinguistic approach reveals links between practices of typifying school-associated language and of characterizing school-associated people.

Citizen Sociolinguistics: The Return of the Repressed

Robert Moore

Relationships between linguists and speakers of languages have been complex over the whole modern period. Aside from the obvious one-way dependency—linguists need speakers; the reverse is in no obvious way true—there are deeper paradoxes, perhaps chief among them the principle that speakers need to be heard (in phonetic detail), but not heard *from*.

Citizen sociolinguistics is located right at the interface between the expert discourse of sociolinguistics developed by (and mostly for) academic researchers, and popular discourses about language variation developed by and circulated among ordinary citizens; furthermore, it tries to trace the way that terms, concepts, discourse genres, texts, and even people circulate back and forth across that permeable boundary. This last task is made easier by the very design and affordances of online social media platforms.

Citizen sociolinguistics, in other words, takes seriously and examines closely the kind of material that modern sociolinguistics has made elaborate efforts to sidestep, ignore, or short-circuit: It seeks to develop new methods of gathering and analyzing the massive amount of freely available data from the internet in which everyday people compile detailed illustrations of and commentaries on their own and others' uses of language (Rymes and Leone 2014). Thus, citizen sociolinguistics, as an approach to research, marks a fundamental break with the epistemic project of traditional sociolinguistics, particularly that of variationism and language attitude research.

In the Martha's Vineyard study, for example, Labov gave advice on how to select a (phonological) variable for study. First, a good variable should be one that is of frequent occurrence; second, it should be "structural"—"the more the item is integrated into a larger system of functioning units, the greater will be the intrinsic linguistic interest of our study"; third, its distribution in the speech community "should be highly stratified ... [and display] an asymmetric distribution over a wide range of age levels or other ordered strata of society" (Labov 1972, 8). But—Labov continues:

> There are a few contradictory criteria, which pull us in different directions. On the one hand, we would like the feature to be salient, for us as well as for the speaker, in order to study the direct relations of social attitudes and language behavior. But on the other hand, we value immunity from conscious distortion, which greatly simplifies the problem of reliability of the data. (8)

So the phonological feature selected for study should be salient to speakers—but not so salient that speakers have ideas of their own about it. In any case it is clear that "immunity from conscious distortion" is not easily gained. In a footnote attached to the above passage, Labov notes that:

> Many ingenious devices are needed to detect and eliminate deceit on the part of metropolitan informants, whether intended or not. On Martha's Vineyard, this is less of a problem, but the effects of the interview situation are evident in the careful style of some informants. (1972, 8n13)

Obviously, we are discussing what Labov calls "the classic methodological problem: the means used to gather the data interfere with the data to be gathered" (1972, 43). "Our goal," says Labov, "is to observe the way people use language when they are not being observed" (61). It's for this reason, of course, that Labov places such high value on "rapid and anonymous observations," such as those of his famous investigation of the (r) variable in New York City department stores (69). In his well-known discussion of "the observer's paradox," Labov recommends the use of "various devices which direct [the speaker's] attention away from speech, and allow the vernacular to emerge," including the "Danger of Death" technique, in which speakers are asked to narrate a near-death experience. Such devices, it is argued, induce in the speaker "a shift of style away from careful speech towards the vernacular" (209–10).

It was in exactly this spirit that Howard Giles and other researchers interested in language attitudes held the matched-guise technique in such high esteem. Matched-guise testing "involves the presentation [to subjects] of tape-recorded voices of one speaker reading the same factually neutral passage of prose in two or more dialects or languages" (Giles 1971, 211). Just as 'the vernacular'—that obscure object of variationist desire (see Coupland 2003; Eckert 2003)—is seen as lurking in the inner recesses of the speaker, requiring for its expression "devices" (See Labov, above) that short-circuit the speaker's self-censorship and "conscious distortion," so too the elicitation of "language attitudes" becomes complicated, and "assumes greater intricacy since such evaluative reactions are concomitantly dependent on a complex matrix of sender-receiver attributes including age, sex and social status" (Giles 1971, 211). Lambert et al. (1965) had claimed that "standard measures of attitudes" produced data inferior to that produced by matched-guise experiments, for the precise reason that the purpose of the data-gathering activity was "often 'transparent' [to the subjects] and is thus conducive to socially-appropriate responses, whereas the true nature of the former technique [matched-guise testing] is unlikely to be detected and in this way undistorted attitudes may be evoked" (Giles 1971, 213). This led Lambert to suggest that "the matched-guise technique was a more efficient instrument 'for evoking "private" or "uncensored" attitudes' towards a particular social group" than other more straightforward methods (Giles 1971, 213). What Labovian variationism shares with language attitudes research is a commitment to that hallmark of modernism in scientific praxis: operationalism (Bridgman 1927). In both literatures, speakers are recategorized as experimental subjects.

Hence this section's subtitle. The emergence of citizen sociolinguistics heralds the return of the repressed: The artist formerly known as the Speaker reappears—but this time neither as a naïve "native" speaker (perhaps induced into a state of maximal unselfconsciousness by the researcher's deployment of elicitation "devices"), nor as the passive bearer of an internalized linguistic competence, nor as an experimental subject, nor as a cultural dope (Garfinkel 1964)—rather, as a citizen sociolinguist, well able and inclined to articulate variously systematic or "anecdotal" ideas about language (and specifically about facts of sociolinguistic variation). To evaluate these statements, stories, performances, expressed opinions, and parodies for their "accuracy" vis-à-vis some sociolinguistic reality to which 'we' (linguists) have independent (and superior) access is to make a category mistake. The material will not allow that—citizen sociolinguists are unreliable narrators. Sweeping generalizations, tendentious claims, pseudo-expert posturing and downright prejudice are all richly on display in online discussions of such matters as those presented here: 'accent,' genre, and nativeness (Moore 2011). But these "biases" become virtues once we ask not about the accuracy of ordinary people's metacommentaries on language, but about the conventions governing their production and reception, and the performative implications of the act of expressing them—which is to say, the conditions under which they become effective (and, perhaps, worth "liking" or "sharing").

Now it becomes important to note that what's interesting about the "ordinary people" whose observations of and comments on language form the data of citizen sociolinguistics is not their ordinariness, but the fact that they can be observed online functioning in roles usually associated with university-based experts, becoming active chroniclers of socially meaningful variation in the language(s) they use and hear around them, even engaging with the discourse (and the data-gathering procedures) of sociolinguistics as an academic discipline. As a cultural phenomenon, citizen sociolinguistics bears witness to the circulation and uptake of erstwhile expert discourses about language in settings apparently far removed from universities and other institutions where these expert discourses originated. And this process of circulation is itself aided by the very same communication technologies where citizen sociolinguistics 'lives.'

To interpret the metapragmatic import (illocutionary force, if you like) of any utterance act in any medium, one must always attend first to its uptake in the event: what happened next? It is in the uptake that we discover whether the just-preceding speech act satisfies its 'felicity conditions' (Goffman 1983). Online discussions, in which it's not only possible but *easy* to react to, respond to, recirculate, and otherwise (explicitly or implicitly) evaluate another's utterance, provide rich attestations of uptake in exactly this sense (Goffman 1976). And the traces of all such intertextual response chains—and the origin, growth, and decline of particular examples, words, and phrases (e.g., as memes)—are open to investigation (see Nie 2015 for an exemplary study of just this type).

In fact, particular online platforms and services (Facebook, Twitter, etc.) do not only develop their own conventions and styles of such metapragmatic uptake through evaluation (e.g., "likes"), recirculation (e.g., retweets), and reanimation—conventions and styles that experts transmit to novices in "socialization" moments—they also become environments in which expertise is displayed primarily through performed mastery of "stylized" uptake (a.k.a., 'curation'). Such online communities, constituted in and by collaborative participation in discursive activity, share many characteristics with 'publics' in the sense of Warner (2002): participants experience mutuality of uptake in an environment of stranger sociability. Online, participants interpellate each other using screen-names and avatars, and calibrate their mutual availability through adopted personae (often many for each user; see Manning 2013).

Unlike dialectology, and in contrast to variationist studies of language change in progress, the ultimate goal of citizen sociolinguistics is not to study variation as a way of understanding larger processes of language change, but to focus on the circulation and exchange of samples of observed speech and metacommentary upon them as *a social activity in its own right*, one that is *centrally constitutive of non-face-to-face online communities*.

Users of social media who participate in online discussions of 'accent' or 'dialect' know that they are being observed. The "devices" that enable the expression of citizens' views of sociolinguistic variation are given, in the form of the digital infrastructures of various social media platforms (and the actual devices people use to access them). The means used to gather the data are identical with the means used to produce the data. Anxieties about the "observer's paradox" disappear when we reorient ourselves to interpreting—and contributing to—publicly available forms of expertise and the technological means for their expression, resignification, and circulation.

Notes

The work presented here and at GURT 2015 grew out of Betsy Rymes's Citizen Sociolinguistics seminar at the University of Pennsylvania's Graduate School of Education in Spring 2014. The authors are grateful to GURT 2015 organizer Anna De Fina for the opportunity to contribute a panel, and to audience members on that occasion for their comments and questions. While this chapter, like citizen sociolinguistics, is a collaborative endeavor, the authors of each individual subsection are responsible in the normal way for any errors of fact or interpretation in their respective contributions.

1. The quotation marks are used here to convey the ideological foundations of nonnative status, in contrast to the self-evident manner in which the term is often used in the field of Second Language Development/Acquisition.
2. All translations/transliterations by author.
3. Trastevere and Testaccio are neighborhoods in Rome.

References

Adam. 2012. "English Lessons with Adam — Learn English with Adam [engVid]." *Youtube*, October 22. Accessed September 2015. https://www.youtube.com/watch?v=ChZJ1Q3GSuI.

Agha, Asif. 2007. *Language and Social Relations*. Cambridge: Cambridge University Press.

American Council on the Teaching of Foreign Languages. 2012. "ACTFL Proficiency Guidelines 2012: English." Accessed March 7, 2016. http://www.actfl.org/publications/guidelines-and-manuals/actfl-proficiency-guidelines-2012/english.

Amin, Nuzhat. 1997. "Race and the Identity of the Nonnative ESL Teacher." *TESOL Quarterly* 31 (3): 580–83.

Aneja, Geeta. Forthcoming. "Rethinking Nativeness: Towards a Dynamic Paradigm of (non)Native Speakering." *Critical Inquiry in Language Studies*.

Bakhtin, Mikhail. 1986. "The Problem of Speech Genres." In *The Problem of Speech Genres and Other Late Essays*, edited by Caryl Emerson and Michael Holquist, translated by Vern W. McGee, 60–102. Austin: University of Texas Press.

Berruto, Gaetano. 1989. "Main Topics and Findings in Italian Sociolinguistics." *International Journal of the Sociology of Language* 76: 7–30.

Bloom, Jedd. 2013. "How to Write an Essay Rap." *YouTube*, February 8. Accessed March 7, 2016. http://www.youtube.com/watch?v=tRpPHylKFCQ_

Bridgman, Percy Williams. 1927. *The Logic of Modern Physics*. New York: The Macmillan Company.

Burgess, Jean, and Joshua Green. 2009. *YouTube*. Cambridge, MA: Polity.

Chomsky, Noam. 1965. *Aspects of the Theory of Syntax*. Cambridge, MA: MIT Press.

Coupland, Nikolas. 2003. "Sociolinguistic Authenticities." *Journal of Sociolinguistics* 7 (3): 417–31.

Doerr, Neriko Musha. 2009. *The Native Speaker Concept: Ethnographic Investigations of Native Speaker Effects*. Berlin: Mouton de Gruyter.

Eckert, Penelope. 2003. "Elephants in the Room." *Journal of Sociolinguistics* 7 (3): 392–97.

Ellis, Rod. 1994. *Second Language Acquisition*. Oxford: Oxford University Press.

Garfinkel, Harold. 1964. "Studies of the Routine Grounds of Everyday Activities." *Social Problems* 11 (3):225–50.

Giles, Howard. 1971. "Evaluative Reactions to Accents." *Educational Review* 22 (3): 211–27.

Goffman, Erving. 1976. "Replies and Responses." *Language in Society* 5 (3): 257–313.

———. 1983. "Felicity's Condition." *American Journal of Sociology* 89 (1): 1–53.

Johnson, Tara Star, Leigh Thompson, Peter Smagorinsky, and Pamela G. Fry. 2003. "Learning to Teach the Five-Paragraph Theme." *Research in the Teaching of English* 38 (2): 136–76.

Jenkins, Henry, Ravi Purushotma, Margaret Weigel, Katie Clinton, and Alice J. Robison. 2009. *Confronting the Challenges of Participatory Culture: Media Education for the 21st Century*. Cambridge, MA: The MIT Press.

Labov, William. 1972. *Sociolinguistic Patterns*. Philadelphia: University of Pennsylvania Press.

Lambert, Wallace E., Moshe Anisfeld, and Grace H. Yeni-Komshian. 1965. "Evaluational Reactions of Jewish and Arab Adolescents to Dialect and Language Variations." *Journal of Personality and Social Psychology* 2 (1): 84–90.

Kachru, Braj. 1985. "Standards, Codification and Sociolinguistic Realism: The English Language in the Outer Circle." In *English in the World*, edited by Randolph Quirk and Henry Widdowson, 11–30. Cambridge: Cambridge University Press.
Kubota, Ryuko. 2002. "The Impact of Globalization on Language Teaching in Japan." In *Globalization and Language Teaching*, edited by David Block and Deborah Cameron, 13–28. London: Routledge.
Leone, Andrea R. 2014. "Ideologies of Personhood: A Citizen Sociolinguistic Case Study of the Roman Dialect." *Working Papers in Educational Linguistics* 29 (2): 81–105.
Lewis, Mark. 2014. "'Follow the Procedure': Online Metapragmatic Commentary on the Five Paragraph Essay." *Working Papers in Educational Linguistics* 29 (2): 45–63.
Long, Michael. 1981. "Input, Interaction and Second Language Acquisition." In *Annals of the New York Academy of the Sciences 379: Native Language and Foreign Acquisition*, edited by Harris Winitz, 259–78. New York: New York Academy of Sciences.
Manning, Paul. 2013. "Altaholics Anonymous: On the Pathological Proliferation of Parasites in Massively Multiple Online Worlds." *Semiotic Review, Issue 1: Parasites.* Accessed 7 March 2016. http://www.semioticreview.com/pdf/parasites/manning_altaholicsanonymous.pdf.
Moore, Robert. 2011. "'If I actually talked like that, I'd pull a gun on myself': Accent, Avoidance, and Moral Panic in Irish English." *Anthropological Quarterly* 84 (1): 41–64.
Mullen, Rebecca, and Linda Wedwick. 2008. "Avoiding the Digital Abyss: Getting Started in the Classroom with YouTube, Digital Stories, and Blogs." *Clearing House* 82:66–69.
nicves1992. 2010. "Ragazze ad Ostia - di N. Veschi e A. Cavaliere." *Youtube*, July 20. Accessed February 13, 2014. http://www.youtube.com/watch?v=sJiEbXTQqos.
Nie, Ted. 2015. "The Viral Spread of 'duang.'" Unpublished manuscript, Tilburg University (Netherlands).
Nota dell'Associazione Culturale Severiana. 2010. "Ostia, Immagine Burina e Degrado Culturale: l'Associazione Severiana contro Vizzani." *Roma Today.* July 23. Accessed February 13, 2014. http://ostia.romatoday.it/ostia/immagine-burina-di-ostia-associazione-severiana-contro-vizzani.html.
Paikeday, Thomas. 1985. *The Native Speaker Is Dead!* Toronto: Paikeday Publishing.
Park, Gloria. 2012. ""I Am Never Afraid of Being Recognized as an NNES": One Teacher's Journey in Claiming and Embracing Her Nonnative-Speaker Identity." *TESOL Quarterly* 46 (1): 127–51.
Rampton, Ben. 1990. "Displacing the 'Native Speaker': Expertise, Affiliation and Inheritance." *ELT Journal* 44 (2): 97–101.
Rymes, Betsy. 2010. "Communicative Repertoires and English Language Learners." In *The Education of English Language Learners: Research to Practice*, by Marilyn Shatz and Louise C. Wilkerson, 177–97. New York: Guilford Press.
———. 2012. "Recontextualizing YouTube: From Macro-Micro to Mass-Mediated Communicative Repertoires." *Anthropology and Education Quarterly* 43 (2): 214–27.
———. 2014. *Communicating beyond Language: Everyday Encounters with Diversity*. New York: Routledge.
Rymes, Betsy, and Andrea R. Leone. 2014. "Citizen Sociolinguistics: A New Media Methodology for Understanding Language and Social Life." *Working Papers in Educational Linguistics* 29 (2): 25–43.
Sanga, Glauco. 1985. "La Convergenza Linguistica." *Rivista Italiana di Dialettologia* 9:7–41.
Selinker, Larry. 1972. "Interlanguage." *International Review of Applied Linguistics* 10:209–231.
Selvi, Ali Fuad. 2010. "All Teachers are Equal, but Some Teachers are More Equal than Others: Trend Analysis of Job Advertisements in English Language Teaching." *WATESOL Caucus Annual Review* 1:156–81.
———. 2014. "Myths and Misconceptions about the Nonnative English Speakers in TESOL (NNEST) Movement." *TESOL Quarterly* 5 (3): 573–611.
Shuck, Gail. 2006. "Racializing the Nonnative English Speaker." *Journal of Language, Identity, and Education* 5:259–76.
Silverstein, Michael. 2003. "Indexical Order and the Dialectics of Sociolinguistic Life." *Language & Communication* 23(3-4):193–229.
SkyTG24. 2010. ""Una bira o famo la colla": dal Tormentone alla Canzone." *Tg24*. July 23. http://tg24.sky.it/tg24/spettacolo/2010/07/23/ostia_tormentone_bira_youtube_facebook_caldo.html.

Taylor, David. 2012. "The Five-Paragraph Essay: Three Formulas for Writing the Basic Academic Essay." *YouTube*, May 27. Accessed March 7, 2016. http://www.youtube.com/watch?v=GwjmMtTVO1g.

Warner, Michael. 2002. "Publics and Counterpublics." *Public Culture* 14 (1): 49–90.

Widdowson, Henry G. 1994. "The Ownership of English." *TESOL Quarterly* 28 (2): 377–89.

Chapter 10

Recasting Diversity in Language Education in Postcolonial, Late-Capitalist Societies

LUISA MARTÍN ROJO, CHRISTINE ANTHONISSEN, INMACULADA GARCÍA-SÁNCHEZ, AND VIRGINIA UNAMUNO

SOCIAL REALITIES OF INCREASING (super-)diversity, mobility, and the corresponding high appraisal of linguistic competences and skills are currently not developing—as was expected—into egalitarian systems and structures in multilingual communities. To the contrary, much evidence of how former inequalities, prejudices, and social and linguistic hierarchies are still active and even amplified abounds in many apparently liberal societies.

This chapter focuses precisely on this issue, examining how various late-capitalist and postcolonial regimes recast new forms of diversity into old molds through the implementation of language-education policies and programs. In what follows we explore the main forces and processes that perpetuate inequality, some of which simply continue outdated dispensations while others present innovations even if still not bringing fundamental change. Particularly, we focus on the impact that neoliberal policies have in schools, the transnational division of labor and the persistence of knowledge, values, and ideologies rooted in the colonial past. The interplay of these processes and their impact on the recent proliferation of language programs, and on how diversity is recast, is substantiated in an illustrative section where we refer to three specific educational contexts which represent different national arrangements: South Africa, the United States, and Argentina. We consider different kinds of language programs, and examine different dimensions of the educational (from linguistic policies to local practices in classrooms) in these settings. Focusing on these three situations, this chapter aims to develop an understanding of what the social, economic, organizational, and even epistemological conditions are that contribute to the perpetuation of inequalities.

Socioeconomic and Educational Processes and Concerns

In the following sections, we attend to the impact of two socioeconomic processes which stand out in the recent proliferation of language programs, also emphasizing how diversity is recast through them.

Schools and the Rise of Neoliberalism as a Prevalent Economic Model

In terms of the first of these determining processes, namely the rise of neoliberalism as a ubiquitous economic model, economists have positioned it around the 1980s, when the classical liberal ideal of the self-regulating market became an ideology, and an extended mode of governance. These features of neoliberalism, Fraser (2003) finds are transforming states into "competition states," fueling myriad deregulation processes, as well as prompting efforts to privatize social services, often by shifting them into the open market. This is also happening in education and schooling.

As part of the neoliberal agenda, education markets are now being expanded while market principles are being applied across education systems. Thus, costs are attached to educational opportunities on a supply-and-demand basis. Liberalization of trade has opened up education, along with other public sectors, to capital accumulation. The result is the global marketing of schooling from primary school through to higher education, which affects all aspects of education and education services.

This process has been evidenced in different geopolitical areas, including not only Europe and North and South America, but also Africa, South Asia, and Southeast Asia. As Macpherson, Robertson, and Walford (2014) observe, the scale, scope, and penetration of the privatization process have taken on excessive proportions. The three most outstanding effects of an agenda that has been set by private, commercial interests are the following: education as a sector gets recast in a manner which increasingly opens it up to profit-making and trade; learners are increasingly conceptualized as consumers; and finally, education, learning, and teaching get conceptualized as consumer goods, but no longer as means for social emancipation (13–15).

Ethnographic research in public schools shows the impact of this dynamic of privatization. Schools face debilitating discourses about the failure of public education, which justify calls regarding the need for growing privatization. In facing such discrediting discourses and the pressure of possible privatization, schools also have to respond to enforced top-down accountability and to incentivized performance targets set for schools, classrooms, and teachers (see Lipman 2011a, 220). As part of this process, public schools are currently confronted with funding cuts. One of the means of managing such curbs is for schools to compete for students and resources among themselves and with subsidized private schools/charter schools. The significant question we will consider then relates to how all this is affecting the role language and language programs play in schools (see Pérez-Milans 2015b; Flubache and del Percio 2016).

The importance of language as a source of symbolic value in a globalized "new economy" points to the need to pay attention to languages in education. There is a proliferation of discourses that celebrate multilingualism and present the maximization of linguistic competencies and skills as a contemporary requirement for guaranteed entry into and mobility within the job market. In spite of the problematization of these assumptions by sociolinguistic research (see Duchêne and Heller 2012; Duchêne 2011), the view that, in the context of globalization, languages "ensure" access to markets and services is deeply rooted. Thus, the need of speakers to expand their linguistic repertoires increases in tandem with their demand for language education, which schools are obliged to provide.

Along with these discourses, and the need to meet market demands, we also need to mention the fact that individuals seek to expand their linguistic competencies by demanding bilingual teaching courses and programs, often paying for certificates that accredit linguistic training and education. These demands become particularly insistent when they are framed in a "neoliberal imaginary" (Rossiter 2003; Urciuoli 2010; see Holborow 2015)—that is, as a set of values, institutions, rules and common symbols through which people imagine their social whole. One of the most powerful features of this "neoliberal imaginary" is that each person is seen as his or her own product, following an ethic of entrepreneurial self-management. As Urciuoli shows in her study of higher education, if neoliberalism in education manifests the main function of an individual as making profit for themselves and/or their organization, then every piece of knowledge (where linguistic knowledge is an important element) they acquire in this process can be interpreted as a skill, an aspect of the self that is potentially productive for prospective employers: "Skills become a form of self-marketing, and students come to imagine themselves as bundles of skills" (2010, 162). As others have claimed, this project of "self-capitalisation" seems to last the individual's whole life (Rizvi and Lingard 2010), and to have a significant impact on their conduct, particularly their linguistic conduct, and their self-perception (see Martín Rojo 2016).[1]

The compelling need to become fully competent in at least one 'international language,' becomes a strong power mechanism in neoliberal economies, and ends up regulating the behavior of individuals and the population in general (see Martín Rojo 2016). Thus, language (self)training becomes an instrument for increasing competency and competitiveness, and fills the void resulting from long periods of unemployment in a precarious job market. All of these responses lead to greater revenues for the language industry while concealing the fact that linguistic competence and skills do not guarantee access to better employment. The research of Duchêne (2011) and Duchêne, Moyer, and Roberts (2013) has shown how multilingualism is valued in labor organizations, particularly in the selection process, but not in promotion or achievement of access to better work conditions.

Within this context, new language educational programs provide powerful strategies for the recruitment of "consumers" and for the legitimation of public schools. Schools with dedicated bilingual and dual-language programs characteristically offer the languages that the marketplace demands, while selecting students whom they consider already the most suitably prepared for access to education and to an increasingly globalized job market (see Pérez-Milans 2015a). This seems to be a worldwide phenomenon, even if its scope and intensity varies according to interregional and transnational divisions of labor.

Schools and the Transnational Division of Labor amid the Prevalence of a Colonial Episteme

The second socioeconomic process we address in order to explain how diversity is recast in schools refers to Wallerstein's division of the "world-system" into core countries, semiperiphery countries, and periphery countries, according to different kinds of markets and market needs (Wallerstein 1979, 2011). Core countries focus on highly skilled, capital-intensive production while the rest of the world focuses on lower skilled, labor-intensive production, and extraction of raw materials. These divisions constantly reinforce the dominance of the core countries. Individual states can gain or lose their core (semiperiphery, periphery) status over time. This chapter reflects on whether different positions in the world-system produce differences in the management of multilingualism, and on whether this could contribute to explaining the persistence of hierarchies of language programs and hierarchies among students within the school system.

Depending on the position of each country, almost predictably different linguistic policies will be found. For instance, Blommaert (2006) notes that peripheral countries invest more in English language development as a way to change their position in the world system than do core countries. Thus, the remarkable movement toward English education attested in the whole European Union ensures its position at the core (see Eurydice 2006, 2008; Relaño-Pastor 2015). Conversely, core countries where English is the language of instruction (such as the example of the United States given below) seem to invest limitedly in multilingual education (Pérez-Milans 2015b). The position of noncore countries on which we report is less clear. For instance, South Africa and Argentina, both identified as semiperipheral countries where histories of colonialism explain the prominence of English and Spanish respectively, are not necessarily equivalent in terms of language policies.

This world-system has historically depended on the supply of cheap labor from the periphery to the core. Pratt (1991) identifies this diaspora as the reversal of the 'colonial spread' in the form of the labor migration of the past twenty to forty years from former colonies into the first world, which has created spaces she calls "contact zones." Schools become then the social spaces where "disparate cultures meet, clash and grapple with each other in highly asymmetrical relations of domination and subordination…and their aftermaths as they are lived out across the globe today" (34).

This diaspora is marked by colonial reminiscences. As van Amersfoort (2008) notes, the social position of immigrants from the former colonies has not only been determined by the legal status of these immigrants, but also by the ideas of race and color that were an intrinsic part of the ideological status hierarchy in the colonies. But reminders of the colonial dispensation go further. Considering education within the frame of coloniality, we find that citizens from former colonies are at times represented as "less capable students," "poorly educated," "from dysfunctional families," "less developed," or "primitive." These are, for example, recurrent, stereotyping characterizations of Central American students in the Madrid Region (Martín Rojo 2010), which are strongly reminiscent of accounts of "Hispanic" students in the United States, or even of accounts of "indigenous" communities in Latin American countries. These social representations can be seen as effects of coloniality, understood as long-standing patterns of exercising power that emerged as a result of colonialism, but that define culture, labor, intersubjective relations, and knowledge production well beyond the strict limits of colonial administrations (Maldonado-Torres 2007).[2]

With relation to these processes, we examine the impact of coloniality within two different contexts. Firstly, the context of increasing mobility that forces schools in multilingual cities to offer programs that teach the languages of instruction to a body of linguistically diverse students who often have had transnational trajectories. Ethnographic studies on the management of linguistic resources within classrooms have shown how, in spite of claims about the commodification of languages, these language programs and the languages of their students are rarely seen as profitable resources (Pérez-Milans 2011). Numerous research reports have also evidenced the existence of hierarchies of ethnic and national groups that shape and are shaped by the unequal distribution of capital in schools (Bourdieu 1991; see Martín Rojo 2010, for an extensive bibliography on this hierarchization of students and languages).

A second context that we examine is that of the revitalization of languages that have been neglected in education as a consequence of a "colonial episteme" of knowledge, ideologies, and values rooted in a colonial past. The analysis shows the limitations of linguistic-rights approaches in language revitalization processes. The case of bilingual education in Argentina (discussed below) allows us to see how introducing a language as a means of instruction is not sufficient; rather, the situation of linguistic domination based on a colonial order and on neoliberal policies has to be challenged. A decolonizing effort requires the production and legitimation of new discourses that recognize the contexts of colonization, raise awareness of the colonized knowledge (Mignolo and Escobar 2009), and change the position of economic dependence and subordination.

We will now examine how both socioeconomic processes mentioned above induce the proliferation of language programs in schools nationally, as well as affect systematic differentiation in the treatment of different languages and students.

Problematizing Bilingual School Programs and Language Instruction across Nation States

In the following sections we consider whether similar processes are taking place across different regions and educational contexts: South Africa, where the profound transformations of 1994 broadened participation of the local population in government, and made explicit its intention to provide improved social opportunities for formerly excluded local, established language communities; the United States, where the schooling of children and youth from historically racialized immigrant populations in multi-ethnic metropolitan areas shows how they come up against a number of social and linguistic inequalities, through which a subaltern social position is assigned to them; and Argentina, where the implementation of bilingual programs illustrates how countries with a recent colonial past seem still to be shaped by the former hierarchies of students, knowledge, and languages.

The main research questions addressed in this analysis are related to the ongoing processes presented above, and can be articulated as follows:

1. What is the role of neoliberal policies in language commodification in education, and in particular in the implementation of language programs and in how they become hierarchically organized?
2. To what extent are language programs in schools still shaped by hierarchies in terms of superior and inferior knowledge (hence of superior and inferior people), rooted in a colonial episteme?
3. To what extent is a postcolonial episteme reinforcing the effects of neoliberalism in language education and vice versa?

The Role of Schools in Implementing Nation-State Policies

The socio-educational context in postcolonial and postapartheid South Africa is informative in considering the question as to which forces and processes, both enduring and new, are central in determining the current ways of handling diversity in language education. This is a country where, since 1996, the linguistic diversity of the population has been acknowledged in one of the most liberal and inclusive language policies in modern constitutional law (see Alexander 2002, 2003). Such language policy, which provides official status for eleven languages, appears to secure state protection of diverse groups in equal measure. However, twenty years beyond the introduction of the currently prevailing language-in-education policy (LiEP), disenabling linguistic and cultural distinctions are perpetuated in practice (Plüddemann 2015). A majority of youngsters who were slighted by a former dispensation find that the new dispensation does not sufficiently protect or socially advance them.

In relation to state funding, the percentage of the gross domestic product (GDP) allocated to education could be an indicator. At almost 6.6 percent of GDP and 18.5 percent of state expenditure dedicated to various levels of education, South Africa has one of the highest rates of public investment in education in the world. This is higher than similar kinds of expenditure in countries financially much more advanced, such as the 5.5 percent of GDP rate of the United States and 6.2 percent of the United Kingdom (World Bank 2012). This is rather confounding given that the outcomes do not appear to be in line with such an indicator of valuing and investing in improved education. One would have hoped to see the effects of such spending in improved throughput rates as well as reduction in unemployment numbers, but that is not the case. However, both Constitutional provisions for multilingualism in schools and the gross state funding of education serve as a means of highlighting certain contradictions and anomalies that can only be explained by referring to a (mostly denied) neoliberal agenda.

First, recent statistics on numbers of learners entering and completing secondary education, and of those gaining access to tertiary educational institutions, point to a disconcertingly high drop-out rate (see StatsSA Census data of 2001 and 2011). This underscores a gap between socially valued knowledge expected and kinds of knowledge actually developed among students. The role of language as the carrier of new and complex knowledge is often obscured, so that inordinately high numbers of learners are constructed not as lagging in L2-acquisition of the medium-of-instruction (MoI), but as generally unfit for the challenges of a socially enabling education. Thus, as predicted in post-colonial theory, the new curricula and teaching practices continue to fail large numbers of learners.

Second, considering the market effects of neoliberal policies, costs of education are increasingly transferred from the state budget to private enterprises. The exorbitant cost of education remains so limitedly addressed that in 2015 and 2016 it was the cause of countrywide paralyzing student protests.[3]

The idealistic aims of the new language policies have not translated into improved management of linguistic diversity. Learning opportunities have become commodified in that schools in affluent areas exact fees additional to the state provision, to the extent that students from lower socioeconomic communities are effectively excluded. The majority of schools with limited resources and no additional parent contributions, serve communities with indigenous African languages as L1s where access to competitive levels of L2-English is rarely in evidence (StatsSA communiqué, April 22, 2015).

Third, due also to policies of the former National Party government, the idea of L1-education for learners from indigenous African-language homes appears tainted. In LiEP development of the 1990s and beyond, no systematic polling of isiZulu/isiXhosa/Sesotho parent communities checked their language-in-education preferences for their children. Where colonial and apartheid systems left parents uninformed on the critical relation between language, learning, and developing new knowledge, the new dispensation appears to do no better. Given a choice of which language(s) should be used as MoI, parents have largely followed dominant discourses on the power of the "international language" in the hope of so assuring access to a system of class privilege for their children (Anthonissen 2013). Thus the impression persists that English, though in some contexts also Afrikaans, guarantees social mobility. This poses little challenge to existing mechanisms of domination.

The new, liberal language policy (1996, 2002) in South Africa conceals the fact that the advantages the former official languages enjoyed continue to work in favor of those established speech communities, and that the limited opportunities that other language communities had had for more than a century would not easily be turned around. In short, official recognition of the effort and cost that would be attached to raising the status of languages such as isiXhosa in the Eastern and Western Cape or Venda in Limpopo to languages of learning, was scant. In practice, the de facto situation after twenty years of democracy is still that (e.g.) isiXhosa-L1 learners are officially provided with mother tongue education for the first three years of schooling, after which a transfer to English as MoI is obligatory. There is insufficient educator training and institutional support for managing the transition to English.

The de facto languages of teaching-and-learning policies indicate that the provisions of the national LiEP of 1996 have, in general, not been actively implemented (Heugh 2007, 188; Plüddemann et al. 2004, 8; Probyn 2005, 161; Sigcau 2004, 243). Secondary school learners from (e.g.) isiXhosa or Sesotho L1 homes have no choice other than English as MoI, while the classroom practices of a majority facilitate neither the development of L1 skills, nor of appropriate levels of English-language proficiency. Classroom practices certainly allow and informally recognize the multilingualism of the learners, but officially this is not provided for: teacher training only very rarely develops skills in the use of various languages (e.g., isiXhosa AND English) for subject teaching. Policy and curriculum provisions mostly gloss over the challenges of early learning through medium of an L2, and do not provide for special attention to development of learners in the use of the MoI as a language in which knowledge is acquired and demonstrated. Effectively, this means that those who attain good levels of academic communication in English with minimal support, are those who will advance educationally. What is more, students are still assessed according to strict and conventional language standards developed within monolingual models of learning languages.

What educational practices that privilege a lingua franca such as English conceal, is the fact that a majority of the population are bilingual and multilingual people and that the dramatic social changes of the past twenty years have brought about new forms of hybridity in language learning, language identity, and language choice. English has in this period become the (only) language of opportunity (90+ percent speak English as L2, with varying levels of proficiency, and a wide variety of forms), so that many choose to change their home language, to give their children an L1 different to the heritage language of the family; or they choose to raise the educational opportunities of their children by sending them to English medium schools from day one. Early access to English education is a middle-class opportunity more open to those with funding for the higher school fees of formerly white-only schools, for transport to and from school, and for care and supervision after school hours, than to others. Low-income families do not have such choices.

In practice, de facto, the language of the classroom in most township and rural schools (e.g.) of the Eastern and Western Cape remains isiXhosa for the full seven years of primary school education—with code-switching between isiXhosa and English for the purposes of doing written work and examinations. In a substantial number of cases these practices continue into secondary school. Limited official and managerial attention is given to how such language practices affect learning and new knowledge construction.

Language policies and programs in schools thus are still shaped by hierarchies of superior and inferior knowledge and so perpetuate discriminating social structures of superiority and inferiority around the world. Neoliberalism in education is increasing these asymmetries and reestablishing old hierarchies by reinforcing the role of English in the global economy and consequently also the position of countries in the world-system. Also, the identified socioeconomic processes limit the resources invested in education, and the access to such opportunity.

Recasting Racial-Ethnic Relationships in a Mobile World

The previous section dealt with how nation-state policies are intertwined with the inclusion of minority and heritage local languages in educational systems. Here we move to discuss a separate but related aspect, inextricably linked to the international division of labor: the inclusion in core countries' schools of immigrant and minority students who speak minority languages. As the sociologist Richard Alba (2013) claims, abundant evidence reveals that most educational systems, including the US system, are failing to meet the challenges of integrating the children of mostly low-status immigrants. Sociological theories underscore these systems' role in reproducing inequality. As a result of an attributed shared racial position, their linguistic practices and school performance may be framed as deficient (see Flores and Rosa 2015 for raciolinguistic ideologies). In relation to this reproduction of inequality, an important underlying question in our discussion of inclusion is about the extent to which racial-ethnic relationships inherited from colonial periods are reactivated within the international division of labor and the expansion of neoliberalism (Grosfoguel 2011). One critical way of understanding how the politics of inclusion regulate racial-ethnic relations in school systems is to consider the implementation of educational policies or curricular programs like the ones examined above. Another crucial dimension in understanding the nature of these relationships among students of different linguistic, racial, ethnic, and cultural backgrounds is to look at the informal politics of inclusion in schools as they are constituted through everyday interactions between teachers and students, and among students themselves. This is particularly important, given that members of the school community have been identified as crucial agents for the successful inclusion of minority and immigrant students. This is the focus of García-Sánchez's (2014) research: firstly, the construction of hierarchical social relations in schools through everyday, seemingly innocuous interactions between teachers and students, and among students themselves; secondly, the ways in which in routine, daily participation in more or less subtle exclusionary interactions, immigrant children are led to feel a lack of recognition, and more generally a feeling that they are not considered legitimate participants in their school communities and educational system.

This second dimension is particularly salient in immigrant children and youth's use of narrative to make sense of their lives and of the everyday, social worlds they inhabit and traverse. The analysis of the stories of personal experiences of Latino immigrant youth in the United States highlights these young students' own perspectives and understandings of their lived experience in relation to larger ideologies that have a long tradition of framing them as a "problem": an integration problem, an educational problem, a delinquency problem, a teen-pregnancy problem, etc. García-Sánchez (2014) has focused specifically on how immigrant children and youth recount experiences of prejudice, by examining the linguistic and other forms of semiosis that the participants discuss when recounting these kinds of experiences. Verbal harassment and overt linguistic forms of ethnic victimization were part of the experiences these young students narrated. A common thread running through the stories, however, is that, in addition to these more blatant forms of expressing prejudice, there are many other subtle semiotic cues directed at them, constructing them as outsiders. For the young participants these subtle forms are at least as powerful, if not more so, than more overt forms in making them feel like second-class, or nonlegitimate members of the school community. The power of veiled insults and exclusionary acts may precisely lie in that they are so concealed and thus difficult to refute.

Many of the youngsters commented on this. For instance, as a coda to their stories, they often mentioned how perplexing these social encounters were because, even though there was no glaring racial aggression, they felt a "negative vibe" or a sense of being treated differently. In particular, a communicative aspect highlighted in this section is children's own descriptions of sensing that something was being withheld from them. Because many conceptualize racism and prejudice as something that is *being done*, it was very interesting to hear that immigrant children and youth also describe it in terms of something that is *not being done*, as something that is denied them, particularly at the everyday interactional level. These narratives illustrate the conversation analytic notion of the "noticeable absent," an etic analytic tool used to explain when an appropriate or preferred next action is not forthcoming (such as not offering an answer to a question). The analyst then shows how this absence is treated as noticeable and accountable by the participants. Many of the narratives analyzed provide striking emic accounts of communicative features that immigrant youngsters perceive as noticeable absents in that they present them either as nonactions for which other social actors are accountable and morally responsible or as absence of a preferred action, given the social context and the kind of activity in question. We reproduce here two examples of, respectively, a Salvadoran (Berenice) and a Mexican (Aurora) immigrant student who each discuss these types of encounters. In example 1, Bernice describes the absence of appropriate greeting and recognition from her head counselor in an out-of-school setting. This is a particularly powerful example because, as Duranti (1997) has pointed out, greetings are taken as morally imperative acts that construct interlocutors as worth recognizing, and as crucial practices that distinguish insiders from outsiders, and valuable from invaluable interactants.

Example 1, Berenice's counselor

Inma — That counselor is coming up quite a bit. (Both laughing)
How did you feel about the counselor?
Berenice — He was very cold with me. He like didn't talk much to me
[...]
See my counselor- my my counselor
and he wouldn't even look into my eyes
because I worked- before I worked at a fast food restaurant
and he would go in there and he wouldn't even look into my eyes
and I was like: "Should I talk to him?"
and I was like: "No, he's not worth it.
He doesn't even deserve my- my- my- ..."
Inma — He would see you and he wouldn't say hello?

Berenice He wouldn't talk to me. He would just go in there
and order what he needed and just be there.
He would even go through the drive-through
and be like he didn't know me and he-
I mean I see a person, even if I don't get to know them,
I see their face and I see them again
and I know who that person is. I try to remember:
"Yes, I've seen her or I've seen him in this place."
But how can you not remember?-

Through a series of parallelistic structures (e.g., "how can you not remember?"), Bernice narratively neutralizes plausible deniability and holds the counselor morally responsible for the absence of recognition and greeting.

In example 2 below, Aurora also describes the absence of what in her opinion should have been the preferred action of their interlocutors, particularly compared to the behavior of the same interlocutors with students of other ethnic and social groups in the same context. Among the things they emphasize is how a detached professional register is adopted and contextualization cues that encode familiarity are avoided; a more colloquial warmth would be communicated to other people in the same social setting.

Example 2, Aurora's principal

Inma What did you mean earlier when you said: Well, the principal was just like that too?
Aurora He was like- towards Mexicans- he was really rude towards Mexicans.
He was really rude.
You'd ask him something and he'd be like- he'd look at you like- you could just feel that he didn't care for the Mexicans and when the- I mean- like the other ones- would go- the- I don't know how to say it- I don't want to say it ((laughing embarrassed))
Inma Just say it
Aurora White people would go and=
=HE would do everything for them=
=AND we would go and he would be like: Later
Inma What things did you bring up to him that he would say later? What would you ask of him?
Aurora Probably in some school activities- and we'd just try to talk to him and he would just be rude- I mean you'd just try to start a conversation with him and he would just be like oh, uh-huh uh-huh and that was it and with, you know the white people he would be like *O::::::::h* you know, really friendly with them and just really like rude with us.

Aurora's quotations of her principal's interactional behavior towards her and Mexicans in general, is particularly interesting in that besides speech, she reports intonation patterns that encode neutral emotion (oh uh-huh uh-huh) versus patterns that encode upgraded positive affect and familiarity (O::::::::::*h*). This is important because, as Besnier (1993) indicates in his analysis of the affective meaning of reported speech, there are many linguistic strategies that narrators can use as keying devices to express their affective point of view and pass judgment on what they are reporting. By emphasizing prosodic elements in her quotations with the main function of communicating affect, in this case school administrators' negative affect, Aurora simultaneously conveys how these practices make her feel wronged and unaccepted. Narratives like these give us some indication of how immigrant youngsters perceive and emotionally react to these types of interactions with their peers and significant others in their social world, such as school personnel.

The examples analyzed show how migrant students who enter core-country schools, as a result of the international division of labor, are not treated as legitimate participants in the educational field. Within a context of neoliberal policies in education, underrating these students will restrict their already limited chances of getting access to the most prestigious schools; those which in turn give access to the best universities in a very competitive system. These examples also broaden our understanding of the role of everyday communicative practices and interactions in the construction of hierarchical ethnic and racial relations in schools, and ultimately, in the inclusion of immigrant and minority children in educational systems. By incorporating the perspectives of immigrant children and youth, who are very often not authorized to speak and who are considered neither legitimate nor capable analysts of their own social realities, these perceptions are authenticated.

Old and New Practices in Bilingual Intercultural Education: The Decisiveness of New Agents

Minority-language programs that appear to recognize the rights of local communities also reproduce language hierarchies which effectively construct indigenous language communities as second-class citizens. The management of these programs illustrates the insensitivity of regimes regarding the rights of groups that have long been excluded from social development. However, new and alternative approaches to bilingual education are emerging in formerly colonized areas where teachers and students question old hierarchies and ways of doing. This confronts us with the question of whether decolonialization and decolonial knowledge are necessary components for imagining and building minority language programs.

In Argentina, one of the political instruments used to guarantee the inclusion of minorities into the public educational system is the Intercultural Bilingual Education program (EIB: Educación Intercultural Bilingüe). Since the 1980s, different kinds of legislation have recognized the right of indigenous peoples to bilingual education. The legislation was prompted by the agitation of indigenous movements after Argentina democratized in 1983 (Unamuno 2015). Since the 1990s, international pressure forced Argentina to recognize the rights of indigenous people to education, land, and health care within a new legal framework that included educational provisions. However, to this day both legislation and official public educational policies consider the EIB to be a mechanism operative only in an educational context where native children are schooled. From an institutional, postcolonial perspective the EIB is not viewed as a model for the development of intercultural and bilingual skills among students; rather, it is presented as coherent with the modernist idea of the nation state where a single language should ideally be uniformly distributed across the population. Thus, the state understands its educational responsibility as one of providing students from indigenous language groups with opportunities to access the dominant, international language, which in this case is Spanish.

Teaching practices in a school in the Chaco region of Argentina illustrate how alternative interpretations of the EIB may coexist with state definitions and show what the implications are. In particular, we argue that new patterns of bilingual language use in EIB-schools have political force because they facilitate the emergence of new groups that are claiming their rights within a contested space in the field of languages and education. The struggle for autonomy in the management of schools has a crucial role in these changes.

The data introduced here comes from a project conducted in a rural school with students from three indigenous groups, namely the Wichis, the Qom, and the Moqoit. Since 2009, researchers from National Scientific and Technical Research Council (CONICET) and from the Center for Research and Training for Indigenous Educational Modality (CIFMA) accompanied indigenous teachers there in the implementation of bilingual practices according to the EIB provisions, also documenting actions that highlighted a tension between two competing definitions of EIB that coexist in schools and are apparent at institutional and interactional levels.

The current institutional EIB definition assumes that bilingualism and interculturality are features of native communities that have to be "normalized." Normalization is achieved by 1) placing bilingual teachers exclusively in initial levels of schooling to prepare young learners for access to Spanish and the mainstream curricula; 2) placing two teachers representing different communities in one classroom: a white teacher appointed to do the primary teaching and an indigenous teacher appointed as an assistant and translator; or 3) segregating children of indigenous and nonindigenous background, placing them in different classrooms. All these procedures reflect the extent to which languages as well as speakers are hierarchized.

Similar to the case examined in the previous section, the hierarchization of languages and speakers is reproduced and reinforced on an interactional level. In everyday school practices bilingual resources have been largely undervalued. The distribution of languages in the classroom is analogous to the position and status allocated to the languages in the program. Although two teachers work together, the role differences of each teacher and the unbalanced amount of time each has for their part of the lesson reinforces the asymmetry. The following example shows how this distribution of space between the participants draws on bilingual resources but eventually has a monolingual aim. Bilingual resources are configured in a monolingual way, in that the two language systems are not seen as connected and complementary, but rather as independent systems of which one is more useful than the other. An excerpt from a Grade 1 classroom interaction will be used illustratively (see table 10.1).

Angelica (MA), the primary teacher, speaks mostly Spanish although, as in turns 13 and 21, she sometimes uses Wichi words, usually instructive expressions such as TAIPHO (sit down) or APUJ (do it/get started). Silvina (MS) is an L1-Wichi teacher who is assigned an assistant role. Figure 10.1 shows the way in which spaces and roles are managed in the classroom, illustrating the significant differences

Table 10.1. Teacher hierarchies

Original	Translation
13. MA: Luisito ¿qué dice ahí? ¿qué está escribiendo ahí Jazmín? APUJ Luisito *una niña se levanta a enseñarle el cuaderno a la MS que está en el lateral derecho de la clase*	13. MA: Luisito what does that say? What are you writing there Jazmin? Luisito DO IT * a girl gets up to show her notebook to MS who is on the right side of the class *
14. MA: {(a LU)¿ah? <XX> ¿qué dice acá Luisito?}	14. MA: {(to LU) ah? what does it say here Luisito?}
15. LU: mate	15. LU: mate
16. MA: muy bien. ma::te	16. MA: very good. ma:: te
17. *Jazmín vuelve a su banco*	17. *Jasmine returns to the desk*
18. LU: casi me caigo [ríe]	18. LU: I nearly fell [laughs]
19. MA: bueno	19. MA: good
20. MA: Bryan. ¿querés pasar a marcar la segunda? pasá	20. MA: Bryan. Do you want to come here to write another one? Come on
21. MS: APASA. BRYAN	21. MS: COME ON. BRYAN
22. MA: decile que marque arriba y abajo	22. MA: tell him to write up there and below
23. MS:*se desplaza del lateral al centro del aula* EH. LAPASACHE ATHANA	23. MS: *moves from side to the center of the room * EH. YOU COME ON NOW
24. *Bryan pasa a la pizarra con poco interés*	24. * Bryan goes to the board with very little interest *

between each teacher's position: while MA is in the center at the front, MS stands on the side. Correlatively, in relation to tasks and activities, MA directs MS's contribution to the lesson (see turn 22 in table 10.1).

This distribution is analogous to the position and status allocated to the languages in the classroom. The amount of time each participant has for their part of the lesson reinforces the asymmetry. Thus, this interaction shows how the distribution of teaching space asymmetrically constructs persons and languages within the bilingual classroom.

Quite recently, however, changes have been observed in daily verbal interactions in indigenous communities and schools which appear to be proposing a different valuation of bilingual resources. New communicative practices challenge the monolingual mindset in public education that restricts indigenous people to their communities, projecting a hierarchy of knowledge, practices, and people that privileges those who have mastered Spanish, and minimizes any social value that indigenous languages and forms of knowledge may have. There are four instances that illustrate how the EIB is being recast according to a second, more egalitarian definition. These can be summarized as 1) "taking the floor," 2) "giving voice" to indigenous language children, 3) reversing dominant language ideologies, and (4) appropriating social media.

In changed practices, newly appointed bilingual teachers challenge the traditional use of bilingual resources in classrooms by more frequently using Wichi in various micro-activities and discursive sequences. The indigenous language is no longer used only for mediation and repairs, nor only in side sequences; increasingly, it is also used for central aspects of the classroom discourse, communicating core content—taking the floor.

In classrooms with Spanish-only teachers, Wichi children are typically described as quiet and passive, as observers who rarely get involved in classroom activities. As the teacher doesn't speak their language and the children are limitedly competent in Spanish, classroom activities are mainly structured in initiation-response-feedback (IRF) exchanges. In these exchanges, Wichi children are addressed either with yes/no questions, or with questions preformatted to facilitate learner's verbal contribution with very little space for creativity.

In bilingual classrooms with Wichi teachers, the communicative patterns are much more interactive, as they invite the pupils to participate, give their opinions, or ask questions. Such discursive exchanges are more diverse, affording children better learning opportunities than otherwise.

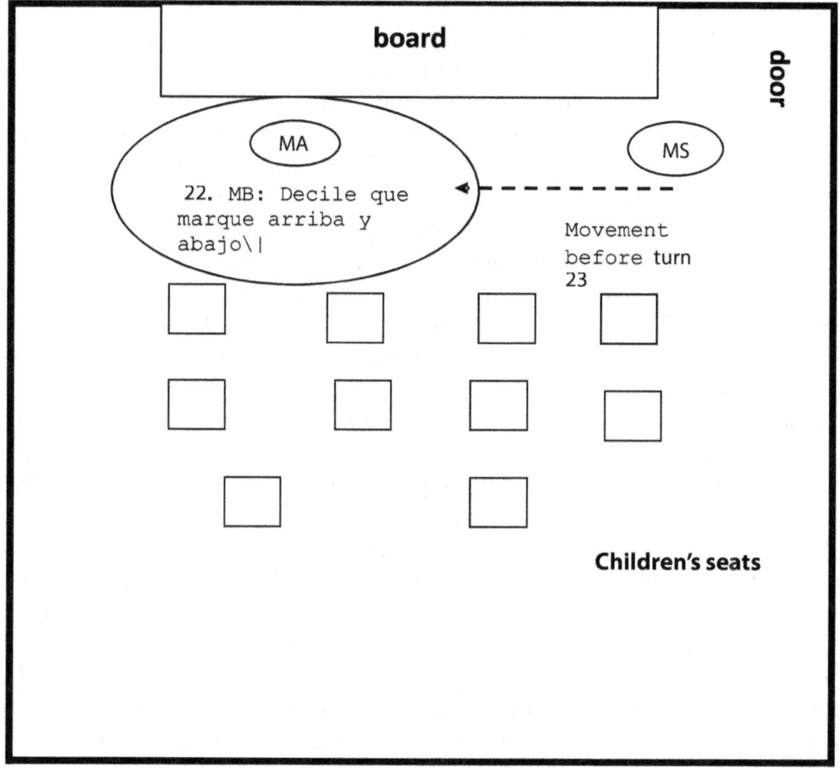

Figure 10.1. Spanish-Wichi bilingual classroom layout

A new bilingual practice in classrooms allows for the more extensive use of the indigenous language, even with Spanish L1 learners. Wichi teachers have been found to use both Wichi and Spanish in their classrooms. Although Spanish is the preferred language for addressing non-Wichi pupils, some explanations will continue in Wichi without translating, thus abandoning the bilingual mode of code-switching and code-mixing. These teacher practices invite non-Wichi pupils to do the same, thus legitimating bilingual repertoires and casting Wichi into a more constructive role than transitional and supportive. This disputes a traditional language ideology and prevailing normative perception that indigenous languages are only for indigenous people.

The phenomenal increase of virtual interaction on social networks like Facebook has changed patterns of bilingualism in that Wichi people interact and so also promote literacy in their L1. Through social networks students expand writing practices and create virtual spaces that are "Wichi." To participate in such virtual conversations, non-Wichi people are pushed to develop their Wichi proficiency. These uses challenge another language ideology in Argentina related to indigenous languages, namely that they belong to the past and that the only authentic uses are ones of orality.

It is important to contextualize these changed patterns of bilingual language use by noting new forms of indigenous organization and the emergence of new social sectors in Argentina. Everyday activities are described in collective terms in relation to new spaces and new positions that native teachers from indigenous communities have claimed for themselves. For example, shared training spaces have been established where native teachers exchange information about their experiences and discuss ways of organizing classrooms and producing teaching materials. Local transformations of educational practices are situated within other social changes. Specifically, there have recently been changes in local power relations and the emergence of new social categories related to language and bilingualism. From these new social categories and positions, legislation has been approved which enables native people to manage the schools in their own communities and legitimates alternative models of education and community participation. Through autonomous community management of schools indigenous teachers can transform the asymmetry long prevalent in the classrooms where they work. Also, colonial practices that persist in schools can be turned around.

Within a neoliberal frame, bilingual programs in minoritized languages are not valued, and their implementation reproduces deep asymmetries. Their design and implementation by the administration has contributed to the reinforcement of educational inequality. However, the analysis of the evolution of this EIB program and of the programs proposed by decolonial and anti-neoliberal movements in Latin America shows how, in order to build and implement bilingual programs that do not subordinate languages and participants, it is necessary to challenge the discrediting and delegitimizing representations of languages, cultures, and communities rooted in a colonial episteme, and to produce new knowledge that shapes and vitalizes new practices. These new kinds of knowledge and practices become possible only when members of the Wichi community have had access to education. However, a more profound transformation seems to be required in order to reinforce Wichi students and teachers' social position, and the autonomy of the community in deciding programs, content, and methods. The state still controls the land and associated means of subsistence (soy, timber, fishing, etc.); it also allows or impedes their appropriation by other groups. Thus, even where there is resistance to limiting structures, the bilingual program still has to struggle against a neoliberal logic (see Baronnet 2009 for the accomplishments in the Zapatista autonomous education system).

Conclusions

The aim of this chapter has been to give insights into how various late-capitalist and postcolonial regimes recast new forms of diversity (often into old molds) through the implementation of language-education policies and programs. In relation to this issue, the authors have emphasized the contradictions between an inclusive national language-in-education policy and classroom practices which effectively deny the multilingual capacities of students and their home communities. Even within the context of political changes oriented to the democratization of society, educational programs still reproduce hierarchies of value, which assign a different value to different languages, ethnic groups, and social classes. Neoliberal policies have contributed to growing inequalities around the globe and to worsening living conditions for the majority of the world's people. Transferring public wealth to private concerns, the conditions of citizens' access to education and other services become restricted. Neoliberal economies also have a strong impact on education, and as a result, the implementation of educational programs is shaped by the demand of schools to be profitable, as well as the demands of students to become productive and gain financial rewards. These demands present education in languages which do not have a crucial role in linguistic and economic markets as a nonprofitable endeavor. Following this logic, national languages are competing with English as languages of instruction in their own countries, and minority language programs are not seen as a priority. However, neoliberal economies and coloniality appear deeply interconnected, and because of that, the implementation of educational programs is also shaped according to colonial heritage both in terms of the maintenance of colonial knowledge and ideologies, and of social relations. Language programs oriented to the linguistic socialization of migrants are not seen as a priority, and do not reinforce the prestige of schools in neoliberal competition for resources.

Furthermore, schools with high numbers of immigrant children and minority-language speakers may overtly seem to be accommodating them, but in practice do not provide them with the linguistic and cultural capital they need. In fact, students report different experiences that indicate covert policies that are severely alienating. The examples of minority-language students in the United States analyzed above broaden our understanding of the role of everyday communicative practices and interactions in the construction of hierarchical ethnic and racial relations in schools, and ultimately, in the exclusion of immigrant and minority children in educational systems. Thus, the resulting social and ethnic relations again reinforce colonial hierarchies of superiority and inferiority among pupils and position migrants and minority students as nonlegitimate participants in education. The way in which the current world-system has historically depended on the supply of cheap labor and low-cost resources from the periphery, presents an order that will not be changed if schools fail to eliminate inequality.

Finally, the management of a bilingual education program in Argentina shows the extent to which minority-language programs reproduce language and social hierarchies, which have the effect of constructing indigenous language communities as second-class citizens. Thus, bilingual programs that apparently intend to improve the life chances and educational choices of students can reproduce language hierarchies that also betray social and racial prejudice. However, when new patterns of bilingual language use are introduced in EIB-schools, significant changes are detected. These changes are facilitating the emergence of new groups who are claiming their rights within a contested space in the field of languages and education. The struggle for autonomy in school management has a crucial role in these changes.

The cases of which this chapter gives account, in fact lead to the conclusion that social processes such as prevalent neoliberalism, the transnational division of labor, and the persistence of coloniality feed off each other. Hence, the need arises to unify social struggles against neoliberalism in education and struggles against the prevalence of a colonial episteme, which (re)produces hierarchies of superiority and inferiority. Neoliberalism is sharpening social differences, and frustrating the access of a significant part of the population to the more valuable resources. Only by curbing privatization of education, and by supporting the autonomy, the participation, and the agency of ethnic and indigenous social movements in their struggles, can new knowledge and inclusive educational programs emerge.

Notes

1. See also Fernández González (2014) for an analysis of the impact of this imaginary in the Spanish educational law.
2. Versus *colonialism*, which denotes a political and economic relation in which the sovereignty of a nation or a people rests on the power of another nation, which makes the dominant nation an empire.
3. See the campaign hashtagged as "Fees Must Fall" which paralyzed teaching and examination processes at virtually all higher education institutions in October and November 2015, and again in 2016.

References

Alexander, Neville. 2002. "Linguistic Rights, Language Planning and Democracy in Post-apartheid South Africa." *Language Policy: Lessons from Global Models.* Monterey, CA: Monterey Institute of International Studies.

———. 2003. *Language Education Policy, National and Sub-national Identities in South Africa. Reference Study for the Language Policy Division.* Strasbourg: Council of Europe. https://www.coe.int/t/dg4/linguistic/Source/AlexanderEN.pdf.

Anthonissen, Christine. 2013. ""With English the World Is More Open to You..." - Language Shift as Marker of Social Transformation." *English Today* 29 (1): 28–35.

Baronnet, Bruno. 2009. "Autonomía y Educación Indígena: las Escuelas Zapatistas de las Cañadas de la Selva Lacandona de Chiapas." PhD diss., Colegio de México.

Besnier, Nikko. 1993. "Literacy and Feelings: The Encoding of Affect in Nukulaelae Letters." In *Cross-Cultural Approaches to Literacy*, edited by Brian V. Street, 62–86. Cambridge: Cambridge University Press.

Blommaert, Jan. 2006. "Language Policy and National Identity." In *An Introduction to Language Policy: Theory and Method*, edited by Tommaso Ricento, 238–54. Oxford: Blackwell.

Bourdieu, Pierre. 1991. *Language and Symbolic Power*. Stanford: Stanford University Press.

Duchêne, Alexandre. 2011. "Néolibéralisme, Inégalités Sociales et Plurilinguismes: L'exploitation des Ressources Langagières et des Locuteurs." *Langage & Société* 136:81–106.

Duchêne, Alexandre, and Monica Heller, editors. 2012. *Language in Late Capitalism: Pride and Profit*. New York: Routledge.

Duchêne, Alexandre, Melissa Moyer, and Celia Roberts, editors. 2013. *Language, Migration and Social (In) equality: A Critical Sociolinguistic. Perspective on Institutions and Work*. Bristol: Multilingual Matters.

Duranti, Alessandro. 1997. "Universal and Culture-Specific Properties of Greetings." *Journal of Linguistic Anthropology* 7:63–97.

Eurydice. 2006. *Content and Language Integrated Learning (CLIL) at School in Europe*. Brussels: European Commission.

———. 2008. *Key Data on Teaching Languages at School in Europe*. Brussels: European Commission.

Fernández González, Noelia. 2015. "Pisa como instrumento de legitimación de la reforma de la LOMCE." *Bordón* 67 (1): 165–78. http://recyt.fecyt.es/index.php/BORDON/article/viewFile/Bordon.2015.67100/17201.

Fraser, Nancy. 2003. "From Discipline to Flexibilization? Rereading Foucault in the Shadow of Globalization." *Constellations* 10 (2): 160–71.

Flubacher, Mi-Cha, and Alfonso del Percio, editors. 2016. *Language, Education and Social Change: A. Critical View on Neoliberalism*. Bristol: Multilingual Matters.

García-Sánchez, Inmaculada M. 2014. *Language and Muslim Immigrant Childhoods: The Politics of Belonging*. Oxford: Blackwell-Wiley.

Grosfoguel, Ramón. 2011. "Decolonizing Post-Colonial Studies and Paradigms of Political-Economy: Transmodernity, Decolonial Thinking, and Global Coloniality. Transmodernity." *Journal of Peripheral Cultural Production of the Luso-Hispanic World* 1 (1): 1–37.

Heugh, Kathleen. 2007. "Language and Literacy Issues in South Africa." In *Global Issues in Language, Education and Development: Perspectives from Postcolonial Countries*, edited by Naz Rasool, 187–218. Clevedon, Eng.: Multilingual Matters.

Holborow, Marnie. 2015. *Language and Neoliberalism*. London: Routledge.

Lipman, Pauline. 2011a. *The New Political Economy of Urban Education: Neoliberalism, Race, and the Right to the City*. New York: Routledge.

———. 2011b. "Neoliberal Education Restructuring." *Monthly Review* 63 (03). http://monthlyreview.org/2011/07/01/neoliberal-education-restructuring/

Macpherson, Ian, Susan Robertson, and Geoffrey Walford, editors. 2014. *Education, Privatization and Social Justice: Case Studies from Africa, South Asia and South East Asia*. Oxford: Symposium Books.

Maldonado-Torres, Nelson. 2007. "On the Coloniality of Being." *Cultural Studies* 21 (2): 240–70.

Martín Rojo, Luisa. 2010. *Constructing Inequality in Multilingual Classrooms*. Berlin: DeGruyter Mouton.

———. 2016. "Language and Power." In *The Oxford Handbook of Language and Society*, edited by Ofelia Garcia, Max Spotti, and Nelson Flores. Oxford: Oxford University Press.

Mignolo, Walter D., and Arturo Escobar, editors. 2009. *Globalization and the Decolonial Option*. London: Routledge.

Pérez-Milans, Miguel. 2011. "Being a Chinese Newcomer in Madrid Compulsory Education: Ideological Constructions in Language Education Practice." *Journal of Pragmatics* 43 (4): 1005–22.

———, ed. 2015a. "Language Education Policy in Late Modernity: Insights from Situated Approaches." *Language Policy* 14 (2): 183–89.

———. 2015b. "Mandarin Chinese in London Education: Language Aspirations in a Working-Class Secondary School." *Language Policy* 14 (2): 153–81.

Plüddemann, Peter. 2015. "Unlocking the Grid: Language-in-Education Policy Realisation in Post-apartheid South Africa." *Language and Education*, 29 (3): 186–99.
Plüddemann, Peter, Daryl Braam, Michele October, and Zola Wababa. 2004. "Dual-Medium and Parallel Medium Schooling in the Western Cape: From Default to Design." *Occasional Paper* 17:1–48.
Pratt, Mary Louise. 1991. "Arts of the Contact Zone." *Profession* 91:33–40.
Probyn, Margie. 2005. "Learning Science through the Medium of English: What Do Grade 8 Learners Say?" *Southern African Linguistics and Applied Language Studies* 23 (4): 369–92.
Relaño-Pastor, Ana María. 2015. "The Commodification of English in 'Madrid, comunidad bilingüe': Insights from the CLIL Classroom." *Journal of Language Policy* 14 (2): 131–52.
Rizvi, Fazal, and Bob Lingard. 2010. *Globalizing Education Policy*. London: Routledge.
Rossiter, Ned. 2003. "Processual Media Theory." *Symploke* 11 (1–2): 104–31.
Sigcau, Nompucuko Eurica. 2004. "Mother-Tongue Education: A Key to Success." In *Researching the Language of Instruction in Tanzania and South Africa*, edited by Birgit Brock-Utne, Zubeida Desai, and Martha Qorro, 239–54. Cape Town: African Minds.
Statistics South Africa. 2001. "Stages in the Life Cycle of South Africans." *Pretoria: Statistics South Africa*. http://www.statssa.gov.za/publications/C2001Stages/C2001Stages.pdf.
———. 2011. "A profile of education enrolment, attainment and progression in South Africa." http://www.statssa.gov.za/publications/Report-03-01-81/Report-03-01-812011.pdf.
———. 2015. "Education Costs Continue to Outstrip Inflation." *Economy Data Stories*, April 22. Accessed on April 2016. http://www.statssa.gov.za/?p=4460.
Unamuno, Virginia. 2015. "Los Hacedores de la EIB: un Acercamiento a las Políticas Lingüístico-educativas desde las Aulas Bilingües del Chaco." *Archivos Analíticos de Políticas Educativas* 23 (101): 1–30.
Urciuoli, Bonny. 2010. "Neoliberal Education: Preparing the Student for the New Workplace." In *Ethnographies of Neoliberalism*, edited by Carol J. Greenhouse, 16–176. Philadelphia: Pennsylvania University Press.
van Amersfoort, Arthur. 2008. "The Legacy of Empire: Post-colonial Immigrants in Western Europe." Migration Citizenship Education: Information Platform 2008, vol. 2008. European Policy. University of Amsterdam Digital repository: Institute for Migration & Ethnic Studies (IMES). http://dare.uva.nl/record/1/301392.
Wallerstein, Inmanuel. 1979. *El Moderno Sistema Mundial. La Agricultura Capitalista y los Orígenes de la Economía-mundo Europea en el Siglo XVI*. Madrid: Siglo XXI Editores.
———. 2011. *The Modern World-System IV: Centrist Liberalism Triumphant, 1789–1914*. Berkeley: University of California Press.
World Bank. 2012. "World Development Indicators 2012." Data Blog. *World Bank*. Accessed on August 3, 2016. http://data.worldbank.org/news/world-development-indicators-2012-now-available.

Chapter 11

Diversity in School

Monolingual Ideologies versus Multilingual Practices

ANNA DE FINA

CONTACT ZONES, OR "SOCIAL spaces where cultures meet, clash and grapple with each other" (Pratt, 1991, 34) have become more and more widespread in the late modern world as globalization has radically increased population flows and transnational exchanges. Thus, even countries that have been traditional sites of emigration rather than immigration, such as Italy, have seen a complete reversal, turning into points of arrival for people from all over the globe. Indeed, economic migration of foreign workers has become one of the most significant phenomena in the social life of modern Italy. Over the past thirty years, the country has transformed itself completely from a site of massive emigration to a destination for millions of immigrants from a wide spectrum of countries and areas, from Eastern Europe, to Africa, to Asia. This change follows economic trends in all of the European Union. But, while in the 1970s immigration was restricted to North European countries that sought foreign workers either from former colonies or from the Mediterranean basin to employ them in construction and factories (see Calvanese and Pugliese 1988), starting in the 1980s a new kind of migration has taken shape (see King 1993; Cole 1997), involving Italy as well as other southern Mediterranean countries. Recent statistics published by Caritas (2012) report that immigrants in Italy in 2012 were about five million and constituted 18 percent of the population, while in 2003 they constituted only 3.4 percent of the total population (Delli Zotti et al. 2011). According to Cole (1997), new migrants come mainly from non-European countries, and are mostly "unsolicited and often unregulated and undocumented" (4). New migrants started targeting Italy due to the absence of tight controls and the existence of a vast informal market. Hence their numbers have been growing exponentially from the 1990s to the present. As noted by Cole and Booth (2007), immigrants' contribution to the economy in Italy depends on local markets (13). While in the North they find employment in the small and medium-sized factories, in other areas (particularly in the South) they perform low-skilled, temporary jobs, mostly in domestic services, in agriculture as temporal workers, and in the tertiary industry.

Italian schools have been deeply affected by these changes, as they have experienced an exponential increase in the number of migrant or migrant-origin children attending. According to the most recent statistics published by the Ministry of Education (2013), in the school year 2012–13, there were 786,630 foreign students (i.e., students who do not have Italian citizenship, independently of where they were born) in Italian schools, having arrived from more than two hundred countries. This number represents an increase of 4 percent with respect to the previous year. The greatest number of immigrant children (276,129) is concentrated in primary schools. More in general, the number of foreign-born children in Italian schools has gone from less than 60 in 1996 to over 600,000 in 2008 (Delli Zotti et al. 2011), to about 8,000,000 today: a dramatic increase.

Italian schools are quite unprepared to face this change and as a result, foreign students are consistently disadvantaged with respect to Italian students. Indeed, 38 percent of foreign-born students are delayed, that is they are attending a level that corresponds to a younger age than their actual age, compared with 11.6 percent for Italian children (Ministry of Education, 2013). In addition, 80 percent of youth of immigrant origin end up in technical and professional schools, which are less prestigious than other types of schools like *licei* (high schools based on a liberal art curriculum). Other than numbers and statistics, very little research exists on immigrant children in Italian schools, probably due to the recent nature of this phenomenon. The study presented here aims at contributing to cover this gap. In particular, I investigate linguistic and interactional practices among children and teachers in a primary education classroom with a significant percentage of migrant children as a window into the analysis of the processes of change that diversity has brought about in Italian schools.

The Study

Because Italian schools have become contact zones par excellence, they are an interesting vantage point for the study of intersections between institutionally and locally driven social processes within contact zones. In particular, it is important to find out how teachers and students manage this new reality of diversity in a country that has traditionally been homogeneous, at least at an ethnic and racial level. The study presented in this chapter was designed to investigate precisely this question. Specifically, I was interested in observing classroom interaction among the children and with the teacher to understand how immigrant children or children of immigrant origins fit within Italian schools, both linguistically and socially, and what kinds of strategies teachers used to teach and integrate them. In this chapter I focus on language ideologies and their relations with language practices. The data come from an ethnographic study conducted in the spring of 2011 in one fifth-grade elementary school in an inner-city area in Palermo: the Istituto Statate Comprensivo Turrisi Colonna. The study consisted of intensive (two or three hours per session) participant observations of classroom activities and breaks, video and audiotaping, and interviews with children and teachers. Observations were carried out between January and March of 2011, but video recording continued until June 2011 with the teacher self-recording during some lessons in April and May of the same year. Turrisi Colonna was chosen as a research site because it is an institution with a high presence of immigrant children. Migration of foreign workers in Palermo has been increasing dramatically in the last twenty years, and there are now about fifteen thousand foreign students in the city schools. In Turrisi Colonna about one third (28.57 percent) of the students are immigrant or immigrant-origin children. Countries from which students originate in the school, according to a 2010 report, were Tunisia, Morocco, Bangladesh, Mauritius, Pakistan, Sri Lanka, Ghana, China, Ivory Coast, Philippines, Ecuador, Cameroon, India, Romania, and former Yugoslavia. As is the case in many other schools of Palermo, teachers and administrators struggle to accommodate the needs of such a diverse population, but they also deal with the very complex social reality of inner-city areas. Many of the children and teenagers who attend the school come from low-income families and often experience difficult social conditions, for example unemployment or incarceration of parents or relatives, forms of abuse of all kinds, and rampant criminality in the area where they live. As a consequence, marginalization and school failure are common.

The classroom that I observed was composed of eighteen students: ten boys and eight girls. Of these, eleven (seven boys and four girls) were born in Sicily of Italian parents, five were born abroad of foreign parents, and two were born in Sicily of Tunisian parents. Among the foreign-born children, three girls were from Bangladesh, one was girl from Sri Lanka, and one boy was from Morocco. Among the Sicilian children, one girl was a special-needs student. The classroom teachers were two women. One taught science and math, while the other taught Italian, history, and foreign language. There was also one teacher devoted to the special-needs student (see table 11.1).

Table 11.1. Class composition

Italian parents	Foreign born	Born in Italy of foreign parents
7 boys	1 boy (Morocco)	2 boys (Tunisia)
4 girls	4 girls (3 Bangladesh, 1 Sri Lanka)	
Total boys = 10 Total girls = 8 (including special needs student)		
2 regular teachers, 1 special needs teacher 18 children age 10/11		

As mentioned, data for this chapter come from recordings of classroom interaction among children, between children and teachers, and interviews with teachers and children. The total number of hours recorded was thirty-six, but the present chapter is based on transcripts that cover about twelve hours distributed across six days of observation. My role in the classroom was that of a participant observer: for the most part I sat next to the children or the teacher and took notes when I was not interviewing, but often I helped the children do their work in class. I placed one recorder on the teacher's desk and another recorder on a student's desk. I moved it from time to time so that recordings would reflect both face-to-face interactions with the teacher and student-to-student conversations. That way I was able to capture what was going on at different levels. As mentioned, I complemented the recordings with interview data.

Language Ideologies and Practices

In this paper I focus on the analysis of language practices and language ideologies as conveyed or openly declared within those practices, and I use such analysis as a point of entry into the study of the insertion of foreign children into Italian schools, which in turn can provide insights into the social roles of Italian immigrants in Sicily/Italy and their relations with the local population within contact zones. I see language practices as one of the most important sites for research into ideologies about self and others, cultural beliefs, and cultural practices (see Fairclough 1989). Such cultural practices lay the foundations for the production and reproduction of social relations and conditions well beyond the school. Indeed, school practices may greatly contribute to the future development of students' material life choices, to their perceptions of self and others, and to their linguistic behaviors (Martin-Jones 2007). The study of the interconnections between school ideologies and practices and the reproduction of social inequalities has a long and established tradition in sociolinguistics, as a great deal of research has shown how school practices may help reproduce inequalities. Teachers and institutional voices may do so among other things, by ignoring students' specific cultural traditions (Michaels 1981; Gee 1987; Hymes 1996), by promoting monolingual and monocultural ideologies (Martín Rojo 2010 and Martín Rojo et al. this volume; Rampton 2006), and by strengthening deficit hypotheses about minorities (Ogbu 2003). As shown by Martín Rojo (2010) for example, in her study of immigrant children in schools in Madrid, school practices indirectly contributed to the construction of inequality by relegating migrant children to insignificant roles in class, by strengthening prejudice about their abilities and potential as students and individuals, by diminishing their self-esteem, and by reproducing social hierarchies and scales among minority groups (see also Martín Rojo et al., this volume). At the same time, relations between local practices and ideologies, mainstream ideologies, social relations, and material conditions cannot be regarded in a mechanistic way, as determined by macro-phenomena of social exclusion and the exercise of power. As argued by Blommaert (2007), interaction and semiotic activities are dynamic and emergent practices that make different scales and levels of indexicality continuously relevant and thus offer participants a variety of ways to convey and negotiate roles and identities. For example, while certain school routines may be the basis for constructing migrant versus local identities based on cultural or ethnic differences, other routines may make relevant a sense of class differences that cuts across ethnic divides. And, while flows of migrants to Italian schools can ultimately be explained in terms of macroeconomic fluxes, how immigrants actually live, express themselves, and contribute to society may vary to a very great extent depending on myriad factors. Even the way they contribute to classrooms may deviate in significant ways from what one would expect. Thus, another guiding principle of this work is that the observation and close study of the local level and of the "interaction order" (Goffman 1983) provides the first and most important step in the study of social phenomena because it allows researchers to tap into participants' own constructions of social reality, into their own unique use of linguistic resources, and into ways in which indexicalities are created and negotiated in specific communities. Such insights can only be attained through ethnographic approaches to data. In the analysis presented below I focus on the following questions:

1. How are linguistic and cultural differences dealt with in class by teachers and students?
2. How are linguistic resources used by teachers and students?
3. What kind of ideological stances are implicit in classroom language practices?

Linguistic and Cultural Difference

Before I discuss how teachers and students deal with linguistic and cultural differences, I will give a general description of the language repertoires available to participants and on the different degrees of access to different linguistic resources.

Given the classroom composition, students' linguistic ability in Italian varied. In particular, while all the boys were perfectly fluent in Italian, two of the girls were not. One girl from Sri Lanka, Sena, had recently arrived in Italy and was in the process of acquiring Italian. She had a teacher who worked with her individually. Sena didn't speak much in the interactions with teachers, but she did speak Italian with her classmates. She was able to carry on a conversation in Italian and to do her homework with the help of the other girls. The second girl, Parveen, was born in Bangladesh and had been in Italy for one and a half years. She had a preference for speaking Bangla and thus I never heard her speaking Italian. She almost exclusively spoke with her girlfriends from Bangladesh and did not interact with the rest of the class. The other two Bangladeshi girls (Bandi and Nandita) were perfectly fluent in Italian.

The three boys of foreign origins were all fluent in Italian. Indeed, the two boys from Tunisia, Rym and Motaz, were born in Palermo, while their parents were born in Tunisia. The Moroccan boy, Medhi, had been in Sicily for three years (see table 11.2).

As in most public Italian schools, a monolingual ideology seems to prevail among teachers. It was clear that the preferred language of communication in student-teacher interaction was Italian. Such preference, which was usually indexed by the absolute predominance of turns in Italian in teacher-student interaction, was

Table 11.2. Foreign-born and foreign-origins children

Gender	Birthplace	Origin	Time in Italy	Italian language competence
Male (Rym)	Palermo	Tunisia	—	Native-like
Male (Motaz)	Palermo	Tunisia	—	Native-like
Male (Medhi)	Morocco	—	3 years	Native-like
Female (Bani)	Bangladesh	—	2 ½ years	Native-like
Female (Nandita)	Bangladesh	—	8 years	Native-like
Female (Parveen)	Bangladesh	—	3 years	Little competence (no Italian spoken)
Female (Sena)	Sri Lanka	—	1 year	In process of learning (spoke Italian with peers)

sometimes enounced by teachers, who insisted that no language other than Italian was to be used during lessons. Thus, Italian was presented as the legitimate language for classroom interactions. Teachers sometimes openly voiced this rule in terms of a prohibition against speaking other languages. For example in the following fragment Parveen and Bani are speaking in Bangla while doing a drawing for a classroom task.

Example 1

1. Ba *Tui jodi eita des tahole eita bujha jabe? Tui eta halka*
2. *kore de eta garho kore de.*
3. Parv *Eita beshi garo! Erokom beshi garo.*
4. T1 Eh! Che lingua stiamo parlando?
5. Ba Come devi colorare.

Translation

1. Ba *Will it be nice if I use this color? If I use a light color in this and a darker*
2. *color on that.*
3. Parv *That's too dark! It's too dark.*
4. T1 Eh! What language are we speaking?
5. Ba The way you have to color.

The teacher's question in line 3 here is to be interpreted as a request to stop using Bangla and talk in Italian and indeed Bani responds by immediately switching into Italian and by explaining to the teacher what she was talking about with Parveen.

It is noteworthy that students themselves used the "Italian-only rule" to suit their own communicative objectives. For example, while the Bangladeshi girls spoke in Bangla a lot of the time among themselves, they sometimes enounced the monolingual norm when they were fighting about something. An instance of this strategy can be seen in the following fragment taken during a verbal confrontation between Nandita and Bani, who are friends but also constantly compete with each other.

Example 2

1.	Na	Parla italiano tu *sc-*
2.	T3	Ah ecco, parla italiano!
3.		Com'è che hai detto?
4.	Ba	Parla italiano.

Translation

1.	Na	Speak in Italian, you *st-*
2.	T3	That's right, speak Italian!
3.		What did you say?
4.	Ba	Speak in Italian.

Here, Nandita is addressing Bani and ordering her to speak Italian. She is most likely going to utter an insult in Sicilian that she often uses when dealing with Bani (*scimunita*: "stupid" in Sicilian), but she self-repairs and does not continue. T3 (who is the special-needs teacher) overhears the conversation and repeats the instruction (it's not clear with what objective) in lines 2 and 3, but she also asks Nandita what she said in order to indicate that she should not use insults. Similarly, Sicilian children would sometimes complain to the teacher when the girls were speaking in Bangla as a form of revenge because they could not understand what was being said. Thus, all in all, we find the "Italian-only rule" as an implicit principle of classroom communication that has been internalized by students.

However, as mentioned in the description of language repertoires, children had access to a variety of languages. Foreign-born children all spoke the language of their home (that is Bangladeshi, Sri Lankan, and Moroccan or Tunisian Arab). On the other hand, all Sicilian children spoke Sicilian (very likely their home language) besides Italian. Within peer talk, all male children (independently of origins) demonstrated a preference for the Sicilian dialect. A clarification is in order here in regards to this variety. Sicilian dialect (as many other Italian vernaculars) is not a dialect of Italian, but a different language altogether. Sicilian is derived from spoken Latin and has been influenced by Spanish, Arab, and other languages of conquerors of the island. There is little or no intelligibility between Italian and Sicilian. Sicilian is regarded as a dialect, as many of the regional languages in Italy, basically because it is spoken locally and by a minority of the Italian population.

Among the foreign-born girls, peer talk was in Bangla, Italian (and occasionally English) when the conversation involved the Sri Lankan girl, and Italian when the conversation involved Sicilian girls. Use of Sicilian dialect among girls (independently of origins) was rare and restricted to speech acts such as teasing and insulting (see the case of example 2). The other official language of classroom interaction was English. Children received three hours of instruction in English per week. They were taught in an extremely traditional way, through reading of texts, translation, and vocabulary repetition. The Bangladeshi girls demonstrated a clear advantage in English with respect to their Sicilian counterparts, but in general, the English taught at school was exclusively seen as a kind of "academic" language, with little resemblance to a live tool of communication (as it appeared to be when children used bits of English in peer interaction).

As noted above, although all the foreign-origin children declared in the interviews that they spoke the language of their home with their parents, only the Bangladeshi girls used Bangla as a language for peer communication. This was in part due to the fact that they were all born abroad, while among foreign-origin boys only one was born in Morocco. The other two were born in Sicily from Tunisian parents and so they preferred to speak Italian and Sicilian. I suspect, though, that the quasi-total absence of Arab in peer interaction was due to fear of prejudice and exclusion. Two episodes that took place in class support this interpretation. One is taken from my ethnographic notes.

One day, I was sitting next to Medhi. I wrote the following in my notes:

> Medhi wants to tell me the time in English and when he does, he says it quite well. Then he repeats it to G. (the teacher), who jokingly asks him to say it in French as well. So I ask him to tell me in Moroccan Arab and he does not respond. When I insist he says 'no' and when I ask why he tells me 'because I am ashamed.'

This exchange is interesting for two reasons. On the one hand we see that the teacher does not take the opportunity to introduce Mohammed's language to the other kids, but only mentions French as a possible alternative for translation. And we should note that French is, with English, the typical foreign language taught in Italian schools. On the other hand, although Medhi's shame to speak his home language may be due to the fact that children do not like to be different from their peers, it can also be read as a lack of confidence in the significance of a language that is not particularly valued, a lack of confidence that we do not see in the case of the girls. The second episode is represented by a telling exchange in the following fragment, which is taken again from a conversation among the immigrant girls. The class is in the computer room. Bani is giving instructions to Sena about the way to Google something on the computer.

Example 3

1	Ba	Scrivi il nome quello che vuoi e poi di Sicilia e viene quello
2	Na	((imitating)) di Sici:::::lia!
3	Ba	Tu stare malata!
4	Na	Malata vatinni tu!
5	Ba	Nandita è una uhm,
6	Na	Se::: a me dda (..) non ci sono
7	Ba	Ma come pa::rli? Sembra come un tunisino!
8	Na	Sì sono tunisina per questo parlo (...)

Translation

1	Ba	Write the name you want then from Sicily and that comes up
2	Na	((imitating)) from Si::::cily!
3	Ba	You be ill!

4	Na	Ill! You go away!
5	Ba	Nandita is a uhm
6	Na	Yea:::h to me there (..) I am not
7	Ba	But how are you speaking? You seem like a Tunisian!
8	Na	Yes I am a Tunisian that's why I speak (...)

Nandita is making fun of the way Bani speaks to Sena. She imitates her with an exaggerated lengthening of the vowels in the word "Sicily" (line 2), so Bani retorts with a frequently used insult: "You are ill!" but notice that she utters it in a kind of 'foreigner talk' (she uses the infinitive of the verb *to be* instead of the present indicative in "You be ill," line 3) that she usually reserves for Sena. Nandita responds also mixing her counter insult with Sicilian ("You go away!"). At this point, Bani makes fun of the way Nandita speaks and tells her that she speaks like a Tunisian, which in this context is clearly an insult (line 7). This episode compounds with Mohammed's reticence in speaking his language, seeming to support the conclusion that Arabic (no matter whether Tunisian or Moroccan given that Sicilians are very likely unable to differentiate) does not enjoy much prestige as a foreign language in Sicily. This status of the language would be consistent with the status of Northern African immigrants to Sicily who are among the most-established immigrant groups, but also among the ones who regularly perform the lowest paid jobs (see Amoruso 2007). There is no space in this chapter to develop such a theme, but I think that our first analysis of the data shows that languages in the classroom are implicitly put in a hierarchical relation in terms of their suitability for institutional communication. In this hierarchy Italian comes first, closely followed by traditional foreign languages such as English and potentially French, while immigrant languages are not admitted. I will turn to the status of Sicilian presently.

This language ideology contrasts with a reality of great linguistic dynamicity in the classroom. No matter how much teachers preach against using languages other than Italian, children show a lively interest in each other's language, a tendency to use 'translingual practices' (i.e., mixtures between different languages, foreigner talk and, in the case of the three immigrant girls, also a great deal of Bangla) in their communications (see Canagarajah 2013). Boys also use a great deal of Sicilian dialect and girls use it too, though in a more aimed way. The tendency to play with languages is not unique to this classroom as it has been noted in other studies of peer interaction among children and teenagers of different language backgrounds (see Lytra 2007; Rampton 2006). Examples of these attitudes and practices can be found in the following fragments. In the first fragment Bani (who is from Bangladesh) is talking to Sena, who is from Sri Lanka. It is to be noted that Bani, Nandita, and Parveen showed a keen liking for Sena and used every occasion to help her with school tasks and to teach her how to do things. It is interesting here however, that Bani seems to be trying to learn Tamil words for numbers from Sena.

Example 4

1.	Se	Che cos'è?
2.	Ba	*Anda sunda munda mala* e poi cosa c'è? Sena!
3.		dillo! *Anda sunda munda mala?* E poi?
4.	Se	*Andu? Ara,*
5.	Ba	*Andu?*
6.	Se	*Ara.*
7.	Ba	*Andu? Ara* significa sei cinque e sei *andu, ara.*
8.		facile: *anda sunda munda mala.*
9.	Se	Facilissimo ((...)) non lo so cos'è
10.	Ba	E dillo il nome
11.	Se	Cos'è?
12.	Ba	Francesco?
13.	Se	Si.
14.	Ba	E il nome lo stesso Francesco guarda eh tu quando eri in Sri Lanka come ti chiami, com'era il
15.		tuo nome? Sena. Quindi pure qui Sena.

Translation

1.	Ba	*Anda sunda munda mala* and then what? Sena!
2.		say it! *Anda sunda munda mala*? And then?
3.	Se	*Andu? Ara,*
4.	Ba	*Andu?*
5.	Se	*Ara.*
6.	Ba	*Andu? Ara* means six five and six *andu, ara.*
7.		easy: *anda sunda munda mala.*
8.	Se	Very easy ((...)) I don't know what that is.
9.	Ba	And say it the name.
10.	Se	What is it?
11.	Ba	Francesco?
12.	Se	Yes.
13.	Ba	And the name is the same Francesco, look eh when you were in Sri Lanka. What is your
14.		name, how was your name? Sena. So it is Sena also here.

In line 4 Bani is taking the role of language learner. She is practicing how to say the numbers in Tamil and she is prodding Sena to say them (see lines 1–2 and 6–7). She has clearly done this before, as she appears to know some of the words already. After they have rehearsed the numbers, Bani proceeds to help Sena find the name of a character that they are working with on the computer, with an additional explanation of how names do not change from one country to the other.

As can be imagined, a great deal of curiosity is also reserved to "bad words" in a foreign language. Thus, children seemed eager to learn how to insult each other in their different languages. The boys, for example, had learned certain insults in Bangla and used them mainly against the girls. Rym (one of the Tunisian children) was particularly aggressive against Bani and Nandita and in a confrontation with her he resorted to Arab to insult Bani so that she would not understand. On this occasion, the trouble between the children had started when Motaz had called Nandita rude because she had asked a question to the teacher. Both Rym and Bani entered the conversation and the exchange between the two quickly developed into a barrage of insults in Tunisian, and later in Bangla. But, interestingly the insults in Bangla were uttered by the boys, who were rehearsing expressions that they had learned, not by the girls.

I reproduce below some fragments of this exchange, which was for the most part not very clearly audible on tape because it all took place while the teacher was explaining the functioning of the human heart.

Example 5

1.	Na	Maestra! maestra! ma il dottore non si è stancato stanca mai?
2.	Mo	Zitta maleducata! (...)
3.	Ba	Maleducato sei tu!
4.	Rym	E sto parlando con te (...)?
5.	Mo	Ha parlato con te?
6.	Ba	Io ho parlato con te?
7.	Rym	*Ummik Qahba*
8.	Ba	Amucca ca @@

Translation

1.	Na	Teacher! teacher! but the doctor never got gets tired?
2.	Mo	Shut up you rude one! (...)
3.	Ba	You are rude!
4.	Rym	Am I talking to you (...)?
5.	Mo	Did I talk to you?
6.	Ba	Did I talk to you?
7.	Rym	*Ummik Qahba* [your mother is a bitch]
8.	Ba	((imitating)) Amucca ca @@

We see that when Rym insults her in Arabic, Bani tries to imitate him and laughs, but she clearly does not know what she is saying. Later on, the boys start using insults in Bangla as well.

Example 6

1.	Mo	Rym !
2.		((to Bani)) Che vuole dire *chootan*?
3.	Ba	Scemo.
4.	Mo	*Cho:tan, ch:otan*!
5.	Rym	*Cho:Otan*
6.	Mo	*Cho:tan*
7.		*Kutar baicha! chotan*! figlio di cane, scemo.
8.	Rym	Tu sei una faccia di *chotan* e tu sei una faccia di *chotan*.

Translation

1.	Mo	Rym!
2.		((to Bani)) What does *chotan* mean?
3.	Ba	Stupid.
4.	Mo	*Cho:tan, cho:tan!*
5.	Rym	*Cho:Otan*
6.	Mo	*Cho:tan*
7.		*Kutar baicha! chotan*! son of a bitch, stupid.
8.	Rym	You are a *chotan* face and you are a *chotan* face.

Here Motaz is trying to learn new swear words in Bangla, and he asks Bani for the meaning of the word *chotan*, then repeats it and adds it to his repertoire, which already included the Bangla insult "son of a bitch." (kutar baicha). Rym promptly uses the word in Bangla for a bit of translanguaging. He mixes it with Italian "faccia" (face), so producing a new insult: stupid face. The boys continue playing and experimenting with these Bangla expressions.

Example 7

1.	Mo	(...) Com'è "ti do uno schiaffo." come si dice?
2.	Ba	(..)
3.	Mo	Va be' non è parolaccia!
4.	Rym	Come si dice kutta ra baccia
5.	Mo	Ah Bani! Bani! come si dice parolaccia?
6.	Ba	Parolaccia
7.		(...)
8.	Ba	*Kutar baicha.*
9.	Ma	*Kutar baicha*
10.	Mo	Bani, Bani, come si dice
11.	Ba	*Tapo*!
12.	Mo	Ah?
13.	Ba	*Tapo*!
14.	Mo	Rym! *Tapo tapo*!
15.		((to Mario and Rym)) Vuol dire ti do uno schiaffo
16.		((to Bani)) Dì! parla!
17.	Ba	No un'altra volta

Translation

1.	Mo	(...) How is "I slap you." how do you say it?
2.	Ba	(...)
3.	Mo	Come on! it's not a swear word!
4.	Rym	How do you say *Kutar baicha.*
5.	Mo	Ah Bani! Bani! how do you say "swear word"?
6.	Ba	Swear word
7.		(...)

8.	Ba	*Kutar baicha.*
9.	Mario	*Kutar baicha*
10.	Max	Bani, Bani, how do you say it?
11.	Ba	*Tapo*!
12.	Mo	Uh?
13.	Ba	Tapo!
14.	Mo	Rym! *tapo tapo*!
15.		((to Mario and Rym)) It means I slap you.
16.		((to Bani)) Say it! speak!
17.	Ba	No! another time.

Again, in this fragment we see that Motaz goes from insulting Bani to using her as a source of information on swear words in Bangla. Bani needs quite a lot of prodding as she appears to be embarrassed about repeating swear words in her language. In a brief conversation with me on this exchange she argued that the boys had not learned the swear words from her, but from Nandita. In any case, at the end she gives in (line 13) and Motaz immediately shares his newly learned expression with two other boys, Rym and Mario. In this fragment we see that Sicilian boys were also attentive to these kinds of 'bad-word learning.' Indeed Mario shows that he also knows the expression "son of a bitch" by repeating it (line 9).

The fragments that we have examined show that there was a clear division in class between languages used in official learning and in teacher-student communication and languages used in peer communication—that is, in communication "front" and "back" regions (Goffman 1959, 106–60). For a discussion, see De Fina (2015) and Blommaert and De Fina, this volume. Figure 11.1 reproduces the language relationships in both communicative environments:

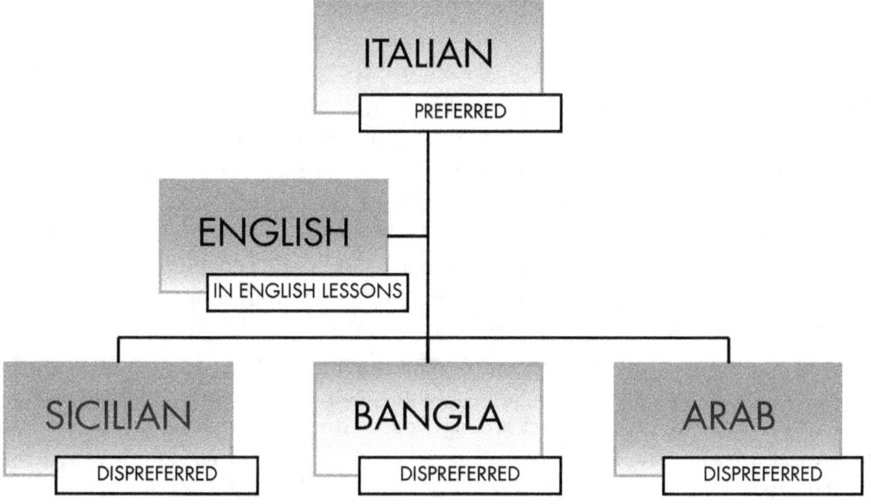

Figure 11.1. Teacher-fronted interaction

Within this hierarchy, Sicilian occupies an interesting place, since it is sometimes allowed and even used by one of the teachers but it is precisely the kinds of uses that the teacher selects for Sicilian that mark it as a language that is not suitable for academic communication. Indeed, while in peer talk dialect is used widely (approximately in 20 percent of the turns counted uttered by the male children) and with a variety of communicative functions, dialect is used by the teacher only in only 1.6 percent of her turns. The teacher uses dialect exclusively to joke, scold, and sometimes mock, as in the following example.

Example 8

1.	T1	((to Antonio)): Quand'è che ti sei andato a tagliare i capelli.
2.	Antonio	*Duminica.*
3.	T1	Du-mi-ni-ca,
4.		((voices)) @@@@@
5.	T1	Du-minica!
6.		Duminica@@@
7.		((voices)) @@@@

Translation

1.	T1	((to Antonio)): When did you go to cut your hair.
2.	Antonio	*Sunday.*
3.	T1	*Sun-day.*
4.		((voices)) @@@@@
5.	T1	*Sun-day.*
6.		*Sunday@@@*
7.		((voices)) @@@@

Here T1 asks Antonio when he had cut his hair, to which Antonio answers in Sicilian dialect: Sunday. T1 repeats the word in Sicilian, dividing it into syllables (line 3) thus conveying that what Antonio said is funny, and in fact the words are followed by laughter by other children. T1 repeats the word a couple of times in a slightly mocking tone. The use and status of Sicilian would merit a much deeper discussion than is allowed in the space of this chapter, but I included this example in order to show that to a certain extent it can be aligned with immigrant languages in terms of it being a dispreferred variety for official communication.

To summarize, the picture that emerges from language use and distribution is that of an extreme dynamism on the side of peer communication on the one hand and of extreme rigidity in teacher-pupil communication on the other. For a representation of language relations in peer-to-peer communication, see figure 11.2, which represents the relative interchangeability of language variety as opposed to their hierarchy in student-teacher communication.

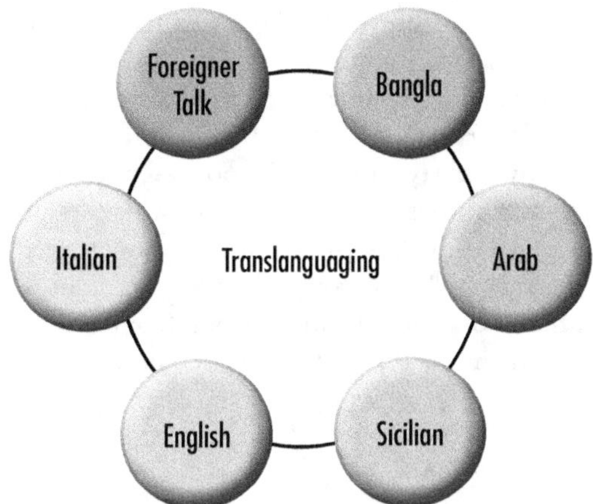

Figure 11.2. Peer group interaction

The management and distribution of language repertoires matches almost exactly the ways in which local and 'foreign' cultures are treated in school practice. Curiosity and interest about 'foreign' cultures is very much the norm among children and teachers and it is conveyed and expressed in nonofficial domains such as breaks and private conversations. See for example the following exchange that took place before the beginning of a lesson. I (Res) saw that Nandita, Bani, and Parveen were exchanging DVDs so I inquired. Marina was overhearing the conversation.

Example 9

1.	Res	Vi scambiare film?
2.	Na	((talking about something else to Bani)) Eh se:: va be'!
3.	Ba	Lei si chiama Shabnum,
4.		lei si chiama Riaz, sono tutte e due (..)
5.	All	@@@
6.	Ba	Lei ora è grossa prima era più bella.
7.		dopo ne porto domani un altro film.
8.	Ma	Sono in Bangla?

Translation

1.	Res	Do you exchange movies?
2.	Na	((talking about something else to Bani)) Ya sure!
3.	Ba	She is called Shabnum,
4.		she is called Riaz, they are both (..)
5.	All	@@@
6.	Ba	Now she is fatter before she was prettier,
7.		then tomorrow I will bring another movie.
8.	Ma	Are they in Bangla?

Here we see that Marina (a Sicilian girl) is attentive to the exchange and curious about the movies. Indeed, she asks if they are in Bangla.

Teachers often made comments to me on how interested they were in the ways that Bangladeshi foods were prepared, for example. The Bangladeshi girls were asked to dance and sing during a carnival party in the classroom. Children asked each other questions about their habits, families, histories, etc., in whispers during breaks or in peer-to-peer communication. But these topics very rarely entered the domain of official business. In my recordings I only found two occasions in which children made reference to their countries of origin during teacher-fronted talk, and in both occasions there was no attempt from the teacher to use such moments to ask questions or to expand on the topics.

Example 10

1.	T1	La mamma si chiama Giovanna Neri, giusto?
2.	Ni	Si (…)
3.	X	Giova::::nna
4.		(…)
5.	Rym	Tua mamma si chiama Neri?
6.		non è tuo padre Neri?
7.	T1	Sono cugini
8.		(…)
9.	Max	Ma i cugini si possono sposare?
10.	X	(…)
11.	Rym	Sì pure da noi in Tunisia si sposano
12.		(…)

Translation

1.	T1	Your mother is called Giovanna Neri, right?
2.	Nino	Yes (…)
3.	X	Giova::::nna
4.		(…)
5.	Rym	Your mum is called Neri?
6.		isn't Neri your father?
7.	T1	They are cousins.
8.		(…)
9.	Max	But cousins can get married?
10.	X	Yes (…)
11.	Rym	Yes also in our country in Tunisia they get married.
12.		(…)

In example 10, the teacher was asking students for their parent's name and Nino was responding (line 2). Rym overhears the conversation and asks Nino whether Neri is not the surname of his father (line 6). At this point the teacher explains that Nino's parents are cousins. This is one of the few occasions in which Rym makes a comment on uses in Tunisia (line 11), but, as we note, there is no follow up from the teacher.

Conclusions

In this chapter I have examined how linguistic and cultural diversity are managed in a fifth-grade classroom in a school in Palermo with the objective of understanding how teachers and students adjust to a reality of multilinguism and multiculturalism unprecedented in a region like Sicily. I focused particularly on language ideologies and found that a monolingual ideology and a lack of stress on cultural diversity are favored in official classroom discourse. On the other hand, I also found that children clearly practiced multilingualism and were interested in multicultural realities. One could say that this contact zone shows how globalization creates arenas where the push and pull of contrary forces can be felt. While there are occasions of encounter between diverse cultures and of experimentation with languages, the school as an institution reflects and perpetuates norms of monolingualism and monoculturalism that dominate many of the arenas where power relations are involved.

Transcription Conventions

Symbol	**Function**
CAPS	louder than surrounding talk
.	at the end of words marks falling intonation
,	at the end of words marks slight rising intonation
-	abrupt cutoff, stammering quality when hyphenating syllables of a word
!	animated tone, not necessarily an exclamation
____	emphasis
::	elongated sounds
italics	utterance in a language other than Italian
(.)	micropause
//	overlapping speech
(())	transcriber's comment
(...)	nonaudible segment or nonidentified speaker
=	no interval between adjacent utterances
X	unidentified speaker

References

Amoruso, Chiara. 2008. "The Second [Unfulfilled] Generation of Tunisians in Manzara del Vallo: Language Lag and Social Exclusion." *Rivista Italiana di Dialettologia* 31:29–60.

Blommaert, Jan. 2007. "Sociolinguistic Scales." *Intercultural Pragmatics* 4 (1): 1–19.

Calvanese, Francesco, and Enrico Puglies. 1988. "Emigration and Immigration in Italy. Recent trends." *Labour* 3 (2): 181–99.

Canagarajah, Suresh. 2013. *Translingual Practice: Global Englishes and Cosmopolitan Relations*. Abingdon, Eng.: Routledge.

Caritas e Migrantes. 2012. "Dossier Statistico Immigrazione 2012." Accessed January 10, 2014. http://www.caritas.it/caritasitaliana/allegati/2908/Dossier_immigrazione2012_scheda_sintesi.pdf.

Cole, James, and Sally Booth. 2007. *Dirty Work: Immigrants in Domestic Service, Agriculture, and Prostitution in Sicily*. Lanham, MD: Lexington Books.

Cole, James. 1997. *The New Racism in Europe. A Sicilian Ethnography*. Cambridge: Cambridge University Press.

De Fina, Anna. 2015. "Ethnography as Complexifying Lenses." *Tilburg Papers in Culture Studies*, paper 146. Accessed February 2, 2016. https://www.tilburguniversity.edu/upload/fdf6bb3c-b036-49fb-a558-ce42026ed3ef_TPCS_146_DeFina.pdf.

Delli Zotti, Giovanni, Donatella Greco, Giorgio Porcelli, Ornelia Urpis, and Chiara Zanetti. 2011. "Children's Voices: Exploring Interethnic Violence and Children's Rights in the School Environment: National State of Art Report." University of Trieste, Department of Social and Political Sciences. Accessed January 24, 2014. http://www.zrs.upr.si/media/uploads/files/IT_STA%20report.pdf.

Fairclough, Norman. 1989. *Language and Power*. London: Longman.

Gallina, Francesca. 2007. "Sociolinguistic Conditions, Perceptions, and Language Use: A Comparison of Scholastic Cycles in Italian Schools." *Studi Italiani di Linguistica Teorica e Applicata*, 36 (1): 173–89.

Gee, James P. 1989. "Two Styles of Narrative Construction and Their Linguistic and Educational Implications." *Discourse Processes*, 12:287–307.

Goffman, Erving. 1983. "The Interaction Order." *American Sociological Review*, 48:1–17.

———. 1959. *The Presentation of Self in Everyday Life*. New York: Anchor Books.

Istituto Comprensivo Turrisis Colonna. "Piano dell'Offerta Forrmativa 2010/2011." Retrieved May 6, 2012. http://www.scuolaturrisicolonna.it.

King, Russell. 1993. "Recent Immigration in Italy, Character, Causes and Consequences." *GeoJournal* 30 (3): 283–92.

Lytra, Vally. 2007. *Play Frames and Social Identities*. Amsterdam: John Benjamins.

Martin-Jones, Marilyn. 2007. "Bilingualism, Education, and the Regulation of Access to Language Resources." In *Bilingualism: A Social Approach*, edited by Monica Heller, 161–82. London: Palgrave Macmillan.

Martín Rojo, Luisa. 2010. *Constructing Inequality in Multilingual Classrooms*. Berlin: Mouton de Gruyter.

Michaels, Sarah. 1981. "'Sharing Time': Children's Narrative Styles and Differential Access to Literacy." *Language in Society* 10 (3): 423–42.

Ministero dell'Istruzione, dell'Università e della Ricerca. 2013. "Gli Alunni Stranieri nel Sistema Scolastico Italiano. Servizion Statistico, October 2013." Accessed February 5, 2014. http://www.istruzione.it/llegati/Notiziario_Stranieri_12_13.pdf.

Ogbu, John. 2003. *Black American Students in an Affluent Suburb: A Study of Academic Disengagement*. Aarhus, Den.: Lawrence Erlbaum Publishers.

Pratt, Mary Louise. 1991. "Arts of the Contact Zone." *Profession* 91:33–40.

Rampton, Ben. 2006. *Language in Late Modernity: Interaction in an Urban School*. Cambridge: Cambridge University Press.

Contributors

(ordered alphabetically by last name)

Geeta Aneja is a fifth-year PhD candidate in Educational Linguistics at the University of Pennsylvania. Her research interests include post-structural approaches to (non)nativeness, nonnative English-speaking teacher (NNEST) identity development, and the role of translingualism in language teacher education. She welcomes correspondence at ganeja@gse.upenn.edu.

Christine Anthonissen is Professor Emeritus in General Linguistics, Stellenbosch University, South Africa. During her tenure as professor, she was variously also Departmental Chair and Deputy Dean (Faculty of Arts and Social Sciences). Her research focuses on discourse studies, critical discourse analysis, and social aspects of bilingualism and multilingualism. Recent work on language policy and practice concerning languages used in education in South Africa relies on neoliberal and postcolonial theories to assist in understanding processes of language maintenance and shift observed in local multilingual communities. She is member of the editorial boards of *Stellenbosch Papers in Linguistics* (SPIL), the *Journal of Language and Politics*, and *Multilingual Margins*.

Adrian Blackledge is Professor of Bilingualism and Director of the MOSAIC Centre for Research on Multilingualism at University of Birmingham, UK. He is the author of numerous articles and books based on his research on multilingualism in education and wider society. His books include *Heteroglossia as Practice and Pedagogy* (2014), *The Routledge Handbook of Multilingualism* (2012), *Multilingualism. A Critical Perspective* (2010), *Discourse and Power in a Multilingual World* (2005), *Negotiation of Identities in Multilingual Contexts* (2004), *Multilingualism, Second Language Learning, and Gender* (2001), and *Literacy, Power, and Social Justice* (2000). He is currently engaged in research funded through the AHRC's Translating Cultures theme, "Translation and Translanguaging: Investigating Linguistic and Cultural Transformations in Superdiverse Wards in Four UK Cities."

Jan Blommaert is Professor of Language, Culture, and Globalization, and Director of the Babylon Center at Tilburg University, The Netherlands, and Professor of

African Linguistics and Sociolinguistics at Ghent University, Belgium. He holds honorary appointments at University of the Western Cape (South Africa) and Beijing Language and Culture University (China) and is group leader of the Max Planck Sociolinguistic Diversity Working Group. He has published widely on language ideologies and language inequality in the context of globalization.

Suresh Canagarajah is the Edwin Erle Sparks Professor of Applied Linguistics, English, and Asian Studies. He teaches language socialization, World Englishes, and academic writing. His publication *Translingual Practice: Global Englishes and Cosmopolitan Relations* (Routledge, 2013) won the MLA, AAAL, and BAAL awards for Best Book.

Angela Creese is professor of educational linguistics at the School of Education, University of Birmingham, and is the principal investigator of the Arts and Humanities Research Council's (AHRC) large Translating Cultures grant, "Translation and Translanguaging: Investigating Linguistic and Cultural Transformations in Superdiverse Wards in Four UK Cities." Her research interests are in linguistic ethnography, language ecologies, multilingualism in society, and multilingual classroom pedagogy.

Anna De Fina is Professor of Italian Language and Linguistics in the Italian Department and Affiliated Faculty with the Linguistics Department at Georgetown University. Her interests and publications focus on identity, narrative, migration, and diversity. Her books include *Identity in Narrative: A Study of Immigrant Discourse* (John Benjamins), *Analyzing Narratives* (coauthored with Alexandra Georgakopoulou; Cambridge University Press) and the *Handbook of Narrative Analysis* (coedited with Alexandra Georgakopoulou; Wiley).

Inmaculada García-Sánchez is Associate Professor of Anthropology at Temple University, Pennsylvania. Her research interests include language and the immigrant experience and language and culture in educational contexts. She is the author of *Language and Muslim Immigrant Childhoods: The Politics of Belonging* (2014) and numerous articles and chapters on immigrant children and youth. She's a past Fellow of the National Academy of Education, and her research has been funded by the Spencer Foundation and the Wenner-Gren Foundation for Anthropological Research, among other sources.

Rachel Hu is a research fellow at the University of Birmingham. She is currently working in the AHRC-funded TLANG project, engaging in linguistic ethnography studies and research of super-diverse cities and communities. Her research interests include social linguistic study of everyday communication, contemporary translation theories and methodologies, and their applications in Sino-British cultural and commercial interactions. Prior to working in the UK, Rachel taught English at Xi'an Jiaotong University, China, for five years with a background in TEFL and applied linguistics research.

Zhu Hua is Professor of Applied Linguistics and Communication and Head of Department at Birkbeck College, University of London. Her main research interests are intercultural pragmatics, language and intercultural communication, and child language development. Her most recent book-length publications on intercultural communication include *The Language and Intercultural Communication Reader* (Routledge, 2011), *Exploring Intercultural Communication: Language in Action* (Routledge, 2014), *Research Methods in Intercultural Communication* (Blackwell, 2016), and *Weaving Intercultural Work, Life, and Scholarship in Globalizing Universities* (Routledge, 2016). She is a joint editor for the book series Routledge Studies in Language and Intercultural Communication.

Andrea Leone-Pizzighella is pursuing a PhD in Educational Linguistics at the University of Pennsylvania. Her research interests are in language ideologies and de facto language policies in the context of the Italian education system. She welcomes correspondence at andleone@gse.upenn.edu.

Mark Lewis is pursuing a PhD in Educational Linguistics at the University of Pennsylvania. He researches language ideologies and representations of language in schools. He welcomes correspondence at markle@gse.upenn.edu.

Luisa Martín Rojo is Professor in Linguistics at the Universidad Autónoma (Madrid, Spain), a member of the International Pragmatic Association Consultation Board (reelected for the period 2012–17), and President of the Iberian Association for Studies on Discourse and Society (EDiSo). She has conducted research in the fields of discourse analysis, sociolinguistics, and communication, mainly focused on immigration and racism. Since 2000, her research has focused on the management of cultural and linguistic diversity in schools, with an ethnographic perspective, analyzing how social inequality is constructed ("Constructing Inequality in Multilingual Classrooms," published in *Sociolinguistic Studies*, 2010), and the role of linguistic ideologies and values (*A Sociolinguistics of Diaspora: Latino Practices, Identities, and Ideologies*, coedited with Rosina Márquez-Reiter, 2014).

Elizabeth R. Miller is an Associate Professor of Applied Linguistics in the English Department at the University of North Carolina at Charlotte. Her research involves adult immigrant learners of English in the United States and focuses on issues related to language ideologies and learners' agency and identity. Her work has appeared in a number of journals, and two of her most recent publications include *The Language of Adult Immigrants: Agency in the Making* (2014) and the coedited volume *Theorizing and Analyzing Agency in Second Language Learning: Interdisciplinary Approaches* (2015), both published by Multilingual Matters.

Robert Moore is a Senior Lecturer in Educational Linguistics at the Graduate School of Education, University of Pennsylvania. He can be contacted at moorerob@gse.upenn.edu.

Anastasia Nylund is Assistant Teaching Professor and Director of the MA in Language and Communication in the Department of Linguistics at Georgetown University. Her work appears in the *International Journal of the Sociology of Language* and *Penn Working Papers in Linguistics*. She is the coeditor (with Deborah Schiffrin and Anna De Fina) of *Telling Stories: Language, Narrative, and Social Life* (Georgetown University Press, 2009).

Markus Rheindorf is Senior Researcher and Lecturer at the University of Vienna, Austria. His research interests include discourse studies, corpus linguistics, genre analysis, and academic writing. He is coeditor of the *Vienna Linguistic Gazette* and founding member of the Society for Academic Writing in Austria. His publications include a diachronic study of argumentation patterns in academic discourse on film and a genre theory–informed analysis of language change in Austrian German. He teaches academic writing and English for Academic Purposes courses at universities in Austria, Germany, and Romania.

Betsy Rymes is Associate Professor of Educational Linguistics at the University of Pennsylvania's Graduate School of Education. Her most recent book is *Communicating Beyond Language: Everyday Engagements with Diversity* (Routledge, 2014). She can be contacted at brymes@gse.upenn.edu.

Fatma Said is a Research Associate in Applied Linguistics at the University of York, UK. She completed her PhD (2015) in Applied Linguistics at Birkbeck College, University of London on the sociolinguistic nature of family mealtime interactions of a multilingual Arabic-English speaking family. Currently, her research centers on the Arabic language, family language policy, language socialization, language ideology, identity, agency, and language maintenance of heritage languages in multilingual families.

Elana Shohamy is a professor of language education at Tel Aviv University in the program of Multilingual Education where she teaches and researches language diversity, coexistence, and language rights. Her main topics of research include language testing and multilingual assessment, language policy, immigration, and linguistic landscape. Among her publications are *The Power of Tests* (Pearson, 2001), *Language Policy* (Routledge, 2006), two edited books on Linguistic Landscape (2009 and 2010), and numerous articles and book chapters on the above topics. Elana is the winner of the 2010 Life Time Achievement Award granted by the International Language Testing Association and the current editor of the journal *Linguistic Landscape*.

Virginia Unamuno is a PhD candidate in philology and specialist in qualitative sociolinguistics. She is Senior Researcher of the CONICET (Consejo Nacional de Investigaciones Científicas y Técnicas) at the University of Buenos Aires. Since 2009, her research has been rooted in the CIFMA at the Argentinean province of Chaco. She teaches sociolinguistics at the University of San Martín (UNSAM) and at the University of Tres de Febrero (UNTREF). Currently, she is leading a research project on new speakers, new uses, and new modes of transmission of indigenous languages in northern Argentina.

Ruth Wodak is Distinguished Professor of Discourse Studies at Lancaster University, UK. Her research interests focus on discourse studies, identity politics, language and/in politics, prejudice and discrimination. She is coeditor of the journals *Discourse & Society*, *Critical Discourse Studies*, and *Language and Politics*. Recent book publications include *The Politics of Fear: What Right-Wing Populist Discourses Mean* (Sage, 2015), *Analysing Fascist Discourse: European Fascism in Talk and Text* (with John Richardson; Routledge, 2013), *Right Wing Populism in Europe: Politics and Discourse* (with Majid KhosraviNik and Brigitte Mral; Bloomsbury Academic, 2013), and *The Discourse of Politics in Action: Politics as Usual* (Palgrave, 2011).

Index

www.ingramcontent.com/pod-product-compliance
Lightning Source LLC
LaVergne TN
LVHW020432080826
844660LV00034B/1404

* 9 7 8 1 6 2 6 1 6 4 2 2 2 *

LINGUISTICS

"The value of this volume is that it goes beyond a simple discussion on super-diversity, including case studies that problematize and complicate the ways in which language, communication, and identity have been interpreted in the past. By embedding these concepts within different and new contexts, it engages readers in the mobility, complexity, and interconnectedness that the case studies so well describe."

—Ofelia García
The Graduate Center, City University of New York

Sociocultural linguistics has long conceived of languages as well-bounded, separate codes. But the increasing diversity of languages most people encounter daily defies this conception, and more recent scholarship complicates traditional associations between languages and social identities. Diversity—and even super-diversity—is now the norm. *Diversity and Super-Diversity* examines this linguistic phenomenon and addresses the theoretical-methodological challenges it poses to sociocultural linguistics. This volume brings together top scholars in the field and stages the debate on super-diversity that will be sure to interest sociocultural linguists, generating discussion and informing future research.

ANNA DE FINA is Professor of Italian Language and Linguistics at Georgetown University. Her most recent publication is *Analyzing Narrative: Discourse and Sociolinguistic Perspectives* (with Alexandra Georgakopoulou)

DIDEM IKIZOGLU is a PhD student in linguistics at Georgetown University.

JEREMY WEGNER is a PhD student in linguistics at Georgetown University.

Georgetown University Round Table on Languages and Linguistics series

www.press.georgetown.edu
Washington, DC

RACE AND
THE REVOLUTIONARY IMPULSE IN

THE SPOOK WHO SAT BY THE DOOR

Edited by MICHAEL T. MARTIN,
DAVID C. WALL, and MARILYN YAQUINTO